The Qur'an and Normative Religious Pluralism: *A Thematic Study of The Qur'an*

THE QUR'AN AND NORMATIVE RELIGIOUS PLURALISM: A THEMATIC STUDY *of the* QUR'AN

Arif Kemil Abdullah

THE INTERNATIONAL INSTITUTE OF ISLAMIC THOUGHT
LONDON • WASHINGTON

THE INTERNATIONAL INSTITUTE OF ISLAMIC THOUGHT
P.O. BOX 669, HERNDON, VA 20172, USA
www.iiit.org

LONDON OFFICE
P.O. BOX 126, RICHMOND, SURREY TW9 2UD, UK
www.iiituk.com

ISBN 978-1-56564-657-5 *limp*
ISBN 978-1-56564-658-2 *cased*

Typesetting and cover design by Sideek Ali

IT IS A TYPICAL feature of human nature, that despite their differences human beings are united, and despite their unity they are different. Moreover, people despite their differences love each other, and despite their mutual love they are different.

Abū Ḥayyān al-Tawḥīdī
Al-Muqābasāt

WHAT I AM CERTAIN OF from my experience of human social life and have learnt from my life-time of study is the following: The thing most worthy of love is love, and the quality most deserving of enmity is enmity. That is, the quality of love and loving, which renders man's social life secure and impels to happiness is the most worthy of love and being loved... The time for enmity and hostility has finished. Two world wars have shown how evil, destructive, and what an awesome wrong is enmity. It has become clear that there is no benefit in it at all.

Bediuzzaman Said Nursi
The Damascus Sermon

Contents

Foreword

SOCIETIES TODAY PERHAPS more so than any time in the past are characterised by religious diversity. A great exchange of views is taking place, partly through interfaith dialogue but also across social media, in a climate of greater international integration – and marked hostility – which seeks to know Islam as never before. Peaceful co-existence is one thing, but tolerance of religious difference, that is of different religious traditions, although almost unanimously agreed upon as a necessary goal, is quite another, causing a dilemma. Whilst theoretically making sense, practical implementation is proving a little difficult, partly because much thought needs to be given to one's own convictions and moral truths in relation to those of others, and partly because, for Islam at least, the right path is clearly defined as belief in God and His Prophet, and this needs to be accommodated in all discussions.

Not surprisingly, some complex theological and other related issues have come to the fore, sparking at times heated debated, and focusing much attention on the field of religious pluralism and Islam's role in relation to not only simply living in tolerance with other faiths, but seeking to understand them through real, positive dialogue:

> But I don't believe that religious dialogue is ever advanced by denying difference. I think there is a kind of arrogance at times in the assumption that 'I can tell you what you really mean'; and I deplore the way in which some of those who use the language of religious pluralism are so ready to tell absolutely every practitioner of every faith on the globe what they're really about. And the recognition of difference seems to me entirely compatible

> with deep mutual respect, with commitment to dialogue, sometimes costly dialogue, and to co-existence.*

Religious pluralism has a variety of meanings and any active engagement with those of other faiths would require at some point discussion of one's worldview and religious truths in relation to those of others. Islam faces a particularly difficult position. Aside from being tolerant and respectful of other faiths, advocating freedom of faith, and peaceful co-existence for all humanity, it has to intellectually engage on matters of religious truth whilst defending the validity of its own Islamic tenets without relegating to perdition all those who deny this. There is an existence of extremes, of perennialist philosophy versus exclusivist interpretation. That is not to say that we are to accommodate all truths relativistic fashion, and not point out error. Far from it. Rather the encounter has to be a highly sophisticated and intellectual one based on respect. Thus, if we separate out what is Islamic from what is cultural or context-based interpretation, we will discover that in the Qur'an we have a great and honourable example of how to live in diversity, of powerful scriptural tenets that lend themselves precisely to engagement with those of other faiths, allowing valuable contributions to be made to the field of religious pluralism. All that is required from Muslims is careful study of these Qur'anic tenets to present them accurately and as they are meant to be understood without projecting them through the filter of historical confrontation or cultural misinterpretation.

Unfortunately, it is easier to be critical and exclusivist, than to find common ground and present truly the inclusive message of the Qur'an. The author criticizes this exclusivist view on the part of certain theologians and scholars, locating their interpretation of controversial Qur'anic verses such as the verse of the sword, in the historical contexts of the Crusades and constant state of

* Former Archbishop of Canterbury Rowan Williams, *Islam, Christianity and Pluralism* (Lambeth Palace, Association of Muslim Social Scientists (AMSS UK), 2007).

defensive action, to argue that shaped in response to onslaughts of various sorts these political readings of Qur'anic texts do not accurately reflect the message being conveyed. Misleading *theological* conclusions, note *not Qur'anic* as is the contention of this study, emerged which were hardline in nature, claiming that Muslims had no obligations towards non-Muslims. Using a thematic, holistic approach to Qur'anic exegesis, as well as linguistically analysing key terms used in Qur'anic verses, he corrects much of this misinterpretation to offer a reading based on the meaning of the verses as they stand and in relation to the comprehensive message of the Qur'an and its humanistic view.

So, in the Islamic and Qur'anic context, we need to be extremely careful, and of course clear, with regards to discussion on religious pluralism and the attitudes Muslims should adopt in relation to this in accordance with the teachings of the Qur'an.

There exist different types of religious pluralisms: *Normative Religious Pluralism* places emphasis on developing an ethico-behavioral pattern towards difference. *Soteriological Religious Pluralism* stresses salvation. *Epistemological Religious Pluralism* focuses on justification or rationality. Finally, *Alethic Religious Pluralism* concerns the nature of truth. According to the author unlike soteriological and alethic pluralism, whose issues are inherently irreconcilable for Muslims (and perhaps for those of other faiths and as such divisive) focusing on core aspects of religious truth and salvation which cannot be compromised on, normative religious pluralism concentrates on terrestrial dimensions and ramifications allowing for seeking genuine understanding, toleration, and peacebuilding. In other words normative religious pluralism does not demand synthesis of religious views, or compromise on matters of doctrine, which is not realistic and for many not feasible, but can foster understanding whilst respecting theological difference.

This work discusses the legitimacy of using normative religious pluralism in relation to the normative teachings of Islam to argue that the former's principles are not alien to Islamic teachings so long as we distinguish between the Qur'an and Sunnah of the Prophet (ṢAAS),* and opinions derived by scholars which are rooted in political contexts or military defence. In terms of the Qur'an analysis is to focus on the commands/teaching contained in the verses, the context of the command/verse, the occasion of revelation, its relation to the overall comprehensive message of the Qur'an (using a thematic approach), and the role of the Sunnah to explain the meaning further. This is the methodology adopted by the author throughout the study.

In doing so the author corrects some highly controversial misquoted, mistranslated, and/or quoted out of context verses of the Qur'an, including as mentioned the verse of the sword and the idea of not taking non-Muslims as friends. In reality, the Qur'an calls for freedom of faith and peaceful co-existence, but condemns oppression, religious persecution, and those who initiate hostilities. *In this way it not only invokes human dignity, but restores it when it is violated.*

> And [thus it is:] had thy Sustainer so willed, all those who live on earth would surely have attained to faith, all of them: dost thou, then, think that thou couldst compel people to believe. (Qur'an *Yūnus* 10:99)
>
> There shall be no coercion in matters of faith. (Qur'an *al-Baqarah* 2:256)

The establishment of a just society which respects all human beings and their rights is essential. In addition, note evidence from the Qur'an and the Sunnah does not support the implementation of a capital punishment for apostasy (*al-riddah*). Rather, textual study points to freedom of belief including the act of rejecting the faith.**

This allows the author to approach the issue of religious pluralism from a strong, clear Islamic perspective which lends much

---

*(ṢAAS) – *Ṣallā Allāhu ʿalayhi wa sallam*. May the peace and blessings of God be upon him. Said whenever the name of Prophet Muhammad is mentioned.

** See Taha J. Alalwani, *Apostasy in Islam, A Historical and Scriptural Analysis* (London: IIIT, 2011). Also AbdulHamid AbuSulayman, *Apostates, Islam and Freedom of Faith: Change of Conviction vs Change of Allegiance* (Occasional Paper 22),(London: IIIT, 2013).

needed clarity to a subject that can quickly lead to confusion in understanding the intrinsic nature of religious diversity, tolerance, and religious truths – and the interplay between them – especially in relation to religious inclusivist and exclusivist positions. The Islamic perspective also calls for genuine engagement not based on false diplomacy or political correctness and makes no false claims to neutral understanding or to blanket relativism.

Dates cited in the work according to the Islamic calendar (hijrah) are abbreviated AH, otherwise they follow the Gregorian calendar and abbreviated CE where necessary. Arabic words are italicized except for those which have entered common usage. Diacritical marks have been added only to those Arabic names not considered contemporary. English translation of quotations taken from original Arabic sources are those of the author unless specified.

Since its establishment in 1981, the IIIT has continued to serve as a major center to facilitate serious scholarly efforts, based on Islamic vision, values and principles. The Institute's programs of research, and seminars and conferences, over the last thirty years, have resulted in the publication of more than four hundred and fifty titles in both English, Arabic and other major languages.

We would like to express our thanks to the author for his cooperation and to the editorial and production team at the IIIT London Office, and all those who were directly or indirectly involved in the completion of this work including Shiraz Khan and Dr. Maryam Mahmood.

IIIT London Office
August 2014

Introduction

We live in a fairly unique time, an age of unprecedented human development. Unlike previous civilisations, marked by clear-cut cultural and religious boundaries, humanity today lives in a vastly diverse world of cultures, ethnicities and faiths. Globalisation has so networked the world and made it inter-dependent and inter-related, that no one person can live in isolation from the next or be indifferent to what goes on elsewhere. It is also said to be an age of secularism. Yet, despite this and despite all the philosophical predictions of the nineteenth and twentieth centuries with regard to the demise of religion, religion in the third millennium has in fact emerged afresh, to play an essential role in shaping and affecting people's conscience and behavior across the world.

Given the fact of globalisation and the revival of religions in a milieu where everyone is practically on everyone else's doorstep, it is vitally important for theologians from all faiths to derive from their own religious sources conceptions of religious pluralism corresponding to the reality of the present world. In other words today's inter-faith issues cannot be solved by resorting to out-of-date conceptions. New efforts are needed in the field of theology to develop up-to-date patterns for peaceful religious co-existence and inter-faith dialogue.

This study is a response to the urgent need and challenge for an effective and positive way to interact with the religious other. It explores the Qur'anic conception of normative religious pluralism with a view to providing answers to questions such as whether the Qur'an itself regards normative religious pluralism as a value system or simply a method through which the Qur'anic worldview can be actualised. What is the main purpose of the Qur'anic endorsement of normative religious pluralism? Is normative Islam always identical with the actions of its adherents? Does an extant negative attitude towards normative religious pluralism emerge from the teachings of Islam or from the context of surrounding circumstances?

The most important key to answering all these questions is Qur'anic exegesis or *tafsīr* which has a decisive religious impact on Muslim consciousness and is a vital prerequisite for Muslim understanding of interfaith relations. The problem is that where once the Qur'anic text was viewed dynamically, allowing for a renewed understanding of religious co-existence and thus preserving the religious identity of Muslims whilst keeping pace with universal human values, this progress over time slowed. Understanding and engagement became historically burdened with methodological and socio-political problems which have carried to this day. These developments include for example, the emergence of certain ethical conceptions from the Qur'anic text in historical contexts different from the present, the usage of the atomistic approach,[1] the excessive implementation of the abrogation claim in relation to some ethical norms towards non-muslims, the exclusive restriction of the general meaning of certain Qur'anic verses referring positively to non-Muslims on the grounds that the general sense of these verses was specified for Muslims only, etc. All these methodological and socio-political circumstances have resulted in exegesis producing meanings which are in reality exclusive with respect to interfaith relations. And these exclusive interpretations have in turn led to the neglect of the humanistic approach[2] with regard to Qur'anic exegesis and hence to the deterioration of religious co-existence.

The main purpose of this study has therefore been to derive from the Qur'an a coherent conception of normative religious pluralism and thus, on the one hand to investigate a progressive way of understanding the Qur'an not only in terms of its own textual and historical contexts, but also in the context of universal human values, and on the other hand, to emphasise both the humanistic approach as well as the dynamic and creative nature of Qur'anic exegesis, *tafsīr*. For this reason, and since the study's area of focus is the Qur'an, Hadith and Islamic jurisprudence (fiqh), will be consulted only to the extent required by the exegetical process, and not as main research areas.

As the classical atomistic approach historically applied to the Qur'an as a main exegetical tool has failed to produce a thematic coherent picture of the organic unity of the Qur'an, the current study uses another approach known as the thematic exegetical method. The purpose of this method is to crystallise coherently the Qur'anic comprehensive conception of a given topic.[3] This is done by gathering together thematically relevant Qur'anic verses in order to study them historically, linguistically and contextually to develop thereby a logical construction[4] presenting clearly the Qur'anic conceptual unity of a topic. Historical analysis of the selected verses concentrates on the authentic occasion of their revelation (*asbāb al-nuzūl*), the authentic interpretations of the Prophet, his Companions and the elderly among the Successors, as it also concentrates on the socio-political environment of the revelation: Makkah or Madinah. By elderly is meant the first generation of successors, they were closest to the time of the Prophet and gained their knowledge from the Companions. This type of analysis ensures that the research does not transgress any authentic, prophetic explanations whilst at the same time providing firm ground for critical examination of historical claims i.e. such as abrogation, for determining abrogation cases in the Qur'an is not based on reasoning, but on authentic, prophetic evidence.[5] Linguistic study of Qur'anic verses reconciles, through syntactical, morphological and rhetorical analysis, the variety of possible meanings with respect to indefinite Qur'anic verses, *mutashābih*. Contextual study of Qur'anic verses involves observation of the particular textual context of a verse being interpreted, the overall Qur'anic context thematically related to the interpreted verse and also the context of the reality of present world, namely human experience. This type of analysis prevents the exegetical process from partial selectivity, since the relevant thematic linkages keep the topic coherent as well as comprehensive and in accordance to universal human values.

The validity of the thematic approach stems from the Qur'an itself, for it is well-established fact among scholars that the revelation itself does not present any given topic, in complete form, in one specific place. Rather, elements of it are fragmented and scattered throughout the text. For this reason, the Prophet himself is reported to have made different references to the Qur'an in order to clarify a given issue or meaning, known as the explanation of the Qur'an by the Qur'an. However, the earliest seeds of the thematic approach to Qur'anic exegetical analysis seem to have been sown in the early 9th century, for well-documented evidence to support this claim can be found in Arabic literature dating from the period. For example, in his encyclopaedic work, *Kitāb al-Ḥayawān*, al-Jāḥiẓ explains and explores various different ideas i.e. that of fire, thematically, that is through a thematic collection of relevant verses on the topic.[6] Use of the thematic method with regard to Qur'anic exegesis can also be traced, to some extent, in later works such as: *Jawāhir al-Qur'ān* by Abū Ḥāmid al-Ghazālī; *Al-Kashf ʿan Manāhij al-Adillah fī ʿAqā'id al-Millah* by Ibn Rushd; and *Risālah fī Lafẓ al-Sunnah fī al-Qur'ān* by Ibn Taymiyyah, etc.[7]

Despite these early steps the thematic method as such was not regarded with much interest nor developed further until the 19th century,[8] when certain western scholars began to apply it with the aim of understanding Qur'anic themes coherently. Thus in 1840 a monograph appeared in Paris entitled *Le Koran: doctrines et devoirs*, containing thematic selections from the Qur'an. This was followed by other similar works.[9] The use of the thematic exegetical approach by western scholars seems to have attracted the attention of some Muslim intellectuals raising their awareness of its significance as an accurate exegetical tool for understanding the organic unity of the Qur'an. For instance, it is thought that Jamāl al-Dīn al-Afghānī was acquainted with one of the earliest thematic studies of the Qur'an, *Le Koran Analyse* written by Jules Le Beaume and published in Paris in 1878.[10] The book was translated by Muhammad Fuad Abd al-Baqi in 1924 and published for the first time in 1935 in Cairo under the title *Tafṣīr Āyāt al-Qur'ān al-Ḥakīm.* It is very likely that al-Afghānī attempted to promote the thematic approach among Muslims because, according to some scholars, a copy of *Tafṣīr Āyāt al-Qur'ān al-Ḥakīm* was later found with his disciple Muhammad Abduh. In addition he is reported to have been criticised by some authorities of Al-Azhar university for his adoption of the thematic exegetical method.[11] Indeed, Al-Afghānī's disagreement with the traditional mindset of some Muslim scholars is a well-known fact. For example, in a lecture entitled *Lecture in Teaching and Learning*, given in 1882 in Calcutta, five years after publication of *Tafṣīr Āyāt al-Qur'ān al-Ḥakīm*, he states:

> The strangest thing of all is that our ulama [scholars] these days have divided science into two parts. One they call Muslim science, and one European science. Because of this they forbid others to teach some of the useful sciences. They have not understood that science is that noble thing that has no connection with any nation, and is not distinguished by anything but itself. Rather, everything that is known is known by science, and every nation that becomes renowned becomes renowned through science. ...The Islamic religion is the closest of religions to science and knowledge, and there is no incompatibility between science and knowledge and the foundation of the Islamic faith.[12]

Resistance to the idea however could not prevent its further development in modern times and thus the first official call for the adoption of a thematic method in the field of Qur'anic exegesis is assumed to have been made by Amin al-Khuli in the 20th century.[13] Consequently, the first PhD work dedicated to the thematic study of the Qur'an was undertaken by Muhammad

Mahmud Hijazi under the title *Al-Waḥdah al-Mawḍūʿiyyah li al-Qur'ān al-Karīm*, [The Topical Unity of the *Qur'ān al-Karīm*], in 1967 at the university of Al-Azhar. From that point onwards, the thematic approach has gradually gained recognition in the field of Qur'anic exegesis all over the world to such a degree that it has been added to the university curricula in many countries resulting in a great deal of thematic research being conducted on a rich variety of Qur'anic topics.

However, the issue of normative religious pluralism has not been thematically studied in its entirety within the Qur'an despite the substantial significance of the subject in the modern era. And whilst it is true that some elements of Qur'anic normative religious pluralism have been studied, they have only been done so as fragmented units, which cannot present an overall coherent picture of Qur'anic guidance with regards to the ethico-behavioral pattern towards non-Muslims. In other instances, authors have often sought to explore broadly Islamic perspectives on religious pluralism as a socio-political phenomenon through approaches differing from the thematic exegetical method. Of course, all these works have positively contributed to the current research either thematically or methodologically. For example, in *Qur'an, Liberation and Pluralism* (1997), Farid Esack in an attempt to understand the Qur'anic position towards non-Muslims in the socio-political context of the Apartheid regime in South Africa sought to strike a balance between two contradictory approaches: the first, used by some liberal scholars, has simply ignored Qur'anic verses denouncing certain features of non-Muslims, whereas the second, characteristic of some conservative scholars, has resorted to exegesis producing exclusivist meanings with respect to interfaith relations. Thus Esack, despite a frequent disregard for the Qur'anic context – a key exegetical tool for disclosing comprehensively the inner thematic structure of a topic – emphasises the valuable idea that Qur'anic exegesis should work in accordance with both the environmental context of an interpreter and universal human values.

Qur'an, Liberation and Pluralism could be seen as the practical application of conclusions and recommendations drawn by Jane D. McAuliffe in her work *Qur'anic Christians* (1991). McAuliffe regards Qur'anic exegesis (*tafsīr*), as the most important key to the Muslim understanding of Christians. However, discovering that interpretation of a Qur'anic text can be a combination of the interpreter's own mind preoccupied with its own socio-political context, McAuliffe suggests that there is an urgent need for creating new interpretive strategies, a conclusion reached after examining a significant part of *tafsīr* literature. In her opinion Christian self-definition, at both sociological and theological levels, does not match the Muslim understanding of Christians. And, according to McAuliffe, the lack of correspondence between the Qur'anic Christians and the living community of people who call themselves Christians is mainly rooted in Qur'anic interpretations, which have a decisive religious impact on Muslim consciousness. Thus, the importance of McAuliffe's study appears in the idea of re-examining the Qur'anic text, which "remains malleable to the interpretive touch, ready to reveal new insights and intimations, ready to generate renewed understandings of these scriptural sources of Muslim-Christian rapprochement."[14] However, it is obvious from the work, that the idea of a thematic approach to the Qur'an is not expressed as a solution able to rectify the inability of classical *tafsīr* literature to create a reasonable model of interfaith relations. Moreover, the author's suggestion for creating new interpretive strategies in accord with a socio-political context, might cause methodological concerns if understood that the Qur'anic text needs to be enforced until it produces a meaning which matches a socio-political status quo.

David Marshall in *God, Muhammad and the Unbelievers* (1999) also analyses the relationship between Muslims and non-Muslims in the Qur'an. Marshall attempts to prove that it is instinctive to God's sincere worshipper to seek to emulate in attitude and in action the divine mind, the problem being that according to him in the case of Islam this declares war on "unbelievers." Is this the model he feels is set forth for Muslims? His implication is clear. However, the simplistic conclusion drawn in this schematic study is misleading as the linguistic indications of the verses are ignored and no account is taken of the historical circumstances which help determine the motivation behind the fighting. Despite this the author advances a significant approach in using thematic observation of the development as well as the improvement of personalities in the Qur'an through constantly changing circumstances.

Unlike Marshall, who draws a clear distinction between believers and unbelievers on grounds of the classical divide between Muslims and non-Muslims, Izutsu (2002) shows in his *Ethico-Religious Concepts in the Qur'an* that the two terms of belief (*īmān*) and unbelief (*kufr*) have very complex semantic structures. These structures are constituted by a wide range of other words and notions that convey subtle shades of meanings; both positive and negative meanings, which depict belief and unbelief respectively, can be manifested in different groups among humans and on different levels of social behavior. Accordingly, the definition of believers and unbelievers in terms of Izutsu's semantic analysis of these two concepts, is not as simple as it appears in Marshall's work. However, the essential thematic point made by Izutsu is observation of two different levels of relationships: between human beings themselves and between human beings and God. The author makes a distinction between them and names the former horizontal relationships related to social ethics, and the latter vertical relationships related to religious ethics. Although Izutsu himself admits that "Islamic thought, at its Qur'anic stage, makes no real distinction between the religious and the ethical,"[15] the divide of relationships into horizontal and, figuratively speaking, vertical relationships is an important formula for understanding the Qur'anic conception of religious pluralism. This is largely because there are a number of key concepts in the Qur'an which are characteristic in the vertical relationships between human beings and God. Applying these concepts to the horizontal relationships between human beings inevitably leads to tensions between them. One example in this regard is the judgement on people's beliefs which, according to Islam, is left exclusively to God, and no one among humanity must possess such a right including the prophets.

Another important study exploring the Qur'anic worldview towards religious diversity is *The Qur'an and the West* by Kenneth Cragg (2006). Basing his argument on the fact that the Qur'an's ambiguous texts are much more numerous than its definitive ones, Cragg's work suggests that certain passages from the Qur'an can be interpreted in different ways whereby the Qur'anic worldview can be accommodated within universal human values. Applying this theory mainly to twelve chosen Qur'anic passages, the author concludes that the Qur'anic sphere concerning humanity is the broadest as well as the most central to the Qur'anic concept of human relations. Thus, Qur'anic passages that seem contradictory to universal ethical values such as mercy and compassion must be interpreted in the light of that broad human sphere in the Qur'an. At this point it is important to notice how Cragg's thematic approach to Qur'anic study differs from that of Marshall (1999).

Doubtless, these works are only examples of some Qur'anic research on issues related to interfaith relations and many other works exist elaborating on different, fragmented elements of normative religious pluralism. Nevertheless, it seems that Muslim scholarship of the Qur'an has been limited, and to some extent reluctant, to research the subject of religious pluralism. One possible reason for this might be the term itself, which is a relatively recent notion that has emerged in the western context as an ideology for reconciliation between conflicting Christian denominations. This implies that a notion or a theory from outside the Qur'anic content be brought to the Qur'an in order to study the Qur'an according to that theory. Such an inductive process, which seeks to understand the Qur'anic position, or infer certain principles from it, moving from external reality to the Qur'anic texts, however has been controversial among Muslim scholars when it comes to the implementation of the thematic exegetical approach. For instance, in his research on the thematic study of the Qur'an, Abd al-Sattar Said appears to suggest that the topic should emerge from the Qur'an itself and the title of the topic be extracted from the Qur'anic words or their derivatives and not be substituted by or confused with modern terms.[16] In comparison, Baqir al-Sadr vividly emphasises the need for conducting a thematic analysis by starting from reality, from human experience, and then moving towards the Qur'anic text. This inductive movement, according to the author, allows on the one hand, examining the Qur'an on religious, social and scientific matters related to actual and contemporary human life, and on the other bringing human experience to the Qur'an for assessment and rectification in the light of the divine guidance.[17] It would appear to be merely a disagreement of emphasis between scholars where one group underlines the Qur'anic text without rejecting the importance of reality, whereas the other places much significance on reality as a way of better understanding the text. In this case, the right approach would seem to be implementation of a thematic analysis of the Qur'an in a twofold process or movement: "To go from reality, from real issues and problems to the sources, and from the sources back to reality. In other words, both inductive and deductive methods should be employed together."[18] This double movement can be recognised in the work of Muhammad Diraz, *The Moral World of the Qur'an*, where the thematic study of the Qur'anic ethical system appears to be a response to moral concerns emerging as a result of grasping the value of freedom as an unlimited notion in the western context. For this reason the author shows that, according to the Qur'an, morality and the whole ethical system collapse without obligation and responsibility.[19]

In fact, the approach of the twofold movement is supported by the Qur'an, where some verses prescribe observation of the universe with the aim of exploring it and drawing lessons from human experience on an inductive basis, whilst other verses provide guidance from the text itself on a deductive basis. In the same way, some Qur'anic verses were revealed as a response to the real issues and problems which occurred during the time of the revelation, whereas others were revealed independently without occasions for their revelation.[20] Thus, in the case of the former, the process commenced from reality, from human experience, which was the occasion for the revelation (*sabab nuzūl al-āyah*) and ended as revealed divine guidance in the form of text. As for the latter, it initially appeared as divine guidance in the form of text to be utilised in reality. Actually, the harmonious relationship between the universe and the Qur'an is something natural, since the Creator of the universe is the One Who revealed the Qur'an, and hence they are both ways of discovering the truth. The first leads to the truth by discovering the divine unchangeable laws (*al-sunan al-ilāhiyyah*) in the universe through human historic, scientific, empirical and socio-political experience in the civilisational process, whereas the second leads to the truth through the divine revelation.

Therefore, applying a thematic approach to the Qur'an to study normative religious pluralism is an attempt to examine the Qur'an for divine guidance in this matter. Although the term religious pluralism has only recently emerged, its implications and associated problems are ancient, dating back to the dawn of humanity. Similarly, it should be pointed out that although the term religious pluralism does not exist in the Qur'an itself, elements and implications of the term do exist throughout the Qur'anic text. Accordingly the current thematic analysis of the Qur'an is a study of a whole process rather than a single notion, since it explores a variety of ethical issues, structural elements and objectives in respect of normative religious pluralism. For this reason, the analysis focuses on the core of the verses related to different issues of normative religious pluralism and thus presents coherently the universal ethical system of the Qur'an in this regard.

To explore the Qur'anic conception of normative religious pluralism on a thematic basis, it is significantly important to understand first the human intellectual experience of religious pluralism in general. This is done by extracting from the current debate on the matter main aspects, problematic areas, suggested solutions and some historical practices.[21] The first chapter therefore, examines current debate on religious pluralism illustrating the complexity of the notion as well as the fact that many other terms are used interchangeably with it. It reveals the existence of different types of religious pluralism; some related to the issues of religious truth and salvation and thus having eschatological dimensions and ramifications; some linked to the ethico-behavioral model towards religiously different people and accordingly based on terrestrial dimensions expressing significance for the peace-building process; others with a reference to religious sources and hence concentrating on the epistemological consequences of religious pluralism. However, the analysis shows that the relevant type of religious pluralism in the Qur'anic content is normative religious pluralism based on an ethico-behavioral pattern towards religiously different people. The chapter also provides some historical practices of normative religious pluralism in order to underline its important aspects.

The second chapter explores thematically some ethical foundations of normative religious pluralism in the Qur'an. These are freedom of belief, human dignity, integrity, the prohibition of reviling what is sacred to others, and forgiveness. By examining the Qur'an's stance towards these ethical foundations, feasible ground is established on which the legitimacy of normative religious pluralism can be based. The chapter's main argument is that these ethical elements are universally prescribed and penetrate the inward dimensions of human behavior thus allowing neither the adoption of exclusivism nor application of normative religious pluralism on the basis of false diplomacy or any hidden strategies of embrace. In other words, the chapter asserts that the universality of the Qur'anic ethical system goes against the claim of exclusivity with regards to one's ethico-behavioral pattern towards religiously different people.

The third chapter examines the Qur'anic view on the three dialectical and most central elements of normative religious pluralism: commonality, diversity, and constructive conversation. The chapter argues that both commonalities and particularities are presented in the Qur'an as facts of nature. On the other hand, the author shows that the Qur'an advances the constructive conversation as an essential means of communication, which is expected to strike the right balance between religious commonalities and particularities, and thus prevent the process of religious pluralism from alternating between one extreme and another. In fact, the chapter provides the second argument against exclusivism as an approach to interfaith relations.

The fourth chapter explores the main objectives of normative religious pluralism in the Qur'an. It is argued that the Qur'an points to four universal objectives of the human relationship: mutual understanding (*taᶜāruf*), mutual engagement (*taᶜāwun*), mutual contribution (*fastabiqū al-khayrāt*), and mutual support (*tadāfuᶜ*). Presented only in the Madinan chapters, as well as in the textual context of religious diversity, the four objectives can be employed to serve as main objectives of normative religious pluralism and hence can be used to construct a compelling argument against exclusivism.

Chapter five focuses on some cases and circumstances which seemingly contradict the Qur'anic ethical system and normative religious pluralism in particular. More precisely the chapter examines the root cause as well as the scope of two Qur'anic prescriptions: that of fighting against non-Muslims and not taking them as "friends" (*awliyā'*). It is argued that the basis of the imperative to fight is not the belief system of others, but rather their oppression and initiation of war on innocent people. Thus, the scope of the Qur'anic imperative to fight is only in relation to people of war. With regard to examining the Qur'anic prescription of not taking the Jews and Christians as *awliyā'* this is analysed and restricted to two aspects: the first purely theological related to the issue of apostasy; the second pertaining to any involvement in partisanship with the Jews and Christians against Islam. The chapter argues against the exclusivist's claim that the differing belief system of others is reason to fight or isolate them.

The case made in this work is logically constructed based on conclusions drawn from collected Qur'anic verses, as important ethical and structural elements of normative religious pluralism, following a thematic approach to the study of the Qur'an. Otherwise, as Diraz importantly points out, the research would appear "as collections of subjects that are unrelated and without structure,"[22] which actually is the case in many thematic studies of the Qur'an.

The final point worth mentioning is that even though a thematic exegetical approach is employed to derive conceptions from the Qur'an, this cannot work independently of the classical atomistic method which concentrates on linguistic as well as historical analysis of Qur'anic verses, for the two approaches are complementary. For this reason and because the research concerns Qur'anic exegesis, the study focuses mainly on three formative and fundamental classical sources of *tafsīr* literature: al-Ṭabarī's *Jāmiʿ al-Bayān fī Tafsīr al-Qur'ān* which provides a rich narrative corpus essential for the historic analysis of the verses; al-Zamakhsharī's *Al-Kashshāf ʿan Ḥaqā'iq al-Tanzīl* which forms the core of the exegetical literature in terms of the linguistic analysis of the Qur'an; and al-Rāzī's *Mafātīḥ al-Ghayb* which provides theoretical and conceptual explanations of the verses. The three classical sources are frequently compared to three modern sources of *tafsīr* literature: 1) Ibn Ashur's *Tafsīr al-Taḥrīr wa al-Tanwīr* which to some extent can be perceived as being the evolved form of al-Zamakhsharī's *Al-Kashshāf*. 2) Tabatabai's *Al-Mīzān fī Tafsīr al-Qur'ān*, which is very useful in respect of the thematic linkages provided between the verses and also in providing good conceptual conclusions. The work is methodologically similar to al-Rāzī's *Mafātīḥ al-Ghayb*. 3) Al-Sharawi's *Tafsīr* which is one of the latest exegetical works in the modern era offering a deep linguistic as well as analytical analysis of Qur'anic verses. However, since the main aim of the study is to examine the Qur'anic conception of normative religious pluralism, and not the conception of certain *tafsīr* literature, the scope of the exegetical sources is broadened in some cases.

1

What is Religious Pluralism?

Religious pluralism is an ambiguous and complex idea. Because of its complex nature giving rise to many meanings incompatible with Islamic teachings, it has triggered deep debate among scholars, as well as heated controversy, to the extent that the subject does not seem to have drawn much research interest in the fields of Qur'an and Hadith studies. However, complexity is not an excuse for complete rejection. Meaning that the merits of the subject should be elucidated, with the topic deconstructed and precisely analysed to discover that which is relevant to Islam and which can be explored thematically in the light of the Qur'an with the aim of determining divine guidance in relation to it.

In what follows some of the most important perspectives of religious pluralism will be presented and then analysed for the purpose of exploring the differences and commonalities between them. The different types of religious pluralism will then be outlined and classified according to the fundaments from which they emerge. This analysis will help to identify and hence incorporate the relevant type and elements of religious pluralism into the Islamic framework.

[1]
Different Perspectives on Religious Pluralism

It would be fitting to start this section with reference to John Hick, one of the world's most famous theorists on the subject of religious pluralism. In *An Interpretation of Religion: Human Responses to the Transcendent* (1989), Hick studies religious pluralism in its broadest terms, suggesting that no one religion has a monopoly on truth or way of life to salvation. Salvation, according to Hick, is a process of human transformation in this life, from natural self-centeredness to a new orientation centred on the transcendent divine reality, God, ultimately leading to fulfilment beyond this life.

Hick builds his theory of religious pluralism on the main idea that divine reality is beyond the scope of human conceptual systems – therefore, there is a difference between God in Himself and God in human knowledge. Since Hick describes God as "ineffable Real," he states that it is only human cognitive responses to God, formed and developed within different historical and cultural situations, that are known to people but that the reality of God is unknowable. So, given that no human being can know the divine reality in and of itself, it follows in Hick's opinion, that all religions are equally valid, representing only different human perceptions of God. The key problem with Hick's theory is that it appears to disregard divine revelation which has manifested itself throughout human existence, choosing to focus on human cognitive responses to the divine reality instead, as the origin of religions. In this way, it is very likely that the legal as well as the practical aspects of religion are ignored.

In his book *Theology and Religious Pluralism: The Challenge of Other Religions* (1986) Gavin D'Costa studies and severely criticises Hick's thesis of religious pluralism arguing: "There is the very real possibility that this new Copernican development in Hick's pluralist paradigm relies on agnostic presuppositions."[1]

This disagreement surrounding the issue of religious pluralism among Christian theologians emerges largely from two traditionally held Christian axioms. The first states that salvation is through Jesus Christ alone, while the second suggests that God desires the salvation of all humankind. D'Costa tries to hold together these seemingly contradictory but most important Christian axioms in order to strike a balance between dealing with the challenges posed by other religions and preserving the central beliefs of Christianity. Thus, D'Costa concludes that all salvation is salvation through the grace of God in Christ. However, a problem arises. Since the Christian Gospel has not reached all people, through no fault of their own, it means that God must somehow offer grace to all those who have never properly encountered the Gospel. This offer, according to the author, must be made available through the religions of non-Christian which "have a limited validity up to the time of a real encounter with Christianity."[2] The meaning of D'Costa's view of religious encounter are reflected in T.S. Eliot's words:

> We shall not cease from exploration
> And the end of all our exploring
> Will be to arrive where we started
> And know the place for the first time.[3]

Hans Küng (1991) argues this idea of religious pluralism is not a solution for achieving peace among religions, but rather a strategy which he terms "the strategy of embrace."[4] Although appearing to suggest toleration, it actually "proves to be a kind of conquest through embrace, a matter of allowing validity through domestication, integration through a loss of identity. No serious religion which seeks to remain true to itself will allow this to happen to it."[5]

So instead of entering into endless discussions concerning matters of truth and salvation, Küng would appear to be moving the question of religious pluralism away from strongly theological issues, to more ethical levels. In his book *Global Responsibility: In Search of a New World Ethic* he views the moral crisis of the postmodern world as an opportunity to gather all religions together under the banner of mutual responsibility to rescue the world from its crisis. However, since religions cannot supposedly succeed in any mutual project before a level of peace is achieved between them, Küng proposes, with regard to religious pluralism, something he terms an "ecumenical strategy."[6] Ecumenical strategy bases itself on the idea that all major religions have potential spiritual and ethical wealth and that a common religious foundation for human values can be established whereby the universal ethical criterion is human dignity. However, it is of paramount importance that each religion realise through self-criticism that "the boundary between truth and untruth is not a priori identical with the boundary between one's own religion and any others."[7]

There is a close affinity between Küng's ideas of religious pluralism and those of Jonathan Sacks in his work *The Dignity of Difference: How to Avoid the Clash of Civilizations*. Sacks sees human dignity as a central aspect of religious pluralism, positing that this dignity should be sought and respected not only in what is held in common between human beings, but also essentially in what is different between them, because it is from matters of difference that tension between religions mostly arises: "we need not only a theology of commonality but also a theology of difference."[8] Furthermore, this new theology of difference should be shaped on the basis of many moral principles likely to lead to a global covenant: responsibility, contribution, compassion, creativity, co-operation, conservation and conciliation.

Sacks criticises Plato's idea (in *The Republic*) that religious truth is universal, that is, the same for everyone at all times. Rather for him religious truth is particular for every religion and it is this which endears one towards one's religion. Therefore, every person must be allowed to live by the faith which he deems true and religion must abandon its historic goal of imposing a single truth on a plural planet. This notion came into being on the Abrahamic faiths encountering Greek and Roman imperialism, and subsequently developing this into an aspiration to conquer or convert the world.

Yet, religious universalism would appear to be the basis on which Seyyed Hossein Nasr constructs his theory of religious pluralism. Although Nasr's thoughts on inter-faith relations appear throughout his works, it is in *The Heart of Islam: Enduring Values for Humanity* (2002) that he gives particular attention to the subject. Nasr's theory of religious pluralism is based on the oneness of God (*tawḥīd*). Not only is this the main axiom of Islam, but, for Muslims, the main axis of all monotheistic faiths. Knowing that Islam is surrender to the One God, Nasr shows that "Islam means not only the religion revealed through the Qur'an to the Prophet Muhammad, but all authentic religions as such."[9] Thus, the author places emphasis on the idea of Islam being inner paths from human hearts to the oneness of God, a process he calls "the universal nature of the truth" or what Frithjof Schuon who influenced Nasr's ideas terms, the "transcendent unity of religions," or what Reza Shah-Kazemi (2006), in turn influenced by Nasr, defines as "metaphysical universalism."

Although Nasr admits that all religions have their own particularities which must be respected, his theory of a universal truth leads him to the conclusion that the criterion of a believer (*mu'min*), and an infidel (*kāfir*), is faith (*īmān*) in the One God, but not a religion (*dīn*). Therefore, "whoever has faith and accepts the One God, or the Supreme Principle is a believer, or *mu'min*, and whoever does not is an infidel, or a *kāfir*, whatever the nominal and external ethnic and even religious identification of that person might be."[10] Consequently, Nasr's statement implies that the first testification (*shahādah*) of Islam "there is no god but God," *Lā ilāha illā Allāh*, makes a person pronouncing it a believer, whereas the second testification "Muhammad is the Messenger of God," *Muḥammadun rasūl Allāh*, defines that person as a believer belonging to the Islamic faith. Nasr's perception of religious pluralism is also advanced in his book as a solution for today's unprecedented historical condition where the whole spiritual legacy of humanity is fraught with the greatest danger.

However, Legenhausen does not seem to be in favor of Nasr's thesis stating that "to accept only some of the prophets ('a)[11] to the exclusion of others, particularly Muhammad (s),[12] with the excuse that it makes no difference because all religions are ultimately saying the same thing, is to fail to heed the divine call."[13] Clarifying further he states:

> According to Islam, the correct religion ordained by God is that revealed to the last of His chosen prophets, Muhammad (s); this and no other religion is required by Allah of all mankind. ...In the present age, general Islam implies specific Islam, and this must be understood if one is not to fall into error about the position of Islam with respect to religious diversity.[14]

Legenhausen's point of view might appear exclusive, but the fact is that he establishes his theory of religious pluralism on the argument that there exists a plurality of religious pluralisms. For example, he calls that type of religious pluralism which refers to the issue of salvation as soteriological religious pluralism, and similarly defines alethic religious pluralism as one referring to the truth of beliefs. Legenhausen also mentions normative religious pluralism pertaining to how adherents treat the followers of religions other than their own.[15] Thus, the author distinguishes different kinds of religious pluralism, and correspondingly defines the position of Islam towards each of them. For instance, in his opinion and as the above quotation makes clear, Islam is exclusivist in terms of alethic religious pluralism, whereas in respect of soteriological religious pluralism he discerns that salvation is possible for non-Muslims through the grace of God, but not because their faith is correct. With regard to normative religious pluralism, the author suggests that "it is the responsibility of true believers to treat the followers of other traditions with acceptance and respect."[16]

More generally, Mohammad Amarah in *al-Islām wa al-Taʿaddudiyyah* [Islam and Pluralism] (1997), comes to the conclusion that pluralism according to Islam is not only the idea of how to tolerate others but is, at first stage, a divine law which functions in the universe in accordance with human nature. Moreover, the author argues that there would not be any meaning to universality, one of the main peculiarities of Islam, without pluralism. Amarah defines pluralism in the Islamic view as justly balanced pluralism, since it avoids all extremes on either side. Thus, the Qur'anic idea of pluralism establishes a right balance between commonalities and the protection of diversity and its peculiarities. This has an important implication when it comes to religious commitment, where it is feared that religious pluralism could lead to a religious melting pot. The author furthers his argument to describe pluralism as a system consisting of two major elements: common ground and diversity based on peculiarities. Therefore, there is no pluralism without common ground between different components, as there is no pluralism without diversity. This theory suggests that to build firm common ground between differences requires a high degree of respect for their peculiarities. Moreover, according to Amarah, Islam regards pluralism as a form of competition to discover the positive sides of human life as well as in the doing of righteous deeds. This conception of pluralism is likely to result in the improvement and development of society.

In another work entitled, *Taʿaddudiyyah al-Ru'yah al-Islāmiyyah wa al-Taḥaddiyāt al-Gharbiyyah* [Pluralism – Islamic View and Western Challenges] (1997), Mohammad Amarah in addition claims that while in the Islamic view pluralism is regarded as a divine law and thus as a value system, Western governments tend to use it as a political means of gaining influence and power in the Islamic world. The author provides examples of how some Western countries have been using at length the idea of pluralism through ethnic minorities in the Middle East, in order to achieve Western political interests. Such a claim seems to underline the importance of examining the ethical parameters of religious pluralism.

In contrast, Hassan Hanafi (1977) challenges these theories of religious pluralism by suggesting that religions should be examined through a hermeneutical process which includes three major sections: criticism, interpretation and realisation. The first concerns historical criticism of the text, to determine the authenticity of Scripture in history. The second defines the meaning of the text and mainly addresses the language and historical circumstances in which the text originated. The third concerns realisation of the meaning of the text in human life, which is the final goal of the Divine Word. Through this hermeneutical process, Hanafi regards the point of religious dialogue to be, in this case, defined as a scientific dialogue, not mere "clerical diplomacy and brotherly hypocrisy."[17]

Religious dialogue, which underpins religious pluralism, is presented in Hanafi's work through the personality of Abraham in the Qur'an. The Qur'anic Abraham represents objectivity and honesty in seeking the truth. Thus, the pattern of Abraham in this respect corresponds to the hermeneutical process advanced by Hanafi. On the contrary, after analysing the Qur'anic concept of land (*arḍ*), the author states that there exist political targets disguised as religious interpretation that disrupt religious dialogue. Hanafi points as an example to Zionism as a major obstacle to interfaith relations. Hanafi's work spreads light on the importance of namely "constructive dialogue," which plays a pivotal role in the process of religious pluralism. Moreover, it provides key conceptions helping to understand some controversial notions in the Qur'an such as oppression (*ẓulm*), unbelief (*kufr*), and jihad. As a whole, Hanafi's work and the suggested hermeneutical process in particular move the discussion of religious pluralism to a more epistemological aspect.

The aforementioned discussion clearly reveals the existence of a multiplicity of theories with regard to religious pluralism. However, apart from Legenhausen, who distinguishes between the different types and demonstrates awareness of the fact that there exists a plurality of religious pluralisms, the rest of the scholars explain religious pluralism on a different basis. Some of the theorists like Hick, D'Costa and Nasr tend to discuss religious pluralism on a pure theological basis, though D'Costa and Nasr's views differ significantly from Hick's, since for them religion is not a social product, as Hick's theory implies, but divine revelation through which God describes Himself to His prophets and thus becomes no longer the "ineffable Real." Other scholars such as Küng, Saks and Amarah, emphasise religious pluralism as an ethical process, and where Küng stresses the importance of the moral and spiritual commonalities, Saks calls for the theology of differences and particularities. For Amarah, the correct approach is to strike a right balance between commonalities and particularities because only in this way can the process of pluralism be achieved. Although, religious pluralism appears to some degree as an ethical issue in Hanafi's theory, its main focus is on the epistemological perception of religious pluralism, where the recognition of religious sources is gained through objective justification of beliefs. Furthermore, Hanafi points to the existence of hidden political agendas in the process of interfaith relations, adding a political meaning to the idea of religious pluralism. In this respect, Amarah also states that religious pluralism or the idea of pluralism in general sometimes is perceived by certain parties as a tool for gaining socio-political power and influence among minorities. It is worth mentioning here that even the religious pluralism advocated by Hick has been criticised on the basis that it emerges from ideological liberalism and thus serves the interests of political liberalism by providing a theological basis for it.[18] D'Costa's theory also contains the idea of religious pluralism being used a tool or strategy for converting people to one's own faith.

Thus we are left with a number of different perspectives coming under the conceptual scope of religious pluralism. These range from the purely theological to the outright political. And between the two extremes is an ethical and epistemological value system, which can even be used as a strategy for religious conversion. So, religious pluralism can be envisioned either as a value system or merely a tool for achieving disguised purposes. Moreover, different types of religious pluralism give rise to different problematic areas which cannot be approached identically. Unless we are able to distinguish between the different types of, and approaches to, religious pluralism, a misleading conception of interfaith relations will result. To avoid this we need to trace the evolution of certain etymological and conceptual aspects underpinning religious pluralism in a little more detail to crystallise the framework of this study.

An Etymological Analysis of the Words "Religion" and "Pluralism"

An etymological analysis of the words "religion" and "pluralism" could help provide some understanding of the multiple concepts of religious pluralism by casting light on the relationship between each of the differently formulated concepts of religious pluralism and the etymologically different definitions of the words "religion" and "pluralism."

The word "religion" in the western tradition appears to have eight main etymological meanings:[19]

1. State of life bound by monastic vows, from Anglo-French *religiun.*
2. Conduct indicating a belief in a divine power, from Anglo-French *religiun.*
3. Religious community, from Old French *religion.*
4. Respect for *what* is sacred, reverence for the gods, from Latin *religionem.*

5. Monastic life, from Late Latin *relegare* to "go through again, read again," from *re-* "again" plus *legere* "read."
6. To bind fast or a bond between humans and gods, from Latin *religare*.
7. Particular system of faith, from *religiens* "careful," the opposite of *negligens*, "negligence."
8. Recognition of, obedience to and worship of a higher, unseen power.

These eight definitions differ in terms of their level of religious exclusivism and inclusivism, respectively. However, all are similar in terms of restricting the meaning of religion to a mere vertical relationship between humans and God or more inclusively gods. Even in the case of the third definition, namely "religious community," the horizontal relationship does not extend beyond the circle of religious members, which appears here as a synonym of religious life in monasteries. Of course, the scope of religion in the western tradition has broadened in modern times. For instance, in his work *Religion the Basics*, Nye concludes that:

> Religion is something that humans do. Religion is an ambiguous term, with a range of meanings and references. In particular, it refers both to specific religious traditions, and also to an aspect of human behaviour which is often assumed to be universal. Religion is a part of everyday life; it is an aspect of culture.[20]

Nye's mention of religion as an aspect of human behaviour broadens the scope of religion by focusing not only on the pure theological aspect of it but on its ethical dimensions as well.

What does religion mean in Islam however? After a thorough etymological analysis of the word *dīn* (religion) in *Islam and Secularism*, al-Attas concludes that in addition to the sincere and total submission to God's will, *dīn* also means "the natural tendency of man to form societies and obey laws and seek just government."[21] It is clear from al-Attas' definition of *dīn*, that it concerns different kinds of relationship. The first is to some extent identical to the western definition of religion, meaning the relationship between man and God. However, the second concerns humanity's horizontal relationships, in a sense related to the whole process of building societies and governing them justly. Although, there would seem to be no further room for expansion of the scope of religion, its definition has been further developed to mean the very essence and core of civilisation. In this respect, al-Fārūqī argues that:

> Religion is the essence and core of civilisation, in that it is the foundation of all decisions and actions, the ultimate explanation of civilisation with all its inventions and artefacts, its social, political, and economic systems, and its past and future promise in history. Religion constitutes the spirit of which the facets of civilisation are the concrete manifestations.[22]

According to this definition, there is no separation between religion and any other aspect of civilisation, to the extent that even one's behaviour towards the environment is regarded as a religion. In other words, it would appear that religion in the Islamic context simply means making a life, where the only limit is intention.

In sum an etymological analysis of the word "religion" reveals, at least theoretically, that a western or more precisely Christian traditional definition of the term, is much more limited than the Islamic one; while the former tends to considerably emphasise the theological aspect of religion related more often to the issue of religious truth, its justification, and religious salvation, the latter underlines religion as an engine of the civilisational process. The term "pluralism," has the following etymological meanings:[23]

1. A term in church administration, from plural, which comes from Old French *pluriel* meaning "more than one" or from Latin *pluralis* meaning "belonging to more than one."

2. A term in philosophy for a theory which recognises more than one ultimate principle.
3. A term in political science for a theory which opposes monolithic state power.
4. Toleration of diversity within a society or state.

These four etymological definitions of the word "pluralism" show the dynamic evolution of the concept during the 19th and 20th centuries. Emerging as a mere administrative term indicating the responsibility of a single person for more than one office in a church, pluralism was later developed further to mean recognition of the condition of multiplicity, as obvious from the second definition. Moreover, according to the third and fourth definitions, pluralism did not remain a static concept in terms of recognition of diversity only, but an ideal opposing ideas of domination and monopoly, as well as promoting an ethical approach toward toleration of difference.

In recent years, pluralism has further developed to mean "the construction of communitarian consensus starting from a situation of extreme particularism."[24] This recent definition adds a new significant element which can be defined as active engagement in the process of pluralism. Such engagement aims to reach, through constructive dialogue, a possible form of communal consensus without violating particularities, which seems to be the most important issue concerning debate on pluralism. Thus, in the light of this definition, pluralistic consensus is not constructed on the basis of commonalities only, but more importantly on representing a balance between commonalities and particularities.

To etymologically define the meaning of pluralism, it is also relevant to state what pluralism is not. Pluralism is neither exclusivism nor monopoly, nor domination or monolithic power. It is an orientation towards multiplicity, the recognition of diversity, the moral acceptance of, and respect for, difference, the search for consensus without violating particularities. In this way, following the dynamic nature of both terms, "religion" and "pluralism," which have evolved from entirely limited notions to universal concepts, it would appear that the concept of religious pluralism relates mostly to both ultimate principles as well as ethical practices and thus should be perceived and implemented as a value system rather than as an instrument for achieving political domination or religious exclusivism.

We can now clearly distinguish two basic, conceptual levels of religious pluralism: theological and ethical. The former pertains to ultimate theological principles such as religious truth and salvation, whereas the latter is linked to ethical practices. The conceptual classification of religious pluralism into theological and ethical levels, however, needs to be further expanded in order to explore a number of concepts used often interchangeably with the notion of religious pluralism and thus to identify more precisely the relevant type and elements of religious pluralism to Islam.

Religious Pluralism with Special Reference to the Concept of Religious Truth and Salvation

The limited definition of religion outlined earlier as entirely related to its theological aspect, leads to a discussion of religious pluralism mainly on the basis of religious truth and salvation, for in the western context it has been in this particular sphere that modern religious pluralism emerged. As Legenhausen remarks, "modern religious pluralism arose specifically in reaction to widespread Christian views about salvation."[25] Yet religious pluralism discussed in this respect poses a serious challenge for especially monotheistic faiths because religious truth and salvation are highly sensitive theological matters and focus of such discussion is largely on the eschatological dimensions and ramifications of religious pluralism. Different concepts used interchangeably with religious pluralism have been developed within its theological sphere. The most important of these are outlined below.

Religious Inclusivism

Religious inclusivism asserts that "one's own group possesses the truth while, other religious groups contain parts of the truth and thus they are less likely to be saved."[26] Although the possibility of salvation for other faiths is not entirely rejected here, the possession of the whole truth is nevertheless limited to one religion only. It is worth mentioning the theory of *Anonymous Christians* at this point from whence the concept of religious inclusivism has emerged. This theory, developed by Karl Rahner in his voluminous work *Theological Investigations* (1966), and serving as the main principle of inclusivism in the Catholic tradition, claims that it is possible for non-Christians to attain salvation, but through Christ and not through their own religions, since despite their rejection of Christianity, they might be committed in reality to those values which are central to the Christian revelation. Such inclusivism is used interchangeably with pluralism in Rahner's writings. He states:

> Pluralism is meant here as a fact which ought to be thought about and one which, without denying that – in part at least – it should not exist at all, should be incorporated once more from a more elevated viewpoint into the totality and unity of the Christian understanding of human existence.[27]

As far as the Christian understanding of human existence is concerned, according to Rahner, it is to understand that non-Christians are actually anonymous Christians. Rahner writes:

> It is nevertheless absolutely permissible for the Christian himself to interpret this non-Christianity as Christianity of an anonymous kind which he does always still go out to meet as a missionary, seeing it as a world which is to be brought to the explicit consciousness of what already belongs to it as a divine offer or already pertains to it also over and above this as a divine gift of grace accepted unreflectedly and implicitly.

The theory of *Anonymous Christians* reflects to a large degree the Islamic point of view with regard to religious truth and salvation. Although Islam recognises the fact that Judaism and Christianity contain parts of religious truth, being earlier revelations, it maintains that the correctness of religious truth cannot be reached with rejection of Muhammad, the last of God's prophets. Consequently, to gain salvation without accepting the whole prophetic circle is something that could happen only through God's grace. As for the element of "anonymity" in Rahner's theory, it very much corresponds to the Islamic concept of *fiṭrah*, human nature, where every human being is regarded has having been born in a state of Islam. Therefore, the point at which different religions converge and diverge, in the case of religious inclusivism, is religious mission or *daʿwah*, the call to Islam. For this reason, the view of inclusivists does not seem to entirely fit the etymological definition of pluralism, since according to them religious truth is not multiple, thus religious domination is seen as a purpose and religious pluralism as an instrument for achieving that purpose.

Religious Relativism

The term religious relativism is often used interchangeably with religious pluralism. On the philosophical level, relativism means that "reality exists only in relation to or as an object of the thinking subject."[28] Consequently, religious relativism maintains that:

> One religion can be true for one person or culture but not for another. No religion, therefore, is universally or exclusively true. Religious beliefs are simply an accident of birth: If a person grows up in America, chances are good that he might become a Christian; if in India, that he will be a Hindu; if in Saudi Arabia, that he will be a Muslim. If what one believes is the product of historical happenstance, the argument goes that no single religious belief can be universally or objectively true.[29]

This perception of inter-religious relations, or religious relativism, is what John Hick actually calls religious pluralism. As mentioned earlier, he defines religious pluralism as "the view that the transformation of human existence from self-centeredness to Reality-centeredness is taking place in different ways within the context of all the great religious traditions."[30] The Relativists' conception of religious pluralism is based on the assumption that it is only human cognitive responses to God, formed and developed within different historical and cultural situations, that are known to people, but that the reality of God is unknowable. The assumption seems to disregard divine revelation however, throughout human history, as a true manifestation, and thus ignores the legal as well as the practical aspects of different religions.

Religious Syncretism

The *Oxford English Dictionary* first affirms the word syncretism in 1615. It is derived from modern Latin *syncr tismus*, meaning the joining, or agreement, of two enemies against a third person.[31] Syncretism also refers to "the system or principles of a school founded in the 17th century by George Calixtus, who aimed at harmonising the sects of Protestants and ultimately all Christian bodies."[32]

As far as religious syncretism is concerned, it is defined as:

> The developmental process of historical growth within a religion by accretion and coalescence of different and often conflicting forms of belief and practice; as understood by Christian theology, the religious attitude which holds that there is no unique revelation in history, that there are many different ways to reach the divine reality, that all formulations of religious truth or experience are inadequate expression of that truth, and that it is necessary to harmonize all religious ideas and experiences so as to create one universal religion for mankind.[33]

It would appear that religious syncretism presents itself as having evolved beyond religious relativism, since the latter separates different claims of truth on the basis of birth place and cultural identity, whereas the former aims to create one belief system through a blending of the different claims. Obviously, religious syncretism is unlikely to meet the requirements of religious pluralism, where the balance between religious commonalities and religious particularities is regarded by religiously committed people as the core issue in the process of religious pluralism.

Metaphysical Universalism

Another suggested form of religious pluralism is metaphysical universalism which attempts to strike a right balance between relativism and exclusivism. In metaphysical universalism there is a clear distinction between faith (*īmān*) and religion (*dīn*). Faith or *īmān*, represents the inner paths from human hearts to the Oneness of God, whereas religion or *dīn*, represents particular religious affiliations and peculiarities.[34] Therefore, religious truth and salvation, according to this theory, are related to faith, *īmān*, not to religion, *dīn*. This in turn means that "whoever has faith and accepts the One God or the Supreme Principle is a believer (*mu'min*), and whoever does not is an infidel (*kāfir*), whatever the nominal and external ethnic and even religious identification of that person might be."[35]

Metaphysical universalism is focused on the philosophical and mystical dimensions of the revelation and thus heavily reliant on esoteric approaches to interpretation. However, separating between *īmān* and *dīn* for the sake of creating a pluralistic platform accommodating other religions in terms of religious truth and salvation, seems an untenable exercise, since for both general and particular Islam, acceptance and belief in all God's prophets is an unconditional imperative. Furthermore, Nasr's separation theory claims that it is faith (*īmān*) in the Oneness of God that defines a person as a believer, which reasoning does not take into account the fact that one of the six main pillars of faith (*īmān*) in Islam is not religion (*dīn*), but a belief in all prophets.[36]

In sum all foregoing theological concepts of religious pluralism, whose roots lie in a particular Christian religious context, seem incompatible with Islam for reasons discussed throughout this section. Thus, religious pluralism applied as full and equal engagement on a purely theological level with reference to religious truth and salvation seems to be out of the question due to all the great religions of the world having developed and adopted their specific doctrines concerning religious truth and salvation. To clarify this assertion, it is worth quoting the statement of Pope Leo XIII in his *Immortale Dei* in which he states:

> To hold, therefore, that there is no difference in matters of religion between forms that are unlike each other, and even contrary to each other, most clearly leads in the end to the rejection of all religion in both theory and practice. And this is the same thing as atheism; however it may differ from it in name.[37]

However, two elements emphasised by the theories can be incorporated into the Islamic framework of religious pluralism. These are religious commonalities and religious particularities. On the one hand, they seem to form the backbone of religious pluralism, and on the other, to pose a great challenge to religions in terms of establishing a right balance between these dichotomic elements.

Religious Pluralism with Special Reference to the Universal Code of Ethics

As concluded in the previous section, there is a little room in Islam for accommodating religious pluralism in the eschatological sphere with regards to religious truth and salvation. This section focuses on the ethical level of religious pluralism. Varieties of different theories have emerged as a result of the debates surrounding the issue of religious pluralism on the basis of the universal code of ethics. Yet, all these different theories can be summarised into three main conceptions interchangeably used with religious pluralism. These are: ecumenism, religious humanism and religious toleration.

Ecumenism

According to the *World Christian Encyclopedia*, the ecumenical movement is "the movement to bring together all denominations and Christian bodies for fellowship, consultation, joint action, and eventually organic union. Ecumenism is, therefore, ecumenical principles and practices as exemplified in the ecumenical movement."[38] Initially, ecumenism was introduced as an idea to unite Christian denominations. However, it has been developed, apparently under the pressure of the challenges of the modern world, to mean cooperation between different religions. Ecumenism in this broad sense is often referred as religious pluralism.

Ecumenism's attempt to bring together the different religions relies on the idea that all major religions have potential spiritual and ethical wealth which lays common religious foundations for human values, where the universal ethical criterion is human dignity. And ecumenism aims by this strategy aims to rescue humanity from the moral crisis of the postmodern world and achieve a global peace.[39]

Ecumenical theory seems to contain a number of important elements, i.e. an ethico-spiritual common ground between faiths, human dignity, and religious cooperation, and also all these pluralistic elements can be incorporated into the study of the Qur'anic conception of religious pluralism. The ethico-spiritual common ground aspect is more akin to being considered an essential component of the structure of religious pluralism, that is commonality, rather than as its foundation. This is largely due to the fact that human dignity should be sought and respected not only in what is common between human beings, but also and most importantly in what is different between them, since the tension between religions mostly arises from differences.

Religious Humanism

Religious humanism is defined by the *World Christian Encyclopedia* as "a modern North American movement composed chiefly of non-theistic humanist churches and dedicated to achieving the ethical goals of religion without beliefs and rites resting upon supernaturalism; sometimes called Christian humanism."[40] By emphasising the importance of universal human values, religious humanism makes an attempt to create a good and peaceful life on both a personal and social level in the diverse world. In this respect it is associated with religious pluralism.

The focus on universal human values has significant implications for this study in terms of considering these values as one of the contexts in which the methodology of Qur'anic exegesis should rest upon. Moreover, core ethical values such as freedom of belief, integrity and forgiveness, are to be incorporated into the exploration of the Qur'anic conception of religious pluralism. However, since religious humanism defines a religion as a social product created by humans with the aim of contributing to people's well-being, it seems to be more closely allied to the idea of secularism rather than religious pluralism. It is important to mention here that although religious humanism emerged initially from a Christian environment, it began to adopt many different forms, including what is called Islamic humanism, which emphasises universal human values, but tends to disregard religious doctrines.

Religious Toleration

Religious toleration means "the attitude of tolerance and acceptance, on the part of a state or a majority church, towards religious minorities."[41] It is obvious that the definition is orientated towards religious minorities, which makes the notion of religious toleration merely one of meaning the absence of religious persecution. However by allowing and accepting religious diversity, religious toleration can lead to either a diverse society or mere religious ghettoes. Nevertheless, the idea of toleration seems inadequate to bridge effectively the divide between different religious communities and engage them in the process of interfaith dialogue. In fact, from the perspective of mutual interaction in society, religious pluralism differs significantly from religious toleration. In this respect, Diana Eck concludes that:

> Pluralism is not just tolerance, but *the active seeking of understanding across lines of difference*. Tolerance is a necessary public virtue, but it does not require Christians and Muslims, Hindus, Jews, and ardent secularists to know anything about one another. Tolerance is too thin a foundation for a world of religious difference and proximity. It does nothing to remove our ignorance of one another, and leaves in place the stereotype, the half-truth, the fears that underlie old patterns of division and violence. In the world in which we live today, our ignorance of one another will be increasingly costly.[42]

Eck's critique of religious toleration raises an important question about the main objectives of religious pluralism. The purpose of interfaith relations should not be limited only to allowance for the existence of diversity, but should be extended to encompass the achievement of mutual understanding, engagement, contribution, and support among different religions. Thus the obvious shortcomings of religious toleration to create common as well as practical goals and objectives for interfaith relations makes it necessary for this study to explore the Qur'anic objectives of religious pluralism.

To summarise, unlike an exclusively eschatological based religious pluralism whose reference point is truth and salvation, an ethically based religious pluralism in contrast mainly focuses on the terrestrial dimensions and ramifications of interfaith relations. Thus, the scope as well as the significance of this latter kind of pluralism, directly related to the peacebuilding process, seems to be much greater than the former. It also appears that religious pluralism based on a universal code of ethics has a better chance of realisation on a much larger societal scale. However, as discussed, all three concepts, used interchangeably with religious pluralism in terms of an ethical code, have their limits. Ecumenism does not provide a solution for differences, religious humanism disregards religion as a divine phenomenon, and religious toleration is reluctant to encourage any mutual engagement for the sake of better interfaith understanding as well as effectiveness.

[2]
The Islamic Framework of Religious Pluralism

What this chapter has shown is that there exists a plurality of religious pluralisms. And the fact that plurality exists is reason for studying the Qur'anic conception of religious pluralism for otherwise we are in danger of being left with extremes of religious exclusivism or religious relativism, neither of which address the issue correctly. Even though many types of religious pluralism can be classified, only three appear to be fundamental. The first type pertains to the issue of religious truth. This type is often referred to as alethic religious pluralism, from the Greek word *alétheia* truth. The second type concerns the question of religious salvation and hence is referred to as soteriological religious pluralism, from the Greek word *sótéria* salvation. Finally, the third type is associated with how to treat people of different faiths to one's own, and thus provides an ethico-behavioural pattern of interfaith communication. This type of religious pluralism is called normative religious pluralism.[43] The relevance of the three types of religious pluralism to Islam will be examined in what follows, which in turn will determine the scope of the research on the Qur'anic conception of religious pluralism.

Alethic Religious Pluralism and Islam

Alethic religious pluralism concerns religious truth. More specifically, it aims at recognising that all religions equally possess the truth. Although religious relativism allows ample room to accommodate this type of religious pluralism, in Islam the conflict is immediately apparent. A universal divine message has been revealed to mankind and Muslims will not compromise on this.

So, alethic religious pluralism is not recognised by Islam. This is because "according to Islam, the correct religion ordained by God is that revealed to the last of His chosen prophets, Muhammad (s); this and no other religion is required by Allah of all mankind. In this sense, Islam is exclusivist."[44] Thus, the prescription of accepting the Prophet Muhammad alongside the rest of God's prophets exists in the Qur'an as a necessary condition for the correctness of faith and religion together. For this reason, belief in God and the Prophet Muhammad is simultaneously a pillar of faith as well as a pillar of religion. There are dozens of Qur'anic verses, whose meaning is clear, requiring belief in the last of God's prophets, Muhammad:

> O ye who believe! Believe in Allah and His Messenger, and the scripture which He hath sent to His Messenger and the scripture which He sent to those before (him). Any who denieth Allah, His angels, His Books, His Messengers, and the Day of Judgment, hath gone far, far astray. (Qur'an *al-Nisā'* 4: 136)[45]

The imperative in this verse is directed towards all people claiming to be believers: "O ye who believe! Believe in Allah and His Messenger." In another verse, this imperative extends further to cover not only those claiming a belief, but the whole of humanity:

> Say: "O men! I am sent unto you all, as the Messenger of Allah, to Whom belongeth the dominion of the heavens and the earth: there is no god but He: it is He that giveth both life and death. So believe in Allah and His Messenger, the unlettered Prophet, who believeth in Allah and His words: follow him that (so) ye may be guided." (Qur'an *al-Aʿrāf* 7: 158)

The description of the Prophet in the verse as unlettered is to leave no room for doubt that the prophet being referred to is Muhammad and not any other. Moreover, the Qur'an explicitly stipulates that any attempt aiming to transgress the integrity of the prophetic circle leads undoubtedly to unbelief:

> Those who deny Allah and His Messengers, and (those who) wish to separate Allah from His Messengers, saying: "We believe in some but reject others": And (those who) wish to take a course midway, – They are in truth (equally) unbelievers; and we have prepared for unbelievers a humiliating punishment. (Qur'an *al-Nisā'* 4:150-151)

Therefore, "to accept only some of the prophets ('a) to the exclusion of others, particularly Muhammad (s), with the excuse that it makes no difference because all the religions are ultimately saying the same thing, is to fail to heed the divine call."[46]

According to Islam religious truth cannot be reached without the acceptance of Muhammad as God's final messenger. This Qur'anic doctrine is affirmed by authentic *aḥādīth*. For example Imam Muslim narrates the following in his authentic collection of Hadith:

> It is narrated on the authority of Abū Hurayrah that the Messenger of Allah (SAW) said: "By Him in Whose hand is the life of Muhammad, he [/she, i.e. anyone] who amongst the community of Jews or Christians hears about me, but does not affirm his belief in that with which I have been sent and dies in this state (of disbelief), he shall be but one of the denizens of Hell-Fire."[47]

Although al-Nawawī explains that it is necessary for all people from the time of Prophet Muhammad onwards to accept his prophethood, he qualifies this by stating that those who have not heard about him and his message, and remain true to their religion based on the Oneness of God, will be forgiven.[48] Whilst al-Nawawī's explanation opens to a certain degree the possibility of a salvation in which the prophethood of Muhammad is not accepted, it firmly closes the door to debating religious truth where his prophethood is rejected.

In fact, where the Qur'an praises certain People of the Book in relation to religious truth, not the normative aspect of life, this is due to their having accepted the Oneness of God, His final messenger Muhammad, and the Qur'an. For instance:

> Not all of them are alike: Of the People of the Book are a portion that stand (for the right); they rehearse the Signs of Allah all night long, and they prostrate themselves in adoration. They believe in Allah and the Last Day; they enjoin what is right, and forbid what is wrong; and they hasten (in emulation) in (all) good works: They are in the ranks of the righteous. (Qur'an *Āl ʿImrān* 3:113-114)

The occasion of revelation of these two verses explicitly shows that the People of the Book praised by the verses were those who had accepted the Prophet Muhammad as the final of God's messengers together with the Qur'an as the last revelation. In this regard, al-Ṭabarānī narrates the following:

> We were told by Muḥammad ibn ʿAbdullāh, who said: we were told by Abū Kurayb, who said: we were told by Yūnus ibn Bakīr, who narrated from Muḥammad ibn Isḥāq, who said: I was told by Muḥammad ibn Abū Muḥammad, the servant, *mawlā*, of Zayd ibn Thābit, who said: I was told by Saʿīd ibn Jubayr or ʿIkrimah, who narrated from Ibn ʿAbbās, may God bless him and his father, who said: when ʿAbdullāh ibn Salām, Thaʿlabah ibn Suʿayyah, Asad ibn ʿUbayd, and other Jews embraced Islam and believed in it, some of the Jewish rabbis, who were people of unbelief, said: "those who believed in Muhammad and followed him are the worst of our people, because if they were among our prominent people, they would never have abandoned the religion of their fathers." At that point, in relation to their statement, Allah Almighty revealed [the verse] "Not all of them are alike" until "[They are in the ranks] of the righteous" (3:113-114).[49]

With regard to the authenticity of al-Ṭabarānī's narration, al-Ḥāfiẓ al-Haythamī in his *Majmaʿ al-Zawā'id* concludes that "all the transmitters [in the foregoing chain of transmission] are trustworthy, *thiqāt*."[50]

Therefore, the occasion of the revelation clarifies that the belief in God and the hereafter, which was adopted by those among the People of the Book praised in the verses, included the acceptance of Muhammad as the final prophet, and the Qur'an as the last revelation. More clearly verse 199 of the same surah (*Āl ʿImrān)* states:

> And there are, certainly, among the People of the Book, those who believe in Allah, in the revelation to you, and in the revelation to them, bowing in humility to Allah. They will not sell the Signs of Allah for a miserable gain! For them is a reward with their Lord, and Allah is swift in account. (Qur'an *Āl ʿImrān* 3:199)

This Qur'anic description is clear in praising those among the People of the Book who in addition to belief in what had been sent to them, also believed in the revelation sent to Prophet Muhammad.

Another Qur'anic verse also affirms that those among the People of the Book who are "well-grounded in knowledge," and "the believers", also believe in what had been sent to the Prophet Muhammad:

> But those among them [the People of the Book] who are well-grounded in knowledge, and the believers, believe in what hath been revealed to thee [Muhammad] and what was revealed before thee: and (especially) those who establish regular prayer and practise regular charity and believe in Allah and in the Last Day: to them shall We soon give a great reward. (Qur'an *al-Nisā'* 4:162)

Similarly the Qur'an praises a group of the People of the Book for their profound recognition of the religious truth revealed to the Prophet Muhammad:

> And when they [some of the People of the Book] listen to the revelation received by the Messenger, thou wilt see their eyes overflowing with tears, for they recognise the truth: they pray: "Our Lord! We believe; write us down among the witnesses. "What cause can we have not to believe in Allah and the truth which has come to us, seeing that we long for our Lord

> to admit us to the company of the righteous?" (Qur'an *al-Mā'idah* 5:83-84)

In sum all Qur'anic praises referring to the truth of the beliefs held by the People of the Book are based on the fact that the people being praised are those who had accepted the Prophet Muhammad and believed in his message. At this point it should be emphasised that for both general and specific Islam a necessary condition for the correctness of faith and hence for reaching religious truth is the acceptance of all of God's prophets, including the Prophet Muhammad:

> Behold! Allah took the covenant of the prophets, saying: "I give you a Book and Wisdom; then comes to you a Messenger, confirming what is with you; do you believe in him and render him help." Allah said: "Do ye agree, and take this my Covenant as binding on you?" They said: "We agree." He said: "Then bear witness, and I am with you among the witnesses." If any turn back after this, they are perverted transgressors. (Qur'an *Āl ʿImrān* 3:81-82)

In the textual context of the above covenant requiring a belief in all God's prophets, the following Qur'anic verse exists:

> If anyone desires a religion other than Islam (submission to Allah), never will it be accepted of him; and in the Hereafter he will be in the ranks of those who have lost (all spiritual good). (*Āl ʿImrān* 3:85)

The existence of verse 85 in the textual context prohibiting separation between God's prophets in terms of belief in and acceptance of them all, leads to the conclusion that following the arrival of Muhammad, the requirement of belief in general Islam, revealed to all God's prophets before Muhammad, became requirement of belief in specific Islam. In this sense, religious truth had taken its final form in terms of a specific Islam revealed for every time and place. Of course, this does not mean that

God's revelations prior to Muhammad were incorrect, but rather that they were revealed for the guidance and salvation of particular peoples and places. In addition, within the message of specific Islam is incorporated whatever is needed from previous revelations, following the era after the Prophet Muhammad to the end of time.[51]

Therefore, Islam does not recognise alethic religious pluralism according to which all religions possess equally religious truth. Failure to accept the integrity of God's prophets and their revelations contradicts, in the Muslim view, religious truth. And there is consensus on this position among Muslim theologians, exegetes, and jurists at both the classical and modern levels. For this reason, there is no room for examining Qur'anic content on the basis of alethic religious pluralism.

Soteriological Religious Pluralism and Islam

Soteriological religious pluralism pertains to the question of religious salvation in the hereafter. According to representatives of this kind of pluralism as different religions equally guide their adherents to salvation all religious people will be saved in the hereafter. Although in the case of Islam, religious salvation in the main is interdependently related to religious truth requiring belief in the Prophet Muhammad, there seems to be a certain degree of possibility for salvation for cases not truly corresponding to religious truth, but saved on the basis of God's will:

> Allah forgiveth not (the sin of) joining other gods with Him; but He forgiveth whom He pleaseth other sins than this: one who joins other gods with Allah, Hath strayed far, far away (from the right). (Qur'an *al-Nisā'* 4:116)

The verse points out that God will never forgive anyone associating other gods with Him, but if He so wills, forgive any other sins. Thus, the question of salvation for those remaining true to belief in the Oneness of God, but who for various reasons fail to acknowledge the Prophet Muhammad, is left to God's will. Although the verse in isolation does not mention belief in the Prophet as a necessary condition for salvation, read in conjunction with other verses, as the following argument will make clear, acceptance of his prophethood becomes unequivocal. At this point, it should be noticed that this verse does not represent a principle on the basis of which definitive statements concerning salvation can be made.[52] All that the verse conveys is that the outcome for those who do not associate other gods with God but who do commit other sins, is left to God's will in the hereafter.

The Qur'an contains two verses which would seem to suggest possible salvation for those who have faith in God as a Qur'anic principle but who do not accept the prophecy of Muhammad:

> Those who believe (in the Qur'an), and those who follow the Jewish (scriptures), and the Christians and the Sabians, – any who believe in Allah and the Last Day, and work righteousness, shall have their reward with their Lord; on them shall be no fear, nor shall they grieve. (Qur'an *al-Baqarah* 2:62)

> Those who believe (in the Qur'an), those who follow the Jewish (scriptures), and the Sabians and the Christians, – any who believe in Allah and the Last Day, and work righteousness, – on them shall be no fear, nor shall they grieve. (Qur'an *al-Mā'idah* 5:69)

One of the purposes for the revelation of these verses was to dispel the social stigma which came to be unfairly attached to those Jews, Christians, and others who had embraced Islam and followed the Prophet Muhammad. As mentioned earlier an authentic narration describes certain religious leaders accusing those of their people who had embraced Islam, as stating: "those who believed in Muhammad and followed him are the worst of our people, since if they were among our prominent people they would never have abandoned the religion of their fathers."[53] In other words the narration would suggest that belief in Muhammad was already a given fact meaning the verses were not referring to Jews, Christians and others on a general level, meaning *all* people of these and other faiths, but rather a specific set of people who had accepted Islam and were following the Prophet Muhammad.

In fact, by mentioning the word *ṣābi'īn* (sabians) the verses dispel any accusations levelled at whosoever embraces Islam, since the Arabic word *ṣābi'īn* derived from *ṣ-b-'a* means to convert from one religion to another new religion.[54] For this reason, Makkan pagans used to call the Prophet and his followers *ṣābi'īn*, on the grounds that they had abandoned polytheism and embraced a new faith (Islam).[55]

Note, Nasr's theory of metaphysical universalism described earlier, relies on these verses to attempt to prove that religious salvation is universal on the assumption that the verses require only belief in God and the Last Day without considering the integrity of Gods prophets.[56] Yet, there is unanimous agreement between classical and modern scholars of Islam that the following part of the conditional sentence, "any who believe in Allah," requires belief in all prophets including Prophet Muhammad.[57] In this respect, Ali states the following:

> The verse [5:69] does not purport to lay down an exhaustive list of the articles of faith. Nor does it seek to spell out the essentials of a genuine belief in Allah, which has no meaning unless it is accompanied by belief in His Prophets for it is through their agency alone that we know Allah's Will and can abide by it in our practical lives. This is especially true of His final Prophet, Muhammad (peace be on him) whose message is universal, and not confined to any particular group or section of humanity. Belief in the Prophethood of Muhammad (peace be on him) is thus an integral part and a logical corollary of belief in Allah. Moreover, it is also an essential test of genuineness of such belief. This becomes clear when the verse is read in conjunction with other relevant verses of the Qur'an. See, for instance, 4:170, 5:16, 21, 7:157, 158, 21:107, 25:1, 33:40, 61:6. See also 2:40, 3:31-32, 4:150-151.[58]

Therefore, the universality of religious salvation cannot be accommodated to the Islamic framework of religious pluralism. Because for humanity as a whole the Islamic conception of belief in God requires also belief in the Prophet Muhammad as clarified by the existence of dozens of Qur'anic verses as well as authentic *aḥādīth* mentioned in the faith section of all hadith collections. Even the expression "grace of God," employed in Karl Rahner's (1966) theory of religious inclusivism as a possible solution for universal religious salvation, is restricted in the case of Islam, to the acceptance of Muhammad as God's final prophet:

> "And ordain for us that which is good, in this life and in the Hereafter: for we have turned unto Thee." He said: "With My punishment I visit whom I will; but My mercy extendeth to all things. That (mercy) I shall ordain for those who do right, and practise regular charity, and those who believe in Our signs – Those who follow the Messenger, the unlettered Prophet, whom they find mentioned in their own (scriptures) – in the Law and the Gospel – for he commands them what is just and forbids them what is evil; he allows them as lawful what is good (and pure) and prohibits them from what is bad (and impure); he releases them from their heavy burdens and from the yokes that are upon them. So it is those who believe in him, honour him, help him, and follow the light which is sent down with him – it is they who will prosper." Say: "O men! I am sent unto you all, as the Messenger of Allah, to Whom belongeth the dominion of the heavens and the earth: there is no god but He: it is He That giveth both life and death. So believe in Allah and His Messenger, the Unlettered Prophet, who believeth in Allah and His words: follow him that (so) ye may be guided." (Qur'an *al-Aʿrāf* 7:156-158)

So, God's mercy, according to these verses, is inclusive for all things in this world. However, to gain God's mercy in the hereafter, requires acceptance of the Prophet Muhammad from all of mankind and particularly the People of the Book, who find mention of the unlettered Prophet in their scriptures. Note, the sentence "those who follow the Messenger" is attached to the previous descriptions of those gaining God's mercy in the hereafter without any grammatical conjunctions. This is a rhetoric method known in the Arabic language as *faṣl* (unsegment) where the grammatical conjunction is omitted due to the existence of complete union between sentences.[59] Thus, the application of *faṣl* between the sentences "those who believe in Our signs – those who follow the Messenger, the unlettered Prophet" (7:156-157), shows that those who believe in God's signs, are the same who follow the unlettered Prophet. Such completeness of faith is determined by the Qur'an as a way of gaining God's mercy and hence religious salvation: "So it is those who believe in him [the Prophet Muhammad], honour him, help him, and follow the light which is sent down with him – it is they who will prosper" (7:157). The word "prosper" here means both happiness and salvation.[60]

It is worth pointing out that the historical roots of soteriological pluralism in Islam seem to date back to the 9th century, when the intellectual institute and academy known as the *Bayt al-Ḥikmah* (House of Wisdom), reached the peak of its activities focusing largely on the translation of mainly Greek scientific works into Arabic. The access to Greek philosophical works resulted in the emergence of symbolic interpretations of the Qur'an. Thus, for the first time in Islam the issue of religious pluralism came to be approached from a philosophical aspect. For instance, al-Fārābī's theory of prophecy, in which he argues that the language of revelation is symbolic in nature and that the prophets receive these symbols from God through their imagination (*takhayyul*)[61] can be considered as the starting point of the esoteric interpretation of the Qur'an and thus, as the root of theories attempting to accommodate both soteriological as well as alethic pluralism to Islam.

Thus, as the discussion demonstrates, overall the doctrine of religious salvation in Islam is interdependently related to religious truth. In this sense, according to Islam, all those believing in the Oneness of God and following God's prophets prior to the advent of Prophet Muhammad, are likely to be saved, for they acknowledged religious truth. And in the same vein, all those who accepted Prophet Muhammad following his prophethood, are likely to be saved. However, there seems to exist a third group remaining true to the Oneness of God (not associating any other gods with Him), but who never acknowledge the prophethood of Muhammad and his final message. Their case is left to God's will. If He wills, He will save them, and if He wills, He will punish them. Therefore, unlike its totally exclusive position with respect to religious truth, the Islamic position appears slightly more inclusive with regard to religious salvation, but not pluralistic. However, since this inclusivism in terms of religious salvation depends only on God's will, the soteriological aspect of religious pluralism is something that cannot be examined or proved in Islam.

Normative Religious Pluralism and Islam

Up to this point our entire discussion has enabled us to determine normative religious pluralism as part of the ethical sphere of religious pluralism, since, as defined previously, this is linked to the ethico-behavioural paradigm of treating religiously different people. In this way, unlike alethic and soteriological religious pluralism, where the locus of discussion revolves around the eschatological dimensions of pluralism, in the case of normative religious pluralism it is the terrestrial dimensions that are of main concern to the participants. Thus, normative religious pluralism is seen as the most central to the peacebuilding process in this world.

Moreover, discussion so far has also enabled us to extract different elements from the ethical sphere of religious pluralism and incorporate these to the particular sphere of normative religious pluralism. This has allowed for a more accurate description of it by placing emphasis on the focus of normative religious pluralism dwelling entirely on human beings. This in turn implies that not only coreligionists, but people belonging to other religions should be treated on the basis of universal human values based on freedom and human dignity. In the same way, this kind of pluralism suggests respect for the religious particularities of differing faiths, and engagement in terms of commonality, to achieve mutual understanding, contribution, and support. Last but not least, normative religious pluralism goes deeper to recognise integrity, affection, and forgiveness towards adherents of other religions as main ethical parameters.

It is obvious from this description of normative religious pluralism how it corresponds to Islam and the Qur'an, particularly since the focus of both is mainly on human beings. On the other hand, the ethical aspects, the structural and constructive elements as well as the objectives of normative religious pluralism, all these components identified through the discussion on the human experience of religious pluralism create a subject area where Islam and the Qur'an can contribute substantially. That is by revealing the divine guidance towards such a subject on both a historical and normative basis. In the following pages some examples, mostly historical, will be presented in order to exemplify more clearly the different aspects of normative religious pluralism before delineating the Qur'anic exploration of it.

The most significant and ethical aspects of normative religious pluralism are freedom and human dignity. These aspects were first witnessed in interfaith relationship settings when the Prophet Muhammad and his adherent, having been rejected by the Quraysh Makkans, were welcomed along with the new religion, in both Abyssinia and Yathrib, later called al-Madinah al-Munawwarah. In Abyssinia, "there was a righteous king called the Negus in whose land no one was oppressed and who was praised for his righteousness."[62] Consequently, Muslims were welcomed by the Christians of Abyssinia and were also "allowed complete freedom of worship."[63] The Prophet and his followers were also welcomed in Yathrib (al-Madinah), where he in turn not only accepted the religious and tribal diversity of the city, but legitimised this by establishing a significant agreement with the different groupings. This document is known as *The Constitution of Madinah.*[64] In fact, the inhabitants of Abyssinia and Yathrib were both descendants of Qaḥṭānī Arabs, who lived as part of a great South Arabian civilisation,[65] *Arabia Felix* (latin meaning Happy Arabia), in which ethical values such as freedom and respect for human dignity were to some degree present. This statement is supported by the Qur'an itself, since it mentions certain facts concerning the Queen of Sheba (*Malikah Saba'*), whose kingdom was in South Arabia. The Queen of Sheba is described in the Qur'an as a very fair, kind and wise person. These features of her character can be discovered in the response she gives to Prophet Solomon, when he sends her a letter inviting her to visit him and submit fully to the one God, Lord of the Worlds. The Queen of Sheba responds:

> (The Queen) said: "Ye chiefs! Here is – delivered to me – a letter worthy of respect. It is from Solomon, and is (as follows): 'In the name of Allah, Most Gracious, Most Merciful: Be ye not arrogant against me, but come to me in submission (to the true Religion).'" She said: "Ye chiefs! Advise me in (this) my affair: no affair have I decided except in your presence." They said: "We are endued with strength, and given to vehement war: but the command is with thee; so consider what thou wilt command." She said: "Kings, when they enter a country, despoil it, and make the noblest of its people its meanest thus do they behave. But I am going to send him a present, and (wait) to see with what (answer) return (my) ambassadors." (Qur'an *al-Naml* 27:29-35)

Significant conclusions underlining the origins of freedom and the respect for human dignity in the case of the Qaḥṭānī Arabs can be drawn from these Qur'anic verses:

1. Although the content of Solomon's letter is not beneficial to her, the Queen of Sheba describes it as "a letter worthy of

respect" (Qur'an 27:29). Ibn al-ʿArabī states in his *Aḥkām al-Qur'ān* that, "the description of the letter as 'worthy of respect' is the most honourable description, since the same description is used for describing the Qur'an."[66] By using such an adjective to describe the letter, the Queen shows her ability to evaluate fairly the methodology through which the letter has been written, and her understanding of international relations, as she reduces possible tension on both levels, internally among her ministers, and externally, between the two countries, respectively.

2. The Queen also demonstrates that she conducts state affairs on the basis of mutual consultation speaking volumes for her character. She states to her ministers: "No affair have I decided except in your presence" (Qur'an 27:32). Far from being a despot she seeks advice from the people surrounding her: "Ye chiefs! Advice me in (this) my affair" (Qur'an 27:32). In adopting this manner she shows respect to others, maintaining their dignity, and "makes them feel confident and capable of making decisions."[67]
3. The Queen of Sheba appears in the Qur'an as a peace-loving person who knows how to lead a peace process. She employs her knowledge of previous human experience in the field of war and occupation and through the method of *istiṣḥāb* "presumption of continuity,"[68] decides to send Solomon not a military presence, but a gift, which is usually given with the aim of achieving closeness and love. She says: "Kings, when they enter a country, despoil it, and make the noblest of its people its meanest thus do they behave. But I am going to send him a present, and (wait) to see with what (answer) return (my) ambassadors" (Qur'an 27:34-35). A truly remarkable woman.

It seems that Qaḥṭānī Arabs were to some extent aware of ethical values such as freedom and human dignity, and it appears they also had knowledge of diplomacy which enabled them to maintain good international relations. In contrast, the mentality of ᶜAdnānī Arabs, northern inhabitants of *Arabia Ferox* (latin for Wild Arabia), was "purely egotistic"[69] and exclusive, which made them, as Dozy concludes, different from Qaḥṭānī Arabs.[70] The Makkans were a part of the ᶜAdnānī peoples, and as such values of freedom and respect for human dignity did not hold a universal dimension for them. Their loyalties were confined only to a certain tribe or more precisely to certain persons known as tribal leaders. For this reason, the Prophet Muhammad and his adherents were persecuted in Makkah at the beginning of Islam and peaceful co-existence was not allowed to flourish. At that point, the Qur'an commenced the process of transforming nomadic egocentric ethics into universal ones. This process can be regarded as a process of enlightenment based on both revelation and reason simultaneously forming thereby a source of critical ideas, including the importance of freedom and human dignity as primary values of society. For instance, the Qur'an from the very beginning of its revelation criticised any attempt targeting religious freedom. Surah *al-ᶜAlaq*, unanimously agreed as the first surah to be revealed,[71] raises the rhetorical question: "Seest thou one who forbids a votary when he (turns) to pray?" (Qur'an *al-ᶜAlaq* 96:9-10).

Three significant points, in connection with freedom, human dignity and normative religious pluralism, can be derived from this Qur'anic question:

1. As Ibn Ashur remarks in his *al-Taḥrīr wa al-Tanwīr*, "the main function of this question is to express astonishment;"[72] that is, astonishment at behavior of this type threatening religious freedom. Since banning or restricting religious freedom is an act of oppression, the Qur'an expresses its astonishment at this in the form of a question. By employing this rhetorical device, which is a type of linguistic metaphor, the Qur'an conveys that this kind of behavior is a phenomenon which contradicts human nature and ethical values.

2. The Qur'an uses the present tense of the verb forbid (*yanhā*, "forbids") while referring to a past event in order to keep that event ever present in people's minds (that is the act of forbidding religious freedom) so that they avoid doing so. According to Ibn Hishām al-Anṣārī, "the Arabs use a verb of present tense referring to a past event, with the aim of keeping that event always present in mind as if it was happening at the moment of mentioning it."[73]
3. More important to note is the grammatical shift (*iltifāt*) from the second to the third person: "Seest thou one who forbids a votary when he (turns) to pray?" Ibn ʿAṭiyyah states that "there is no argument among the interpreters of the Qur'an about to whom 'one who forbids' and 'a votary' refer. They all agree that the former refers to Abū Jahl,[74] whereas the latter refers to the Prophet Muhammad."[75] In this case, where "the addressee is the Prophet,"[76] the normal grammatical way of expressing the above meaning would be to say: "seest thou one who forbids *you* (Muhammad) when *you* turn to pray," but instead of saying: "who forbids *you* (Muhammad)," the Qur'an states, "who forbids *a votary*." As Ibn al-Athīr in his *Al-Mathal al-Sā'ir* comments, "the shift from one form to another is done only when it is required for some special reasons"[77] we can conclude that there is a reason for this grammatical shift (*iltifāt*) from the second person (Muhammad) to the third person (a votary). In this respect, al-Zamakhsharī's explanation that the linguistic shift (*iltifāt*) "is a habit of speech of the Arabs seeking to raise the interest of the listener,"[78] should not be regarded as the special reason for the shift (*iltifāt*) in this case. Actually, the grammatical shift from the Prophet to a votary is required for the process of transforming extant nomadic egocentric ethics into universal ones. By concentrating on a votary instead of the Prophet, the Qur'an from the very beginning of its revelation announces religious freedom as a value system, which cannot be monopolised by anyone. Therefore, the main function of the

> linguistic shift (*iltifāt*) here is to emphasise disapproval of forbidding or restricting religious freedom, whether for the Prophet or any other worshiper, as everyone's dignity should be respected. As can be seen, this rhetorical approach, known as shift (*iltifāt*), implies subtle meanings, which might be the reason why Ibn al-Athīr calls it "the core of the rhetoric, *balāghah*."[79/80]

Another important aspect of normative religious pluralism is the establishment of right balance between religious commonalities and particularities through constructive conversation. This aspect was clearly implemented by the Prophet through the foundation of *The Constitution of Madinah*, which on the one hand declared different religious groups as one nation, *ummah wāḥidah*,[81] but on the other hand preserved their religious particularities. Thus, the inclusive concept of "one nation," *ummah wāḥidah*, based on the recognition of religious particularities confirms the Prophet's approval of normative religious pluralism, which appeared in different manners in that society. For instance, Ibn Hishām mentions that a Christian delegation from Najran visited the Prophet in the mosque, *al-Masjid al-Nabawī*, in Madinah, with the aim of discussing points of doctrine including the nature of God. In spite of doctrinal disagreements, the Prophet received them warmly, allowed them to perform their prayers in the mosque, and signed a treaty with them.[82] Of course all these early interfaith interactions were geared towards achieving mutual understanding, mutual engagement, contribution and support between religiously different people.

The early achievements of such important objectives of normative religious pluralism are documented in non-Muslim sources dating back to the 7th century. For example, this is Patriarch Ishôyahb III, writing to his correspondent Simeon of Rewardashir around the year 650, during the heat of the intra-Christian controversy of the time:

> As for the Arabs, to whom God has at this time given rule (*shultānâ*) over the world, you know well how they act toward us. Not only do they not oppose Christianity, but they praise our faith, honour the priests and saints of our Lord, and give aid to the churches and monasteries.[83]

Furthermore, it would appear that essentially important is to conduct the whole process of normative religious pluralism on the basis of integrity, compassion and forgiveness. Such ethical qualities could gain interfaith relations further strength and mutual trust, as this seems to have been the case in different aspects of life throughout the history of interfaith relations. For instance, with respect to academic debate and interfaith dialogue some non-Muslim sources relate that during the reign of the Abbasid Caliph, al-Ma'mūn, inter-faith dialogues regularly took place in Baghdad. One of these debates documented, is that held by Theodore Abū Qurrah with a number of Muslim scholars in the presence of Caliph al-Ma'mūn himself.[84] Abū Qurrah was "a monk of the monastery of Mar Sabas in Judea, and for a while he also served as the bishop of the Melkite community in Ḥarrān in Mesopotamian Syria."[85] Although he was not a Muslim, he was deeply respected by the Caliph for his ideas. This is obvious from some of the expressions al-Ma'mūn directed towards Abū Qurrah during the debate, i.e.: "By God you are right, Abū Qurrah! By God you have done well Abū Qurrah and have put your opponents to shame!"[86] It appears that al-Ma'mūn's purpose behind the platform of debate was to encourage people to seek knowledge rather than to seek to dominate by their opinions. It is reported that before a debate the Caliph would say: "This is a *majlis* [council] characterised by justice and fairness. No one will commit excesses in it. So present your argument and answer without dread. There is nothing here except by that which is better."[87] The result of al-Ma'mūn's integrity and objectivity is expressed by Abū Qurrah himself where the Christian monk and scholar prays for the Muslim ruler in the following words:

> May God strengthen the Commander of the Faithful, the *imām* al-Ma'mūn, the victorious leader, the fortunate caliph, the beloved master, whose assault is terrible, the one who is gracious to the one rejected, and counsel of the one assisted, possessor of remarkable compassion, courage granted, and a community sought...May God inspire in him patience, mercy and justice for all his subjects![88]

Integrity as an important ethical aspect of normative religious pluralism is also attested to in Muslim academic writing towards religiously different people. In this regard, Hilary Kilpatrick remarks:

> It is rare for members of the dominant religion in a society to write about aspects of a subordinate religion in the same society in a non-polemical spirit. Yet the *diyārāt* works, books about monasteries compiled in Iraq and Egypt in the fourth/tenth century, reflect an attitude on their Muslim authors' part of remarkable openness towards Christian customs and institutions; they exemplify such a non-polemical approach. For this reason they deserve to be taken account of in any discussion of Arab Christianity during the ʿAbbasid period.[89]

This mutual trust and respect between Muslims and non-Muslims is historically also apparent in more social aspects of life. It is reported that one day when "the caliph al-Muʿtazz felt thirsty out hunting, one of his companions suggested they should visit a good friend of his, a monk at the Mār Mārī monastery, and when they arrived, they were given cool water to drink, a meal, and entertaining conversation."[90]

Given this how is it that some Muslims from the past as well as today have chosen to adopt an exclusive approach even in respect of normative religious pluralism? The answer could be partly due to specific historic circumstances and partly to a lack of distinguishment between differing types of religious pluralism, alethic, soteriological, and normative. They would seem to be of the opinion that, "one has no obligations whatsoever toward those who are not of one's faith, that their blood is permitted to be shed and their property taken."[91] This exclusive attitude towards those of different faiths is likely to have been triggered by a chain of historical interfaith conflicts, for instance, the transgression of the mutually signed pact of the *Constitution of Madinah* by Jewish tribes in the 7th century;[92] the coalition between Byzantine Christians and the northern Arab Christians against Islam in the 7th century;[93] and John of Damascus' public pronouncement of Islam as heresy in the 8th century. In his work *Concerning Heresy*, John of Damascus, one of the most prominent and influential Christian scholars of the time, regarded the Prophet Muhammad as heralding the era of the Antichrist and also claimed that Muhammad had plagiarised the Qur'an from the Bible.[94] This was the first anti-Islam polemic written by a member of Byzantine Orthodoxy. Other elements causing division were the religiously motivated Crusades against Muslims in the 11th, 12th and 13th centuries and afterwards. All these interfaith conflicts, which took place during the formative period of Islamic sciences and the conceptual perception of interfaith relations, might have created good reasons for religious exclusivism and hatred to grow and flourish even outside the context of war and oppression, which seem to be the only reasons justifying the transgression of normative religious pluralism in Islam. On the other hand, the Muslims' counter-attack and reaction to historical interfaith conflicts as well as inability to recognise different types of religious pluralism has resulted in misleading conclusions among many non-Muslims that Islam teaches no respect for religiously different people.

In sum, due to the problematic areas outlined, it is vital that we return to the authentic sources of Islam for solutions to questions of interfaith relations, especially since the normative teachings of these sources have been contaminated by irrelevant historical, methodological and ideological issues.

[3]
Conclusion

Religious pluralism is a complex concept accommodating a multiplicity of definitions with considerable discrepancy between them in terms of their themes, scopes, and problematic areas. Inability to distinguish between all the different types of religious pluralism will lead to confused understanding and misleading conclusions if the appropriate type of pluralism is not isolated and relevant approaches corresponding to that type are not adopted. Both alethic and soteriological religious pluralism emerged from the specific context of Christianity as a result of theological discussions exploring religious salvation. However, since religious truth and consequently religious salvation claims are considered as irreconcilable and thus inherently divisive, religious pluralism reduced to that particular level becomes an unmanageable issue. In this respect, the best solution might be to concentrate on the terrestrial dimensions and ramifications of religious pluralism, namely normative religious pluralism, which is the most relevant type with respect to Islamic theology and the Qur'anic content.

Thus, the following chapters will explore the Qur'anic conception of normative religious pluralism elaborating on elements mentioned in this chapter: ethical foundations of normative religious pluralism, its structural and constructive elements, and its objectives.

2

Ethical Foundations of Normative Religious Pluralism in the Qur'an

It should be mentioned from the outset, that with regard to "ethical foundations", the title of this chapter, the Qur'anic scope of the "ethical" is too broad to categorise on a simple level, to the extent that Izutsu remarks that "Islamic thought at its Qur'anic stage, makes no real distinction between the religious and the ethical."[1] This breadth of the Qur'anic ethical world poses a challenge for selectivity. However, based on the ethical problematic areas raised in the previous chapter, the selection can relatively be limited to five main ethical foundations of normative religious pluralism: freedom of belief, human dignity, integrity, the imperative of no vilification of what is sacred to others, and forgiveness. An exploration of Qur'anic guidance with respect to these ethical features allows critical examination of exclusivist claims which reject any moral obligation in relation to peaceful people of differing faiths, allowing their blood to be shed and their properties to be destroyed.

[1] Freedom of Belief

The universality of freedom as an unchangeable human value

should be methodologically taken into consideration in the process of Qur'anic exegesis. Freedom in general and freedom of belief in particular are inviolable human rights, since they reflect the unchangeable characteristics of human nature. Thus, to recognise the right of freedom is tantamount to the recognition of human nature. Apart from human nature, freedom does not have other affiliations such as geographical, political or religious. Due to this fact, freedom is considered as an irreplaceable value in the East as well as in the West. For the East, this fact is made clear in the well-known declaration of Caliph ʿUmar ibn al-Khaṭṭāb: "How dare you enslave people, whereas they were born free?!"[2] In the same way, Jean-Jacques Rousseau in the West opens his famous treatise *The Social Contract* with the following statement which has become an inalienable part of western civilisation: "Man was born free, and everywhere he is in chains. One believes himself the master of others, and yet he is a greater slave than they."[3] Moreover, Rousseau argues that there is a firm relationship between freedom and morality. He remarks:

> To renounce one's liberty is to renounce one's essence as a human being, the rights and also the duties of humanity. For the person who renounces everything there is no possible compensation. Such a renunciation is incompatible with human nature, for to take away all freedom from one's will is to take away all morality from one's actions.[4]

The interrelationship between freedom and morality increases the level of human responsibility towards the preservation of this right globally. Transgression of the right of freedom leads inevitably to serious interfaith tension and ulitmately massacre. For this reason, the famous Islamic scholar and exegete, *mufassir*, Bediuzzaman Said Nursi emphasised in the context of interfaith conflict between Muslims and Christians that:

> Their freedom [of Christian people] consists in leaving them in peace and not oppressing them, for this is what the *Sharīʿah* enjoins. More than this is

> their aggression in the face of your bad points and craziness, their benefiting from your ignorance... The freedom of non-Muslims is a branch of our own freedom.[5]

Nursi's statement implies that in order for one to enjoy one's own freedom one has to struggle to gain the freedom of the other. This principle deserves to be considered as a golden rule in respect of normative religious pluralism, i.e. "the freedom of the other is my own freedom." Therefore, the right of freedom is equally valued all over the world as an inviolable human right, which makes its exploration in the case of the Qur'an vital in order to dispel any exclusive claims and historical doubts concerning it.

The Word Freedom in the Qur'an

The Arabic word for freedom,[6] *ḥurriyyah*, does not exist in the Qur'an directly as a noun, but its primary root *ḥ-r-r* and other derivatives of it do exist. Tracing the derivatives of the root morpheme *ḥ-r-r* in the Qur'an, it becomes clear that six derivatives have been mentioned in thirteen different Qur'anic places. These six derivatives of the root *ḥ-r-r* are: *taḥrīr, muḥarrar, ḥurr, ḥarr, ḥarūr, ḥarīr*. Before analysing these Qur'anic words, it is important to firstly examine the definition of the root *ḥ-r-r* in one of the earliest works in the field of lexicography: *Muʿjam al-Maqāyīs fī al-Lughah* written by Abū al-Ḥusayn Aḥmad ibn Fāris ibn Zakariyyā.

Ibn Fāris distinguishes between two major meanings of the root *ḥ-r-r*, stating: "*ḥ-r-r* has two main meanings: the first being what goes against slavery and has neither defect nor shortcoming, *mā khālafa al-ʿubūdiyyah wa bari'a min al-ʿayb wa al-naqṣ*, whereas the second is the opposite of cold, *khilāf al-bard*."[7] Even though, some scholars have made attempts to derive from the second meaning of the root *ḥ-r-r* significance related to freedom (*ḥurriyyah*) such attempts seem to be rather exaggerated and thus implausible. Therefore, the Qur'anic words derived from the root *ḥ-r-r* meaning "hot" (such as *ḥarr, ḥarūr, ḥarīr*) are unlikely to work in comibnation with the word freedom (*ḥurriyyah*).

As far as the rest of the derivatives, related to the first meaning of the root *ḥ-r-r* mentioned by Ibn Fāris, are concerned, it is important to discover what Ibn Fāris meant by the definition of *ḥ-r-r* as something that "goes against slavery and has neither defect nor shortcoming, *mā khālafa al-ʿubūdiyyah wa bari'a min al-ʿayb wa al-naqṣ.*"[8] In this case, it is relevant to look at the work of another lexicographer who lived in the generation immediately following Ibn Fāris and who seems to have been influenced by him. Al-Rāghib al-Aṣfahānī developed a definition of *ḥ-r-r* by making a clear distinction between the social and the metaphysical meaning of freedom, *ḥurriyyah*. In his *Mufradāt Alfāẓ al-Qur'ān* he states:

> A free man, *al-ḥurr*, is the opposite of a slave, *al-ʿabd*, and freedom, *al-ḥurriyyah*, is divided into two kinds. The first one refers to the person who is literally not a slave. This meaning is referred to in the Qur'an: 'The free for the free.' (Qur'an *al-Baqarah* 2:178). In the same way, the Qur'an uses the word *taḥrīr* to mean literally the process of giving a slave his freedom, as it is mentioned in the Qur'an: 'Give a slave his freedom' (Qur'an *al-Mā'idah* 5:89).
>
> As far as the second kind of freedom, *ḥurriyyah*, is concerned, it is referred "to the person who is not dominated by such ugly qualities as greed and the desire for worldly possessions."[9] This meaning of freedom, *ḥurriyyah*, is derived from the Qur'anic word *muḥarraran*: 'I do dedicate unto Thee what is in my womb for Thy special service' (Qur'an *Āl ʿImrān* 3:35). *Muḥarraran* here means freed from all worldly affairs and specially dedicated to God's service.[10]

These foregoing definitions of the root "*ḥ-r-r*" show that the Qur'an uses the derivates from this root to refer mainly to two different levels of freedom, *ḥurriyyah*. The first is the legal aspect of freedom dealing with slavery meaning the actual physical possession of the slave by wealthy people. The second is the ethical aspect of freedom which deals with the intellectual as well as the metaphysical character of human nature.

In fact, the Qur'anic word *muḥarraran*, from which the second aspect of freedom is derived, defines the concept of freedom in the light of the Oneness of God. By relating the concept of freedom to the Oneness of God, the Qur'an seems to aim at protecting this human right from any possible violation and to maintain it in its highest level of quality. It is very likely that Fakhr al-Dīn al-Rāzī was aware of this fact when he wrote: "Freedom is a natural feature of human nature...Whenever the bodily connection of the soul is the weaker, and the intellectual one the stronger, the soul possesses more freedom and vice versa."[11] According to al-Rāzī's conclusion, it would appear that no one is truly free unless he devotes himself totally to God. Such a concept of freedom is confirmed also by the Prophet who said: "Perish the slave of dinar, perish the slave of dirham."[12]

It should be stressed here, that Islam emphasises the right of freedom on both its levels, the physical and intellectual, respectively. However, the intellectual aspect of freedom is more underscored, since the consequences of its violation are far more dangerous than the ramifications emerging from violation of the physical aspect. It is interesting to mention in this respect al-Ghazālī's understanding of the fact. He remarks that "to enslave the intellectual freedom of man is more dangerous than actual slavery, since the enslavement of intellectual freedom aims to enslave not only man's body, but also his heart and mind."[13] It is obvious from Ghazālī's statement, that he was aware of the political implications of the idea of freedom as he seems to have also been aware of the right of the individual to maintain and protect his freedom. Thus, al-Ghazālī's definition of freedom suggests an understanding of the Arabic term *ḥurriyyah*, which comprises an appreciation of its subtle meanings together with a comprehension of freedom's various other implications, centuries before the age of European enlightenment. For this reason, Franz Rosenthal would appear to be not entirely accurate, when he concludes that "Arabic did not possess a truly workable term to express the full force of [the] concept of "freedom" until, in modern times, western influence gave a new meaning to [the] old *ḥurriyyah*."[14]

Thus analysing the root morpheme *ḥ-r-r*, in terms of its derivatives in the Qur'an, we see that the Qur'an recognises both the physical as well as the intellectual aspects of freedom. Moreover, in order to guarantee and perpetuate the right of freedom, the Qur'an attributes the concept of freedom to the Oneness of God and thus indicates that nobody among human beings has the right to enslave others physically or intellectually.

Qur'anic Indications of Freedom of Belief

Freedom of belief is a fundamental right supported by the Qur'an in a number of verses. Examining all Qur'anic statements on this subject however it would seem that we can focus on two main verses to show that Islam recognises complete freedom of faith: *al-Baqarah*:256 and *al-Aḥzāb*: 72.

Surah al-Baqarah Verse 256

> Let there be no compulsion in religion: Truth stands out clear from Error: whoever rejects evil and believes in Allah hath grasped the most trustworthy handhold, that never breaks. And Allah heareth and knoweth all things. (*al-Baqarah* 2:256)

An exegetical examination of verse 2:256 will follow. This will focus primarily on four main aspects: a) historical context; b) linguistic structure; c) thematic linkage between the verse and its textual context; d) modern context (the world today world and its reality).

Methodologically speaking, it is important to initially outline the historical context of the verse (the occasion of its revelation or *sabab al-nuzūl*), to allow for greater accuracy and a more comprehensive understanding. In this respect, the historical context in which verse 2:256 was revealed provides us with a reliable historical source of information. In this regard al-Wāḥidī, in his work *Asbāb al-Nuzūl*, reports from Ibn ʿAbbās that:

> The children of some of the al-Anṣār's women used to die young. Prior to Islam their superstitious mothers would consequently take an oath to devote their children to Judaism if they remained alive. Thus, those children who became Jews followed Judaism even after their parents from the al-Anṣār had embraced Islam. However, when the Jewish tribe Banū Naḍīr was expelled from al-Madinah, some of the al-Anṣār wanted to force their Jewish children to embrace Islam in order to stay with their Muslim families in al-Madinah. At that point, God revealed the verse "Let there be no compulsion in religion."[15]

This narration is also transmitted by al-Ṭabarī, Abū Dāwūd, al-Nisā'ī and others. In terms of the authenticity of the narration, al-Albani concludes that "it is an authentic narration, *ṣaḥīḥ*."[16]

So, this being the occasion for the revelation of verse 2:256, it is apparent that the verse was revealed in the historical context of a religious conflict between the Jews and Muslims of Madinah. It was a religiously diverse society. Another point which can be derived from the narration is that it was parents who were attempting to force their children to convert from Judaism to Islam. Even so, despite the nature of familial ties and what others might consequently see as mitigating circumstances providing reason enough for a possible violation of freedom of belief, this was not accepted by the Qur'an which categorically states: "there is no compulsion in religion" (2:256). And this clear and unequivocal Qur'anic position with regards to freedom of faith, prohibiting compulsion in religion, whether among family members, and in the context of interfaith conflict, is absolute, promoting freedom of belief to be a universal value and inviolable human right.

Yet, there have been claims by certain quarters that verse 2:256 was abrogated by Qur'anic verses prescribing fighting against the "unbelievers." Al-Ṭabarī attributes such a claim to Ibn Zayd,[17] while al-Nuḥās reports Sulaymān ibn Mūsā to have been among those who favored the abrogation claim for

2:256.[18] Ibn Ashur, in contrast, reasons that taking into account that the verse was revealed after the conquest of Makkah, then verse 2:256 abrogated "the verses prescribing fighting against those who refuse to embrace Islam."[19]

Clearly the issue of abrogation (*naskh*) in the Qur'an is controversial.* Even in the case of this one single verse (2:256), there exist two opposing claims. One reason for the controversy is problems arising from the definition of abrogation itself. Prior to al-Shāfiʿī's *Al-Risālah*, *naskh* was used in its broadest sense to mean both specifying the meaning by different linguistic approaches as well as the substitution of an earlier rule, *ḥukum*, with a chronologically succeeding one.[20] With regards to the latter, that is substitution of an earlier rule, it should be stressed that the way in which this type of abrogation is determined in the case of the Qur'an is not through reasoning, ijtihad, but through an authentic hadith attributed to the Prophet himself.[21]

Another issue, which should be taken into consideration while discussing abrogation in the Qur'an, is the condition that scholars have set as necessary for the acceptance of any claim of abrogation. This condition requires existence of an absolute contradiction between two or more verses together with absence of any possible way in which the verses in question can be understood together.[22] In this respect Abū Zahrah states that: "Together with a number of scholars, we participated in writing a work of Qur'anic exegesis entitled *Al-Muntakhab*. In our entire work on the Qur'an, we did not find any two verses that can be regarded as contradictory to each other."[23] This complete lack of any contradiction leads Abū Zahrah to conclude: "We adopt the same attitude of Abū Muslim al-Aṣfahānī[24] and say that there is absolutely not any case of abrogation in the

* Abrogation in the Qur'an is a controversial issue. For a detailed and comprehensive understanding of abrogation in the Qur'an, please see Israr Ahmad Khan, *Theory of Abrogation: A Critical Evaluation* (Research Management Centre, International Islamic University Malaysia, Kuala Lumpur, 2006). Also see Dr. Taha J. Alalwani, *Naḥwa Mawqif Qur'anī min al-Naskh* [Towards a Qur'anic Position on Abrogation] (Egypt: Maktabah al-Shuruk al-Dawliyyah, 2007), in which he rejects the concept of abrogation entirely. [Editor].

Qur'an."[25] This conclusion is also confirmed by the late Muhammad al-Ghazali.[26]

In addition the Prophet did not force anyone in his entire life to embrace Islam. He invited people to the message of God and then left matters of faith to their own volition.

In view of these conclusive arguments the claim of abrogation with regard to verse 2:256 is rejected, as is the very concept of *naskh* itself. Hence verse 2:256 was not abrogated, in the sense of freedom of belief having been substituted by its opposite, coercian to accept Islam. The reasons are clear: a) there is no authentic *aḥādīth* attributed to the Prophet in this respect. b) there is no contradiction between the verse pertaining to freedom of belief and those concerning the imperative to fight. Indeed as will be discussed in more detail later, the motivation underlying the latter was not the belief system of those of other faith. c) The abrogation claim clearly contradicts the purpose of abrogation stated by the Qur'an itself in surah *al-Baqarah*:

> None of Our revelations do We abrogate or cause to be forgotten, but We substitute something better or similar: Knowest thou not that Allah Hath power over all things? (*al-Baqarah* 2:106)

As can be seen, the purpose of abrogation, according to the Qur'an itself, is to substitute something for another thing that is better or similar to the abrogated subject, and by no means to substitute something for something that is worse. Thus, it is unacceptable to claim that the Qur'an has abrogated the right of freedom of belief in order to substitute it for fighting and compulsion.

Having outlined the historical context of verse 2:256, we next turn to examining its linguistic structure. A rhetorical approach employing a laconic style, *al-'Ījāz bi al-qaṣr*, gives us a concise statement statement using few words to express a rich and deep meaning. Indeed al-Rummānī in his work *al-Nukat fī Iʿjāz al-Qur'ān*, defines this approach as a main feature of the Qur'an proving its miraculous nature.[27]

A linguistic exploration focusing on the Arabic text, *lā ikrāha* "Let there be no compulsion," gives us gramatically expression of a generic negative (*nafī istighrāq al-jins*), which indicates a complete negation of the idea of compulsion in all its forms.[28] Accordingly, it makes the scope of the prohibition of compulsion in religion fall inclusively on all human beings. In this regard, it should be emphasised that restriction of the scope of the prohibition as applying only to the People of the Book and those who are subject to paying the *jizyah*, as al-Ṭabarī has suggested,[29] contradicts the Islamic concept of the terrestrial test through which all human beings are examined before God.[30] Moreover, the view that the scope of the prohibition is limited to those who are subject to paying the *jizyah* is untenable, since the verse prescribng *jizyah* (9:29) was revealed in connection to the expedition of Tabūk which took place in 630 CE /9 AH[31] approximately five years after the revelation of verse 2:256, which was revealed when the Jewish tribe Banū al-Naḍīr was expelled from Madinah in 625 CE/4 AH.[32] On the other hand, the issue of fighting pagans (appearing to be the most frequent argument presented in favor of the restriction of the prohibition of compulsion) is misdirected, for it was motivated by their aggression towards Muslims and constant war mongering, and not by their belief system.[33]

Another linguistic point supporting argument for the universality of freedom of belief occurs in the sentence following the intial statement: "Let there be no compulsion in religion: *Truth stands out clear from Error*" (2:256, *italics mine*). This sentence functions here as a justification for prohibiting compulsion.[34] In other words, compulsion in religion is prohibited because Truth (*rushd*) is clear and Error (*ghay*) is clear. So, compulsion is prohibited and freedom adopted because in the context of the former Truth disappears and Error appears, whereas in the context of the latter Truth, becomes clear. These dialectical relations between freedom and compulsion can be further elaborated by reviewing the verse once more:

> Let there be no compulsion in religion: Truth stands out clear from Error: whoever rejects evil and believes in Allah hath grasped the most trustworthy handhold that never breaks. And Allah heareth and knoweth all things. (*al-Baqarah* 2:256)

The verse apparently presents us with three main dialectical dichotomies: compulsion-freedom; truth-error; and evil (*ṭāghūt*)-God. The first dichotomy sets off a dual chain reaction, which can be illustrated as follows: freedom → truth (*rushd*) → God; compulsion → error (*ghay*) → evil (*ṭāghūt*). Thus, as the three dialectical dichotomies indicate attaining final goals is dependant on their starting point, and this being so to attain God we would need to start from freedom, whereas evil will be the end result of compulsion as the starting point. We can therefore deduce precisely that coercian in matters of belief will in all likelihood lead people only to evil.

Historical and linguistic contexts aside, we now move onto examining thematic links. It is methodologically important to study the Qur'an in terms of its own context in which a verse occurs as failure to do so could lead to a distortion of its correct meaning. In this respect, examining Qur'anic verses which eventually lead up to the verse "Let there be no compulsion in religion," we see that these verses concern the issue of fighting (*qitāl*). In particular, the verses preceding 2:256 refer to a battle in which the believers among the children of Israel fight a force led by the formidable warrior Goliath (Jalūt) who is killed at the hands of the young prohet David. The purpose of the battle was to defeat oppression, as clear from the verse:

> They said: "How could we refuse to fight in the cause of Allah, seeing that we were turned out of our homes and our families?" (Qur'an *al-Baqarah* 2:246)

The occurrence of the verse "Let there be no compulsion in religion" (2:256) following soon after the account of this event is a clear indication that the purpose of the fight was not geared towards converting people from one faith to another.[35] On the other hand, the promotion of the freedom of belief in the textual context discussing oppression shows again that the purpose of fighting, *qitāl*, is to free people from oppression and allow them to exercise their human rights, regardless of their religion, ethnicity or nationality.

As far as the verses succeeding the verse "Let there be no compulsion in religion" are concerned, they present three different narratives. The first concerns a dispute between Abraham and a ruler granted power by God, where the main argument concerns the oness of God; the second refers to a man who God causes to die for a hundred years, and who is then raised up again; and the last concerns Abraham's request to God to show him how He gives life to the dead. The main argument of the second and third narrative is that it is only God who causes life and death.

What is significant in the case of these three narratives is that their central argument is supported and proved through compelling evidence and experience. This initself thematically confirms the Qur'anic rule of no coercian in faith in the sense that the way to persuade people of a certain belief should be through constructive argument, and not by force or compulsion.

Therefore, within the Qur'an's own context the verse "Let there be no compulsion in religion" corroborates the right to freedom of belief in two ways. Fist, the context disapproves of using force in respect of belief and second it demonstrates this by encouraging the use of compelling arguments and experience as a mean to persuade people of a certain belief.

Another context to be consulted with respect to no coercian in matters of faith is that of today's world and civilisational reality in terms of human rights and values. In other words, the relevant question here is what importance does today's world attach to the right of freedom? To answer this question, it seems appropriate to refer to one of the core sources exploring historically human experience in the civilisational process. This is Arnold Toynbee's *A Study of History*, wherein the author concludes that the right o freedom of choice is a criterion for the rise and decline of civilisations: "A broken-down society would prove to have forfeited a salutary freedom of choice through having fallen under the bondage of some idols of its own making."[36] So, the consideration of freedom of choice in the context of today's world as a criterion for the rise and decline of societies, does not allow exegetes to fail to recognise the right of freedom of belief as a universal right in the case of the verse "Let there be no compulsion in religion" (2:256).

In sum an exegetical study of verse 2:256 at the historical, linguistic, thematic and civilisational levels, has shown that the right of freedom of belief is endorsed by the Qur'an as a universal right and value, which cannot be subject to abrogation or restricted to a certain group of people.

Surah al-Aḥzāb Verse 72

The second Qur'anic verse to be exegetically examined with reference to freedom of belief is verse 72 of surah *al-Aḥzāb*:

> We did indeed offer the Trust to the Heavens and the Earth and the Mountains; but they refused to undertake it, being afraid thereof: but man undertook it. He was indeed unjust and foolish. (Qur'an *al-Aḥzāb* 33:72)

Once again the first step is exploration of the historical context of the verse. As obvious from the name of the chapter *al-Aḥzāb*, referring to the siege of Madinah by confederates, the surah is a Madinan one.[37] However, apart from the fact of the verse having been revealed in a multicultural society which Madinah was, it seems difficult to trace any other historical facts related to the verse. This is because there does not seem to exist any historical occasion for its revelation. It is important to point out that the perception of some scholars that every Qur'anic verse must refer to a special occasion appears to be a methodological mistake in the field of Qur'anic exegesis. This view has led to Qur'anic texts being burdened with historical events having no relation to the texts in question. In fact, the number of the verses which refer to special occasions is restricted as "most of the Qur'anic stories, past events mentioned in the Qur'an, and even the texts referring to the hereafter, have been revealed initially without special occasions."[38] Furthermore, verse 33:72 relays information concerning an event which took place before the revelation of the Qur'an, so it is also clear why there is no special occasion for its revelation. Therefore, the key to its understanding is the linguistic text itself and its relation to the Qur'an's own context. In this respect, al-Salih importantly remarks that "the exploration of the relationship between the verse and its textual context compensates for the lack of special occasion or confirms it in the case of its availability."[39]

Following this line of reasoning we begin with a linguistic analysis of the verse's content. The crux of this is the word *al-amānah* or trust. *Al-amānah* has caused controversy among exegetes, historically being interpreted in a variety of ways since no prophetic explanation exists in direct relation to it. For example, al-Ṭabarī narrates a number of different meanings of "trust" such as obedience to God, loyalty to humankind, and Adam's trust towards his son Qābīl. However, after mentioning all these he concludes that "the most relevant understanding of "trust," *al-amānah*, is to be left to its general meaning including all religious obligations as well as the obligations towards people."[40] Unlike al-Ṭabarī, al-Zamakhsharī restricts meaning to the obedience of God.[41] In a similar way, al-Rāzī defines the meaning of "trust" as "the commandment of God, *al-taklīf*."[42] Yet, as the commandment of God is not exclusively related to human beings but includes the rest of the universe, al-Ālūsī distinguishes between the fulfilment of the commandment of God by force and fulfilment by choice. He states that "the commandment of God (*al-taklīf*) was accepted by man on the basis of his own choice and without compulsion."[43] Likewise, its undertaking was rejected by the heavens, earth and mountains. By this reasoning he implies that freedom of choice would appear to be a more suitable meaning of *al-amānah* than the commandment of God, for it is fulfilled equally by those who accepted the trust as well as by those who rejected it.The sense of meaning al-Ālūsī gave to *al-*

amānah was later developed by Ibn Ashur to mean "intellectual power, *al-ᶜaql*."[44]

Finally, the latest definition of *al-amānah* has been formulated by al-Sharawi, who seems to have summarised the previous definitions and thus formed a more explicit concept of "trust". He concludes that "trust, *al-amānah*, means the ability of human beings to choose their actions. Therefore, the trust, *al-amānah*, which was offered by God to his creatures, is the freedom of choice or the ability of these creatures to choose whether to believe or disbelieve."[45]

In sum *al-amānah* has witnessed significant evolution in its definition, both in terms of the sense of meaning given to the term as well as understanding of it. This commences with a classical understanding focusing on obedience to God in terms of His commandments. Yet the issue remains that this would mean by implication that the heavens, earth, mountains did not follow God's commandment refusing to undertake "the trust" (*al-amānah*) something which is unacceptable, as the Qur'an itself repeatedly confirms that the universe continuously praises and glorifies God. For this reason, al-Rāzī seems to have been puzzled over how human beings, the universe, and angels obey God's commandment, stating that they all obey God in different ways, and pointing to the angels' obedience of God as being similar to the way human beings eat and drink.[46] This last observation by al-Rāzī implies that apart from human beings, all other creatures obey God on the basis of instinct without any involvement of free choice or will. Therefore, providing that all creatures share the ability to obey God, the interpretation of *al-amānah* as obedience is unconvincing, since the "trust," in the verse exclusively belongs only to human beings. In fact the point, on which al-Rāzī seems to have been puzzled and could not designate appears to be what succeeding exegetes, and particularly al-Sharawi, have defined as a free choice or free will.

On the whole, the most reasonable designation for the word "trust" (*al-amānah*) seems to be free choice or free will, which means the ability of humans to choose through an intellectual power whether to believe or disbelieve in the commandment of God. Thus, it is this ability that was offered to the heavens, the earth, and the mountains, and which they refused to undertake because of its eschatological ramifications, that mankind accepted. Given to them directly by God as a gift, *al-amānah* was also a fundamental feature of the terrestrial test carrying tremendous eschatological responsibility. For this reason, human free will or the ability of humans to choose freely is metaphorically determined in the verse as "trust."

Not only has verse 33:72 related freedom of choice to human beings but also rhetorically illustrated God's approach through which He presents this great "trust" to them. This approach is expressed in the verse by the word offer, *ʿarḍ*, which means that freedom of choice itself was initially offered by God to man on the basis of freedom of choice, far from any compulsion. The important emphasis given to freedom of choice and its consequences is signified by the ending of the verse which presents two nouns (*ẓalūm* and *jahūl*) in *ṣīghah al-mubālaghah* form (that is, forms of intensification/hyperbolic forms) to give intensification of meaning: "...He [the human being] was indeed unjust (*ẓalūm*) and foolish (*jahūl*)" (33:72). Those among mankind who fail to choose in accordance with the requirements of Allah are *ẓalūm* (to God); and they are also *jahūl*, because they did not utilize the freedom of choice granted them in a way that guarantees them perpetual happiness.

To further support the argument that verse 33:72 refers to humans beings as inherently endowed with freedom of choice, which serves as a foundation of freedom of belief, we need to examine some thematic relationships within the surah. In this respect, there seems to be an important clue to understanding the dichotomy between freedom of belief and compulsion in the fourth verse:

> Allah has not made for any man two hearts in his (one) body: nor has He made your wives whom ye divorce by *ẓihār* your mothers: nor has He made your adopted sons your sons. Such is (only) your (manner of) speech by

> your mouths. But Allah tells (you) the Truth, and He shows the (right) Way. (Qur'an *al-Aḥzāb* 33:4)

The verse clearly underlines the fact that man cannot live in two different universes. Actually, the reality that "Allah has not made for any man two hearts in his (one) body," implies the inability of the method of compulsion to create any real intellectual pattern going against the endowed freedom of choice. Analogically, the verse provides two examples: one's wife cannot become one's mother nor can one's adopted child become one's real child. Therefore, given that the importance of certain beliefs or certain actions is based on what is in man's heart, the use of force and compulsion appears to be not only pointless but also deceptive. In this respect, one of the purposes of the verse in particular, and the whole of surah *al-Aḥzāb* in general, is to criticise hypocrisy, which is one of the main topics of the chapter.

Moving to the Qur'anic textual context preceding verse 33:72, we see another thematic relationship in terms of the eschatological consequences of man's terrestrial freedom of choice:

> Verily Allah has cursed the Unbelievers and prepared for them a Blazing Fire – To dwell therein forever: no protector will they find, nor helper. The Day that their faces will be turned upside down in the Fire, they will say: "Woe to us! Would that we had obeyed Allah and obeyed the Messenger!" And they would say: "Our Lord! We obeyed our chiefs and our great ones, and they misled us as to the (right) Path. Our Lord! Give them double Penalty and curse them with a very great Curse!" (Qur'an *al-Aḥzāb* 33:64-68)

These verses convey the terrible regret expressed in the hereafter by those who failed to obey God in their earthly life, as well as their great wish that they had obeyed Him. This combination of regret and wish, expressed by the words *yālaytanā* ("woe to us") functions in the eschatological context as a metonymy of regret.[47] In other words, the Arabic word *layt*, woe, indicates one's wish to do what one had a choice to do in the past, but failed in doing. Thus, this metonymy laconically expresses the Qur'anic concept of freedom of choice as pertaining to not only people's right to choose freely their belief in this world but also their accountability for that choice in the hereafter. In fact, it is this issue of eschatological accountability which may be the reason underlying the heavens, earth, and mountains' refusal to undertake the trust offered.

To summarise, our analytical study of verse 33:72 has demonstrated that the verse itself and the context in which it exists prove the distinguished nature of human beings as possessors of free will. In fact, freedom of choice, according to the verse, is the main boundary distinguishing human beings from the rest of creation. Therefore, this ability to choose freely, the right of freedom of belief in this world, is seen as tantamount to constituting what a human being actually is.

Freedom of Belief versus Oppression: The Dialectics of Opposites in Three Qur'anic Stories

The Qur'anic attitude towards the right of freedom of belief can also be dialectically examined by analysing three stories critically presented in the Qur'an. These are known as: "the makers of the pit of fire" (*aṣḥāb al-ukhdūd*); "the sorcerers of Pharaoh" (*saḥarah Firᶜawn*); and "the companions of the cave" (*aṣḥāb al-kahf*).

The first was revealed in surah *al-Burūj*, in the context of Makkan socio-political circumstances. The story concerns a pre-Islamic community of monotheistic believers burnt to death for no other reason than their belief in God. The act of killing people because of their faith has been criticised by the Qur'an and defined as a crime:

> Woe to the makers of the pit (of fire), Fire supplied (abundantly) with fuel: Behold! They sat over against the (fire), And they witnessed (all) that they were doing against the Believers. And they ill-treated them for no other

> reason than that they believed in Allah, Exalted in Power, Worthy of all Praise! – Him to Whom belongs the dominion of the heavens and the earth! And Allah is Witness to all things. Those who persecute (or draw into temptation) the Believers, men and women, and do not turn in repentance, will have the Penalty of Hell: They will have the Penalty of the Burning Fire. (Qur'an *al-Burūj* 85:4-10)

The Qur'anic statement "and they ill-treated them for no other reason than that they believed in Allah" (85:8), clearly demonstrates that the root cause of the persecution and slaying of these people was their belief system. Therefore, the Qur'anic criticism of such a kind of religious oppression dialectically reveals the Qur'anic endorsement of the right of freedom of belief.

The second Qur'anic story known as "the sorcerers of Pharaoh," *saḥarah Firᶜawn*, has been revealed in three different but all Makkan surahs: *al-Aᶜrāf, Ṭā Hā*, and *al-Shuᶜarā'*. The story is about a group of extremely skilful sorcerers ordered by Pharaoh to prove Moses' message to be false. However, after seeing clear evidence proving his message to be true, the sorcerers declare their submission to God. At this point Pharaoh violates the sorcerers' right to choose their faith, and threatens to slay them by cutting off their hands and feet on opposite sides and then crucifying them. This threat is depicted in the Qur'an as follows:

> So the magicians were thrown down to prostration: they said, "We believe in the Lord of Aaron and Moses." (Pharaoh) said: "Believe ye in Him before I give you permission? Surely this must be your leader, who has taught you magic! Be sure I will cut off your hands and feet on opposite sides, and I will have you crucified on trunks of palm-trees: so shall ye know for certain, which of us can give the more severe and the more lasting punishment!" (Qur'an *Ṭā Hā* 20:70-71)

Although the sorcerers' acceptance of Moses' message was based on evidence and experience, their right to freedom of belief was violated by one of the most evil figures (aside from Satan) in the Qur'an, Pharaoh. In fact, Pharaoh's coercian in matters of faith is constantly criticised throughout the Qur'an dialectically proving the right to freedom of belief.

The third story appears in the Makkan surah *al-Kahf*. The story is known as "the story of the companions of the cave," *qiṣṣah aṣḥāb al-kahf*. The Qur'anic account refers to a group of young monotheistic believers religiously persecuted and threatened with death by stoning if they refuse to abandon their religion. The Qur'an describes the persecutors' attitude towards religious diversity as follows:

> "...And let him behave with care and courtesy, and let him not inform any one about you. For if they should come upon you, they would stone you or force you to return to their cult, and in that case ye would never attain prosperity." (Qur'an *al-Kahf* 18:19-20)

The approach of compulsion and punishment in respect to the religious other is presented in the verses as an exclusive and oppressive pattern of behavior. The Qur'anic disapproval of such a pattern dialectically approves its opposite behavioral paradigm based on freedom of belief and inclusivism.

Therefore, the three Qur'anic stories, historically revealed in the oppressive context of Makkah, exemplify the dark side of human experience towards religious diversity. Analysis of the stories reveals the crucial point being criticised by the Qur'an to be religious persecution and punishment (whether by burning, crucifying or stoning) in response to determining one's belief system. More importantly, by revealing these stories in the Makkan context, the Qur'an on the one hand criticises Makkan oppression, and on the other dialectically prepares the ground as well as the mindset of Muslims for the establishment of a new multicultural society in Madinah based on freedom of belief and religious pluralism.

In sum, an examination of the different aspects of freedom of belief discussed in this section reveals the Qur'an to define this right as a value as well as a foundation of man's earthly test. Such is the significance of the right to freedom of belief, that it has been added to the main objectives of Islamic law, *Maqāṣid al-Sharīʿah al-Islāmiyyah*.[48] Therefore, ethico-behavioral patterns of religious compulsion and disregard for the right to freedom of belief in any Muslim context should not be regarded as a normative teaching of Islam, but as a cultural transformation of Islam.

[2]
Human Dignity

Although freedom of belief alone could allow for the existence of diversity, it is inadequate to create a sincere encounter of different religious commitments. This is largely because freedom is often perceived as a personal value. For this reason, in order not to be reduced to a vehicle for creating segregated religious communities, normative religious pluralism should rest on another universal value, which pertains equally to the nature of all human beings. This universal value is human dignity and will be examined next as the second Qur'anic foundation of normative religious pluralism.

Human dignity can simply be defined as "the worth of being human."[49] This short definition can be further clarified by Immanuel Kant's conclusion on human dignity, wherein he states: "Act so that you treat humanity, whether in your own person or in that of another, always as an end and never as a means only."[50] Therefore, the dignity of a human person is humanity itself, which according to Kant, should be the final target of human treatment.

Needless to say, the importance of human dignity has become, at least theoretically, one of the foundational bases of the modern world and hence there will hardly be a quesion left unanswered on the subject. In particular, once human rights became one of the main concerns of the United Nation, a vast amount of literature on human dignity was produced, to a degree that there now exists in Geneva an entire library on the subject. Our analysis however will focus on Qur'anic exegesis with a particular focus on human dignity as a universal foundation of normative religious pluralism. For thorough exposition of the Qur'anic attitude towards human dignity analysis will concentrate on two different levels, the first concerning the anthropological aspect of human dignity in the Qur'an, and the second examining some Qur'anic doctrines forming an ideological framework for preserving human dignity.

An Anthropological Analysis of Human Dignity in the Qur'an

At the outset, it should be clarified that by anthropological analysis in this context is meant exploration of the Qur'anic view on the genesis of human beings and their status among other creatures. By exploring anthropologically the Qur'anic view on the genesis of humans, this particular section of the research aims to show the relationship between human dignity and the inclusivity of God's love and compassion.

God's extreme care of human beings in the process of creation appears mainly in three points connected to human dignity. First, the Qur'an states that man has been created in the best of moulds: "We have indeed created man in the best of moulds" (Qur'an a*l-Tīn* 95:4). This means that a human being has been created in the best physical, spiritual and intellectual form.[51] Secondly, the process of man's creation has been conducted directly by God's hands, something also underpinned by God's criticism of *Iblīs* when he refuses to honor man (whom God created with His hands) by prostrating to him:

> (Allah) said: "O Iblīs! What prevents thee from prostrating thyself to one whom I have created with my hands? Art thou haughty? Or art thou one of the high (and mighty) ones?" (Qur'an *Ṣād* 38:75)

Finally and most importantly, God breathed of His spirit into man:

> But He fashioned him in due proportion, and breathed into him something of His spirit. And He gave you (the faculties of) hearing and sight and feeling (and understanding): little thanks do ye give! (Qur'an *al-Sajdah* 32:9)

These three aspects of man's creation show that man has been created by God with extreme and special care. God's care of the creation of man suggests the universality as well as the inclusivity of God's love and compassion towards all people. This fact, in turn, promotes the inviolability and the respect of human dignity to a universal value. This assertion is supported by the following authentic hadith:

> A believer is that person, who loves others and is loved by others, and there is nothing good about a person who does not love others and is not loved by others, and the dearest people to God are those who are most beneficial to other people.[52]

The statement of the Prophet that "the dearest people to God are those who are most beneficial to other people" underlines, on the one hand, the vertical relationship between God and those who care about His human creatures, and on the other emphasises the universality of human dignity and its foundational role in respect of the ethico-behavioral pattern of human relations.

The Qur'anic attitude towards human dignity is also manifested in the highest status that human beings enjoy among the rest of God's creatures. In this respect, the Qur'an says:

> We have honoured the sons of Adam; provided them with transport on land and sea; given them for sustenance things good and pure; and conferred on them special favors, above a great part of Our Creation. (Qur'an *al-Isrā'* 17:70)

God's great care and love for humanity appears again in this verse. However, this time the inviolability of human dignity is emphasised in a more particular sense. For instance, the past tense verb "honoured" is preceded by the word *laqad*. According to Arabic grammar a past tense verb preceded by *laqad* expresses a certainty and affirmation. This means that there must not be any doubt as to the fact of the dignity of all human beings having been honoured directly by God Himself. What is important to note here is that when it comes to the dignity of a human being, the Qur'an makes no distinction between people on the basis of their differing affiliations and identities. Instead, it states in a very inclusive way that "We have honoured the sons of Adam" (Qur'an *al-Isrā'* 17:70).

The universally honoured status which the Qur'an confers on human dignity can also be found in the prophetic ethico-behavioral model which serves as a practical reflection of the verse. In this respect, Jābir ibn ʿAbullah narrates:

> A funeral procession passed in front of us and the Prophet stood up and we too stood up. We said, "O Allāh's Apostle! This is the funeral procession of a Jew." He said: "Whenever you see a funeral procession, you should stand up."[53]

In another similar case, ʿAbd al-Raḥmān ibn Abū Laylā narrates that:

> Sahl ibn Ḥunayf and Qays ibn Saʿd were sitting in the city of Al-Qādisiyyah. A funeral procession passed in front of them and they stood up. They were told that that funeral procession was of one of the inhabitants of the land i.e. of a non-believer, under the protection of Muslims. They said, "A funeral procession passed in front of the Prophet and he stood up. When he was told that it was the coffin of a Jew, he said: 'Is it not a living being (soul)?'"[54]

This normative teaching of the Prophet in connection to the dignity of religiously different people, reveals two important points which deserve attention. The first pertains to the exclusive question raised by Muslims in both texts that why should they stand up given that the dead person was a Jew or generally, a non-believer. This query reflects the challenging process of transforming an exclusive mentality into a universal one. It seems transforming the pre-Islamic perception of the other into a new understanding of human relations was a long term educational process.

The second point relates to the Prophet's method of teaching Muslims how to respect others. In fact, the Prophet established the ethico-behavioural model of treating others on a universal basis. The reason for respecting others was clearly stated by the Prophet in the form of a counter-question: "Is it not a living being, *'a laysat nafsan?'*." Therefore, the main reason for respecting people is the fact that they are human beings. For this particular reason, the Prophet not only respected the dignity of people during their life, but also after their death.

According to the Qur'an, the dignified status of humans, given to mankind directly by God, is based on the fact that people have been created as intellectual beings endowed with knowledge, wisdom and free will.[55] At this point, it is important to look into some Qur'anic verses in order to understand the relationship between the intellectual nature of human beings and their dignity. The Qur'an remarks that when God initially informs the angels that He is going to create a new being called man, the angels appear to have disliked the project on the grounds that man would likely cause violence and bloodshed on Earth. However, once having witnessed man's intellectual power the angels suddenly change their attitude and bow down to him:

> Behold, thy Lord said to the angels: "I will create a vicegerent on earth." They said: "Wilt Thou place therein one who will make mischief therein and shed blood? Whilst we do celebrate Thy praises and glorify Thy holy (name)?" He said: "I know what ye know not." And He taught Adam the names of all things; then He placed them before the angels, and said: "Tell me the names of these if ye are right." They said: "Glory to Thee, of knowledge we have none, save what Thou Hast taught us: In truth it is Thou Who art perfect in knowledge and wisdom." He said: "O Adam! Tell them their names." When he had told them, Allah said: "Did I not tell you that I know the secrets of heaven and earth, and I know what ye reveal and what ye

> conceal?" And behold, We said to the angels: "Bow down to Adam" and they bowed down. Not so Iblis: he refused and was haughty: He was of those who reject Faith. (Qur'an *al-Baqarah* 2:30-34)

These verses reveal that man was able to dispel the accusation of being violent and thus to defend his dignity through use of his intellectual power.[56] However, what should be borne in mind is that man's dangerous potential to commit violence and shed blood becomes reality when his intellectual power is neglected and his dignity is violated.

This relationship between human intellectual power and dignity is remarkably underscored by Sacks in his work *The Dignity of Difference*, where he concludes that "education is the single greatest key to human dignity."[57] In the same way, the Bible states that:

> And God said; Let us make man in our image, after our likeness: and let them have dominion over the fish of the sea, and over the birds of the heavens, and over the cattle, and over all the earth, and over every creeping thing that creepeth upon the earth. And God created man in his own image, in the image of God created he him; male and female created he them. (Genesis 1:26-27)

In his interpretation of the Biblical verses, Saint Thomas Aquinas argues that the creation of man in God's image means that the human person is an intelligent being. Thus, according to the Bible also there exists a relationship between God's creation of humans, their intellectual nature, and human dignity.

The foregoing discussion on the relationship between the intellectual power of humans and their dignity shows that these two features are interdependently related. It means that the dignity of human beings is related to their ideologies, beliefs and way of thinking. Therefore, to respect the dignity of man means to respect also their ideological differences. Moreover, knowing that God has honoured mankind by endowing him with intellectual power, it is worth seeking wisdom in the face of the different other. In stark contrast, disregard of and rudeness towards other people's beliefs means violation of their dignity, which in turn can easily trigger man's inherent potential negativities.

In sum, our anthropological analysis of human dignity in the Qur'an reveals that human dignity is a universal right and value, inviolable and to be respected, emerging from God's love, care, and compassion towards man. Furthermore, the relationship between intellectual power and dignity requires people to respect differences on the one hand, and to seek intellectual exchange across the lines of these differences on the other. In this way, being interdependently related to the intellectual power of mankind, human dignity forms a universal foundation of normative religious pluralism.

Qur'anic Doctrines Concerning The Preservation of Human Dignity

Here focus will be on the broadest Qur'anic doctrines forming a framework likely to accommodate any elaborations concerning the preservation of human dignity. In fact, it can be assumed that the whole theory of the higher objectives of Islamic law, *maqāṣid al-sharīʿah*, which serves as an ideology for dignifying a human being, rests on these Qur'anic doctrines. The purpose of the discussion is to prove once again that according to the Qur'an, dignity is an inviolable human feature which stands above human ideology, thus constructing a universal foundation of normative religious pluralism.

The preservation of human dignity "has been a central concept in the Arabic culture since the pre-Islamic period."[58] In this respect, a great deal of data regarding the value of dignity can be found in pre-Islamic poetry, although this dignity was confined to a certain subject, identity, or social status. This narrow view created social destabilisation primarily because the modus operandi was to preserve the dignity of some by violating and destroying the dignity of others. The Qur'an importantly confirmed the value of human dignity and simultaneously made it clear that the dignity of all human beings was inviolable so moving away from the prejudice of the pre-Islamic concept and broadening its scope to include all humanity. Moreover, in order to preserve human dignity from any possible violation, the Qur'an set universal doctrines, guiding the ethico-behavioral model of treating others.

The first of these Qur'anic doctrines (aimed at preserving human dignity) relates one's deeds directly to personal responsibility: "Namely, that no bearer of burdens can bear the burden of another" (*al-Najm* 53:38).

This verse is mentioned five times in five Makkan surahs: *al-Najm*, *Fāṭir*, *al-Isrā'*, *al-Anʿām*, and *al-Zumur*.[59] And the fact that it appears only in Makkan surahs is testament to the Qur'an's early concern to preserve human dignity from any possible violation. In this respect, al-Zamakhsharī argues that the verse comes as a response to the following Qur'anic verse:

> And the Unbelievers say to those who believe: "Follow our path, and we will bear (the consequences) of your faults." Never in the least will they bear their faults: in fact they are liars! (Qur'an *al-ʿAnkabūt* 29:12)[60]

This statement asserting that one can bear the consequences of the deeds of others is an attempt to negate the notion of personal responsibility. The negation of personal responsibility means a loss of sovereignty over life, which in turn appears as tantamount to the loss of dignity, and to prevent the dignity of a human being from such violation, the Qur'an established the basic principle of personal responsibility in 53:38.

According to Rashid Rida, this verse is "considered as a major principle of all revealed religions throughout the history of mankind, and it also constitutes one of the most central foundations of the reform of human personal as well as collective life."[61] This is because the destiny of man should rest in their own hands and everyone should be the author of his or her deeds and life by bearing a personal and moral responsibility before God.[62] In fact, the realisation of the importance as well as the dimensions of personal responsibility, as imparted by the verse, constructs a major principle for preserving human dignity by implying that nobody should become the victim of other people's faults.

Another Qur'anic doctrine preserving human dignity is the belief that the earth belongs only to God, and that He created it for the benefit of all human beings equally. The Qur'an says:

> It is He Who hath created for you all things that are on earth; Moreover His design comprehended the heavens, for He gave order and perfection to the seven firmaments; and of all things He hath perfect knowledge. (Qur'an *al-Baqarah* 2:29)

Al-Sharawi's comment on this verse is that "it comes to draw our attention to the fact that the earth is the property of God and that we do not own anything except as trustees on behalf of God during our earthly life."[63] On the other hand, Abū Ḥayyān al-Andalusī states that the words "for you," *lakum*, are related to the whole of mankind and that the preposition "for," the letter *lām* making the word *la*, functions as a reason for the creation of the earth. In other words, it means that for the benefit of the whole of mankind God created the earth.[64]

The fact that the earth belongs to no human being but only to God and that He is the Merciful Sustainer of the whole of mankind forms an inviolable right to life for every human being regardless of their different identities. In this respect, the Qur'an makes it clear that the right to life cannot be violated for ideological reasons:

> And remember Abraham said: "My Lord, make this a City of Peace, and feed its people with fruits, – such of them as believe in Allah and the Last Day." He said: "(Yea), and such as reject Faith, – for a while will I grant them their pleasure, but will soon drive them to the torment of Fire, – an evil destination (indeed)!" (Qur'an *al-Baqarah* 2:126)

The Prophet Abraham's perception of God's mercy towards

human beings in this world was corrected by God.[65] So, religious affiliation or identity does not matter when it comes to exercising the right to life, but rather it is "God's mercy which covers the whole of mankind and provides all with essential needs for [a] secure life."[66] The Qur'an underscores more vividly, the fact that all people receive God's favor and that this is not closed to anyone:

> Of the bounties of thy Lord We bestow freely on all – These as well as those: The bounties of thy Lord are not closed (to anyone). (Qur'an *al-Isrā'* 17:20)

Fakhr al-Dīn al-Rāzī comments on this verse: "God provides all people with everything they need for a dignified and pleasant life. God's bounty is open to all and restricted to none. This is because the earth is a place where human beings are examined before God."[67]

In sum, Qur'anic doctrine asserts that the earth belongs to God alone but has been created for the benefit of all mankind. This grants every human being therefore an inviolable right to life. This Qur'anic position preserves human dignity and implies that no one has the right to monopolise the life of others. Moreover, to emulate God's mercy towards people, believers should make an effort to contribute positively towards creating a dignified and pleasant life for all human beings regardless of their religious differences.

Another clear Qur'anic doctrine preserving human dignity is removal of any intermediaries between God and man. According to the Qur'an, every single person regardless of his/her identity and social status can freely connect, without any need for special authority, with God.

> When My servants ask thee concerning Me, I am indeed close (to them): I listen to the prayer of every suppliant when he calleth on Me: Let them also, with a will, Listen to My call, and believe in Me: That they may walk in the right way. (Qur'an *al-Baqarah* 2:186)

Although this verse occurs in the context of verses explaining fasting, this does not mean we restrict its scope to Muslims only, the direct relationship between God and man referred to is inclusive of all human beings. It is important to note that the word "servants," *ʿibād*, used in the verse can refer to all human beings, as is the case in the following verse:

> He is the Irresistibly Supreme over His servants. And He is the Wise, Acquainted with all things.[68] (Qur'an *al-Anʿām* 6:18)

There is no disagreement among scholars over the meaning of the word "servants," *ʿibād*, used in this verse. They are unanimous that it refers to all human beings. Moreover, Abdel Haleem goes further to translate "servants," *ʿibād*, in this verse as God's creatures.[69] Therefore, providing that the word servants, *ʿibād*, is used in the Qur'an in an inclusive way, it cannot be used as a reason for limiting the principle of direct relation exclusively to Muslims. In other words, God's encouragement to His servants, *ʿibād*, to seek a direct relation with Him is meant for all people, though the primary addressees might be considered Muslims, seeing as the verse is presented in the context of fasting:

> Ramadan is the (month) in which was sent down the Qur'an, as a guide to mankind, also clear (Signs) for guidance and judgment (Between right and wrong). So every one of you who is present (at his home) during that month should spend it in fasting, but if any one is ill, or on a journey, the prescribed period (Should be made up) by days later. Allah intends every facility for you; He does not want to put to difficulties. (He wants you) to complete the prescribed period, and to glorify Him in that He has guided you; and perchance ye shall be grateful.

> When My servants ask thee concerning Me, I am indeed close (to them): I listen to the prayer of every supplicant when he calleth on Me: Let them also, with a will, Listen to My call, and believe in Me: That they may walk in the right way. (Qur'an *al-Baqarah* 2:185-186)

Ibn Jarīr al-Ṭabarī mentions a possible occasion for the verse's revelation explaining: "a person came and asked the Prophet whether God was close to people in order to whisper to Him or He was far from them so to raise their voices while speaking to Him."[70] Muhammad Abduh comments on this: "It is very likely such a question to have been raised by Arabs or Bedouins, since they were accustomed to seek intermediaries between them and God."[71] So, it can be assumed that in allowing mankind to freely communicate with God, in that context, Islam ushered in a new phenomenon. In this respect Henry Corbin remarks in his *History of Islamic Philosophy*:

> The first thing to note is the absence in Islam of the phenomenon of the Church. Just as Islam has no clergy in possession of the "means of grace," so it has no dogmatic magisterium, no pontifical authority, no Council which is responsible for defining dogma.[72]

In fact, the absence of any special authority serving as an intermediary between man and God plays an important role in preserving human dignity, since such authority could be corrupted and thereby become a source of injustice and oppression destroying the dignity of human beings.

Furthermore, according to the Qur'an, when people commit a sin or feel guilty over any wrongdoing, they do not need to confess their sin to anyone pretending to possess the "means of grace." All that they need to do is turn directly to God and beg forgiveness:

> Say: "O, my Servants who have transgressed against their souls! Despair not of the Mercy of Allah: for Allah forgives all sins: for He is Oft-Forgiving, Most Merciful". (Qur'an *al-Zumar* 39:53)

Ibn Ashur explains that "O, my Servants" in this verse refers primarily to pagans.[73] The direct relationship offered by God to man is for every human being, and everyone is given the privacy to confess his/her sins to God alone in order not to expose their dignity to humiliation. In a similar way, according to the verse, human sin should be seen as an opportunity for compassion, forgiveness, and change, instead of accusation, hatred and enmity.

It will be seen that these Qur'anic doctrines hence emphasise three essential elements for human existence: man's deeds, life, and relationship to God. Due to all three's critical importance for man's earthly as well as eschatological existence, they have been meant by God to be strictly characteristic of every single human being. Thus, the doctrines form a framework for preserving human dignity in such a way, that no one person has the right to monopolise any other person's deeds, life, and relationship to God.

Overall, the examination demonstrates that the Qur'an does not require a special religious affiliation with regards to respect for human dignity and its inviolability, and more importantly, determines this respect for human dignity as a natural right and universal value. Thus, an ethico-behavioral pattern oriented towards humiliation of the dignity of religiously different people contradicts the normative teaching of the Qur'an.

[3]
Integrity

Integrity towards religiously different people was identified in the previous chapter as an essential ethical element, which protects the process of normative religious pluralism from becoming mere diplomacy. Furthermore, integrity can be regarded as the most central inward dimension of normative religious pluralism. Due to this importance it is essential to examine the Qur'an's stand towards integrity and establish whether it approves treating those of different faith with truthfulness despite their differing beliefs.

The Qur'an's universal ethical system in general, and its attitude towards freedom of belief and respect for human dignity in particular, indicate that integrity towards non-Muslims is a naturally obvious stance to observe. Consequently, such behavior cannot be transgressed or contradicted by other normative teachings of Islam, except in the case of religious persecution, killing and oppression (to be discussed in detail in chapter five). Although the Qur'anic position is plainly obvious nevertheless for the purpose of clarity, it is important to conduct further exegetical examination.

People should use integrity towards those of other faiths and the most central Qur'anic verse in regard to this is:

> Allah forbids you not, with regard to those who fight you not for (your) faith nor drive you out of your homes, from dealing kindly and justly with them: for Allah loveth those who are just. (Qur'an *al-Mumtaḥinah* 60:8)

Analysis of the verse reveals that it encompasses three main aspects which allow an accurate and comprehensive conclusion to be derived with respect to the issue of integrity towards the other. The first is the historical aspect and this is related to the debate on the current status of the verse, whether it has been abrogated or not. The second is linked to the question of the identity of those who are meant to be treated with kindness and justice. The third concerns focus on the meaning of the verb *tabarrūhum*, translated as "dealing kindly."

With regard to the first aspect – the issue of abrogation – its worth pointing out that abrogation has been so excessively applied by some classical sources of Qur'anic exegesis, that there seems to have existed a tendency to regard as abrogated any positive Qur'anic verse concerning the religiously different other. And verse 60:8 is no exception. For instance, al-Ṭabarī reports Ibn Zayd and Qatādah having adopted the attitude of abrogation with regard to it, so according to Ibn Zayd: "The above verse has been abrogated by the verses ordering Muslims to face by their swords pagans and slay them if they refuse to accept Islam."[74] Qatādah asserts much the same pointing to: "Then fight and slay the Pagans wherever ye find them" (Qur'an *al-Tawbah* 9:5)[75] as having abrogated verse 60:8.

To critique the abrogation claim we need to first clarify (as discussed earlier) that the term abrogation (*naskh*) prior to al-Shāfiʿī's *Al-Risālah* was used in its broadest sense to mean both specifying as well as substitution. By specifying is meant elucidating the meaning of Qur'anic general words by different linguistic approaches, and by substitution is meant substitution of an earlier Qur'anic rule, *ḥukum*, with a chronologically successive one (as is claimed for verse 60:8 by i.e. Ibn Zayd and Qatādah).[76]

To state that the treatment of people on the basis of kindness and justice has been replaced by a new rule ordering their bloodshed, largely due to their different belief system, needs to be firmly underpinned by clear evidence. However, in respect of verse 60:8, which allows Muslims to treat peaceful people with kindness and justice, there does not exist a single piece of authentic evidence from the Prophet indicating that the verse has been abrogated. This might be the reason behind al-Ṭabarī's statement that in the case of verse 60:8 the claim of abrogation is unacceptable.[77]

On the other hand, those scholars who support the occurrence of abrogation have set a clear condition for its acceptance. The condition requires an absolute contradiction between two or more verses and the absence of any possible way of reconciliation.[78] However, according to Abū Zahrah such a condition is not applicable to the Qur'an. He states: "Together with a number of scholars, we participated in writing a work of Qur'anic exegesis entitled *Al-Muntakhab*. In our entire work on the Qur'an, we did not find any two verses that can be regarded as contradictory to each other."[79]

Therefore, the question arising is whether the kind and just treatment of people, expressed by verse 60:8, contradicts the Qur'anic imperative of fighting? The answer lies in the textual context of 60:8. Verse 60:9 immediately following 60:8 states:

> Allah only forbids you, with regard to those who fight you for (your) Faith, and drive you out of your homes, and support (others) in driving you out, from turning to them (for friendship and protection). It is such as turn to

> them (in these circumstances), that do wrong. (Qur'an *al-Mumtaḥinah* 60:9)

This verse explicitly clarifies that the prohibition of kind treatment is directed against those who are engaged in fighting Muslims and driving them out of their homes. In contrast verse 60:8 clearly allows Muslims to treat with kindness and justice those people who do not initiate war against them or expel them from their homes. In this way, there is no contradiction between the imperative to fight and the prescription of inclusive kindness towards people, since the former applies only to the people of war, while the latter is related to peaceful people in general.

Therefore, the abrogation claims made by Ibn Zayd and Qatādah in respect of verse 60:8 are untenable, for they contradict the textual context of the verse, the Qur'anic normative principles of warfare, the character of the Prophet, and universally accepted human values. Such claims are also not supported with any authentic evidence. Moreover, the point which is to be noted is that these abrogation claims are attributed to exegetes of the third exegetical generation of the Successors, but not to the Prophet or the Companions. This fact suggests the possibility of the claims having been employed later in the history of interfaith relations as evidence underpinning exclusive attitudes towards religiously different people.

Turning to the second aspect of the analysis of 60:8, which concerns the question of who the people meant to be treated with kindness and justice are, it appears that once again a number of exclusive claims have been made. For instance, Mujāhid claims that the people meant to be treated with kindness and justice are those who had embraced Islam in Makkah, but did not immigrate to Madinah.[80] On the other hand, al-Rāzī states the following:

> There is a disagreement about who are those people that 'do not fight you.' However, most of the scholars see that those are the people of covenant, *ahl al-ʿahd*, who signed an agreement neither to fight against the Prophet and

> Muslims nor to help anybody against them. Actually, it was the tribe of Khuzāʿah that signed an agreement neither to fight against the Prophet nor to drive him out of his homeland. For this reason, those people were treated with kindness and loyalty until the covenant came to its end.[81]

Another opinion mentioned by al-Rāzī is that those people who are meant to be treated with kindness and justice, are women and children.[82] Finally, for Ibn Zayd and Qatādah the people referred to are the peaceful pagans, although for them the verse has been abrogated.

Reviewing the varying opinions, it is evident that all are restricted and thus exclusive in some respects. Mujāhid, Ibn Zayd, and Qutādah's opinion is limited in terms of religious affiliation and thus exclusively restricts treatment with kindness and justice only to Muslims. As for the opinion ascribed by al-Rāzī to most scholars, it restricts treatment with kindness and justice only to people of the covenant, where this kind treatment is limited to the end of the covenant. In this respect, the opinion is exclusive in terms of time and also suggests that the general state of human relationships is war, except in the case of existing a covenant. Whereas, according to the second opinion mentioned by al-Rāzī, kind and just treatment is limited only to women and children and thus is exclusive in terms of gender and age.

Hence the feature common to all exclusive based opinions is the act of giving specific meaning to the general staement (and meaning) of verse 60:8. However, according to one of the most important rules of Qur'anic exegesis, both legal regulations, *al-aḥkām al-sharʿiyyah*, and reports, *al-akhbār*, retain their general meaning until there comes reason and evidence for giving them a specific one. In the same way, occasions of revelation, *asbāb al-nuzūl*, do not make specific the general meanings of the Qur'anic words.[83] For this reason, throughout his exegetical analysis relying heavily on these rules of Qur'anic exegesis al-Ṭabarī concludes on 60:8 that the people to be treated with kindness and justice are all people of all nations and religions, who neither fight against Muslims nor expel them from their homes. This is due to the fact that the verse should remain in its general sense, since there is nothing to specify it.[84] In favor of this inclusive opinion are scholars such al-Zamakhsharī and Ibn Ashur.[85]

Therefore, the Qur'anic exegetical rules lead us to the conclusion that the scope of verse 60:8 inclusively covers all peaceful people and thus encourages Muslims to deal with all human beings on the basis of kindness and justice. Conversely, the scope of the verse cannot accommodate only those people who initiate war against Muslims or drive them out of their homes.

Having proved that verse 60:8 has not been abrogated and that it has an active meaning, as well as being inclusive in scope, it is important to study the meaning of the verse with particular focus on the verb *tabarrūhum*. This has been translated as "dealing kindly" but of course its subtle and accurate meaning has been lost in translation, because Qur'anic Arabic has great depth of meaning and when translated from Arabic into any other language, nuances conveyed by the original are not always fully transmitted. An approximation can only be given.

The verb *tabarrūhum* is a key word for understanding the Qur'anic attitude towards integrity as a central ethical element in the process of normative religious pluralism. In order to examine the meaning of *tabarrūhum* in depth, we need to first methodologically explore the Qur'anic usage of this word. In this regard, it should be mentioned that the root morpheme of *tabarrūhum* is *b-r-r*, the infinitive *barra*, and the noun *birr*. The adjective of *barra* is *barrun*, and the plural of this is *abrār* or *bararah*.

To examine the Qur'anic usage of the root *b-r-r* we begin with surah *al-Baqarah* in which the meaning of *birr* is defined in two separate places. The first Qur'anic definition of *birr* occurs in the following verse:

> It is not righteousness (*birr*) that ye turn your faces towards East or West; but it is righteousness (*birr*) – to believe in Allah and the Last Day, and the Angels, and the Book, and the Messengers; to spend of your substance, out of love for Him, for your kin, for orphans, for the needy, for the wayfarer,

> for those who ask, and for the ransom of slaves; to be steadfast in prayer, and practice regular charity; to fulfil the contracts which ye have made; and to be firm and patient, in pain (or suffering) and adversity, and throughout all periods of panic. Such are the people of truth, the God-fearing. (Qur'an *al-Baqarah* 2:177)

In this verse the noun of *birr* is translated as "righteousness," whereas in 60:8, where the word exists in the form of a verb (*tabarrūhum*), it has been translated as "dealing kindly." This again proves the complexity of the word in terms of its translation from Arabic. However, observing the Qur'anic definition of *birr* in verse 2:177, we see that the Qur'an begins definition of *birr* by a process of elimination. The verse states that the meaning of *birr* is not that people turn their faces towards East and West, but *birr* is that people remain true and sincere towards God, themselves, and their fellow-men. In this respect, Asad remarks that in the verse "the Qur'an stresses the principle that mere compliance with outward forms does not fulfil the requirements of piety."[86] Therefore, according to the verse, *birr* is a notion based on the inward dimensions of humanity's dealing with God, people, themselves, and others. Thus, *birr* requires that any action should proceed from truthfulness and integrity. Accordingly, *birr* loses its true meaning if implemented on the basis of formalism.

In the Qur'an's second definition of *birr* (correcting the wrong perception some had adopted concerning it at the time of the Prophet) it points out:

> ...It is no virtue (*birr*) if ye enter your houses from the back: It is virtue (*birr*) if ye fear Allah. Enter houses through the proper doors: And fear Allah. That ye may prosper. (Qur'an *al-Baqarah* 2:189)

Birr here is translated into English as "virtue." What is more important, however, is the fact that the Qur'an underlines again the meaning of *birr* in terms of its inward dimensions. The historical background of the verse makes known that some people at the time of the Prophet had a perception that it was unlawful to enter their houses from the front and proper door after performing pilgrimage and this tradition or rather superstition was regarded as a sort of *birr*. Thus, they insisted on having special entrances at the back of their houses, from where pilgrims could enter.[87] However, the Qur'an corrects this wrong perception by emphasizing the meaning of *birr* to be not about the method of entering houses, but about fearing God. In this way, the Qur'an once again stipulates that *birr* cannot be restricted to the outwards dimensions of certain actions.

The root *b-r-r* exists also in the form of an adjective in two verses of surah Maryam:

> And kind (*barran*) to his parents, and he was not overbearing or rebellious. (Qur'an *Maryam* 19:14)

> "(He) hath made me kind (*barran*) to my mother, and not overbearing or miserable." (Qur'an *Maryam* 19:32)

Barran in both verses has been translated as "kind" and is mentioned in relation to the prophets Yaḥyā (John) and Jesus, respectively. Both prophets are described as *barran* in terms of their dealing with their parents. In this case, *barran* indicates a sincere and respectful way of dealing with parents. For this reason, it is known among Arabs that the expression *birru al-wālidayn* (commonly used by them) indicates a sincere and respectful relationship between children and their parents. The Qur'an uses the adjective *barran* to describe prophets Jesus and Yaḥyā's sincere and respectful behavior towards their parents. Semantically thus the meaning of *barran* conveyed is not one of double standards or formalism, meaning in turn that this latter type of behavior towards non-Muslims, who are peaceful to us, is not accepted.

As mentioned earlier the adjective of *barra* is *barrun*, and the plural of this is *abrār* which is used as a description of the inhabitants of Paradise: "As for the Righteous (*abrār*), they will be in bliss" (Qur'an *al-Infiṭār* 82:13). The inhabitants of Paradise are described as *abrār* due to their sincere and truthful compliance with God's commands.

In the same way, Angels are described as *bararah*, which is a second plural form of *b-r-r*: "Honourable and Pious and Just" (Qur'an *ʿAbasa* 80:16). *Bararah* has been translated here as "pious and just." The description of Angels as *bararah* is due to their sincere and truthful worshiping of God.

Therefore, the root morpheme *b-r-r* in its different grammatical forms has been translated into English as: "dealing kindly," "kind," "righteousness," "righteous," "virtue," "pious and just." However, as the analysis has shown the Qur'anic usage of *b-r-r* indicates also honesty and truthfulness in actions. Conversely, the Qur'anic usage of *b-r-r* has also shown that the meaning of this word cannot accommodate double standards, hypocrisy, and false diplomacy in terms of relationships. Correspondingly, the lexicographer Ibn Fāris confirms that one of the meanings of *b-r-r* is truthfulness, *ṣidq*, as well as honesty in love.[88]

In sum analysis of verse 60:8 has demonstrated that its status is *muḥkam* (not abrogated) and that it is inclusive in terms of human relationships. Thus, the verse prescribes an ethical norm of treating peaceful people on the basis of love and integrity. Moreover, the occurrence of the word *tabarrūhum* in the verse excludes any dishonest, manipulative, and false diplomatic behavior to be enacted towards other people, reaching its culmination at the end of the verse, wherein the treatment of religiously different people on the basis of integrity is defined as a way of gaining Gods' love.

[4]
The Prohibition of Reviling What is Sacred to Others

To revile and to critique are two different things especially as concerns establishing the Qur'an's fundamental message of the Oneness of God. It is crucially important that an accurate distinction be made between Qur'anic descriptive and prescriptive data, particularly while deriving from the Qur'an conceptions of interfaith relations. This is because the Qur'an describes the issue of unbelief and unbelievers for the purpose of providing guidance by revealing the difference between belief and unbelief, but does not prescribe harmful actions towards these people and their belief system, except in the context of oppression and war. In the same way, the Qur'an, with the aim of guidance, repeatedly describes idols and gods other than Allah as not having any power and influence over people's life, but does not prescribe violent action against them, except when belief in these idols or gods is oppressively imposed on people, as in the case of prophet Moses' destruction of the statue of the calf. For this reason, although the Qur'an and Hadith descriptively inform us that Jesus was a human being and only one of God's prophets, and that he was not crucified, neither the Qur'an nor the Hadith prescribe destruction of the cross, which is regardedby Christians as a sacred symbol of their faith. In fact, Prophet Muhammad reveals that Jesus himself, with whom the cross is associated, will come to Earth to destroy it. In this regard Abū Hurayrah reports that the Prophet said:

> The Hour will not be established until the son of Mary (i.e. Jesus) descends amongst you as a just ruler; he will break the cross, kill the pigs, and abolish the Jizya tax. Money will be in abundance so nobody will accept it (as charitable gifts).[89]

The question which might arise in this case is why did the Prophet then destroy the idols around the Kaʿbah. In this respect, it should be mentioned that there exists not a single authentic piece of evidence proving that the Prophet took any action against Makkah's idols before conquering the city. Authentic evidence recorded by al-Bukhārī however shows ʿAbdullāh ibn Masʿūd reporting the following:

> When the Prophet entered Makkah on the day of the Conquest, there were

> 360 idols around the Kaʿbah. The Prophet started striking them with a stick he had in his hand and was saying: "Truth has come and Falsehood will neither start nor will it reappear."[90]

The Prophet's destruction of these idols cannot be regarded as some sort of Islamic normative teaching which allows abuse of what is sacred to others, since on the day the idols were destroyed scarcely anyone remained in Makkah and its surrounding areas who held them as sacred. Thus they were no longer needed in this context. ʿAmr ibn Salimah reports that: "...When Mecca was conquered, then every tribe rushed to embrace Islam..."[91] Moreover, on this day of conquest the leader of Makkah's pagans Abū Sufyān embraced Islam and proclaimed his loyalty to the Prophet Muhammad.[92] Al-Barā' reports that in the same year of the conquest of Makkah, during the battle of Ḥunayn: "...Abū Sufyan ibn al-Ḥārith was holding the white mule of the Prophet by the head, and the Prophet was saying: 'I am the Prophet undoubtedly, I am the son of ʿAbd al-Muṭṭalib.'"[93]

Even if we want to assume that a number of pagans still remained, we should be aware of the fact that the main religious context in Makkah, after its conquest, was Islam and hence the Kaʿbah, which was note initially established as a sign of the Oneness of God by the prophets Abraham and Ishmael, was not a place for idols. Actually, it is even dubious whether the pagans of Makkah had ever perceived of their idols as being sacred but rather viewed them simply as a means to gain benefit. For instance, the Prophet revealed that Makkah's pagans knew very well of the truth of the prophets Abraham and Ishmael. In this regard, Ibn ʿAbbās narrates the following:

> When Allah's Apostle arrived at Makkah, he refused to enter the Kaʿbah while there were idols in it. So he ordered that they be taken out. The pictures of (the Prophets) Abraham and Ishmael, holding arrows of divination in their hands, were carried out. The Prophet said: "May Allah ruin them (i.e. infidels) for they knew very well that they (i.e. Abraham and Ishmael) never drew lots by these (divination arrows)"...[94]

William Watt reaches a similar conclusion with regards to the idols of Makkah not constituting anything sacred for the pagans: "The nomadic Arabs are said to have had many gods, but these do not seem to have meant much to them."[95]

Therefore, the Prophet's removal of the idols from the Kaᶜbah cannot be employed as legal evidence supporting the act of reviling what is sacred to non-Muslims, since once Makkah had been conquered, no pagans remained. Second, the Kaᶜbah was not initially built as a place for idols. Third, the Makkan idols do not seem to have been held as sacred in that context.

As for the Qur'anic account which informs us that Abraham destroyed the idols worshipped by the pagans of his tribe, such action also carries no legal implications for Muslims, since the story occurs before the prophethood of Abraham is established, at a time when he was a youth (see Qur'an 21:60).

Now, unlike the Qur'anic descriptive data pertaining to what is sacred to non-Muslims, the Qur'anic prescriptive ethical principles in this respect seem to go further to secure not only the dignity of religiously different people, but to secure also the dignity of what is regarded as sacred to them.[96] On this subject, the Qur'an prescribes to Muslims not to utter any abusive word or to take any insulting action towards what is sacred to others:

> Revile not ye those whom they call upon besides Allah, lest they out of spite revile Allah in their ignorance. Thus have We made alluring to each people its own doings. In the end will they return to their Lord, and He shall then tell them the truth of all that they did. (Qur'an *al-Anᶜām* 6:108)

Interestingly, no abrogation claims have been made for this verse in the sources of Qur'anic exegesis, and the reason for this absence is understandable, since according to the verse, there is an interdependent relation between reviling what is sacred to others and the revilement of Allah. Therefore, it is clear that any abrogation claims would be insensitive to the possibility of Allah being reviled. Where the difficulty lies however is in the exegetical understanding, in some quarters, of the root cause of the prohibition forbidding the abuse of what is sacred to others.

Generally speaking, exegetes agree that verse 6:108 has not been abrogated and hence its ruling remains valid for all generations.[97] Consequently, this means that it is not permissible for a Muslim to abuse what is regarded as sacred to others. Yet, the motivation for the prohibition has been defined in a great number of Qur'anic exegesis sources as diplomacy, rather than as an unchangeable ethical value. For instance, al-Zamakhsharī regards the reviling of what is sacred to others basically as true behavior and even as a way of worshipping God, but since there is a fear that such behavior could lead to a revilement of Allah, it is prohibited.[98] In the same vein al-Rāzī observes:

> If somebody asks: knowing that it is a principle of worshipping God, how the revilement of idols could be prohibited? The answer is that: although, this is a way of worshipping God, it is prohibited, since it results in reviling God and His Prophet, and results also in emerging many other evils.[99]

Moreover, al-Qurṭubī states:

> Providing that unbelievers are strong and powerful, and thus it is feared that they would revile Islam, or the Prophet, or Allah, then it is not permissible for a Muslim to revile the religious symbols of unbelievers, their religion, or churches...In this way, the verse 6:108 serves as evidence that a possessor of a certain right should abandon his or her right, if it harms the religion.[100]

Another opinion has been strongly linked to the process of inviting people to Islam (*daʿwah*). For example, Ibn Ashur assumes that the prohibition of reviling idols allows Muslims to fully engage in calling pagans to Islam, and thus to prove their paganism as wrong.[101] More vividly, al-Sharawi devotes his entire commentary on verse 6:108 to the process of calling people to Islam, arguing that the verse conveys a necessary method of *daʿwah*. In other words, the reason for the prohibition, according to al-Sharawi, is accommodation to human nature in the interests of inviting others to Islam. He observes that encouraging others to embrace Islam is so extremely difficult a task that any additional behavior insulting those we are inviting would make it impossible.[102]

To summarise these opinions it would appear that reviling what is sacred to others is considered a Muslim's right, naturally true behavior, and a principle of worshipping Allah. The only reason it is avoided is to avert any reprisal in the form of revilement against Allah and to protect *daʿwah* efforts from being affected negatively.

In other words this position is considered a diplomatic one rather than an unchangeable ethical value. The prohibition of reviling what is sacred to others contradicts in my opinion previously discussed foundations of normative religious pluralism, namely freedom of belief, human dignity and integrity. At this point, in order to judge whether the prohibition is based on a Qur'anic ethical value or diplomacy, it is important to explore verse 6:108 linguistically.

The first thing to note is that the verse begins with a command to Muslims not to revile those whom people call upon besides Allah. The verb conveying this prohibition is in the imperative form – *lā tasubbū* – the meaning of which is not confined to revilement, but goes further to mean humiliation.[103] In fact, there is a clear difference between the act of criticising what is sacred to others on the basis of compelling arguments, and the act of humiliating what is regarded sacred thorough use of emotively rude language and insulting words. Of course, it is the latter which is the focus of *lā tasubbū* and thus is prohibited by the Qur'an. So, the question arises how on earth can emotional humiliation of what is deemed sacred to others be regarded as a principle of worshipping God? The implication being that the Qur'an and the Prophet would otherwise allow Muslims to abuse what others hold sacred and thus knowingly insult and humiliate them. Obviously, statements of this kind contradict the overall Qur'anic context, Islamic ethics, and the behavior of the Prophet. For this reason, observing that the imperative of 6:108 is ethically not applicable to the Prophet because he would never have done so anyway, Ibn Ashur remarks that *lā tasubbū* is directed at Muslims, not the Prophet, since his great character would never allow for the abuse and humiliation of others.[104]

Another core issue in terms of the linguistic analysis is the use of the relative clause "those whom," *alladhīn*. It is commonly known that the relative clause *alladhīn* is used in the Arabic language to refer only to intellectual beings. However, in verse 6:108 *alladhīn* is used with reference to idols, which the Qur'an principally defines as having no intellectual power. Why has this been done? Ibn ʿAṭiyyah was the first to partly answer this question, suggesting that *alladhīn* here is used to underscore the conviction of unbelievers that their idols have intellectual power when in fact they obviously don't.[105] This subtle divine consideration for the convictions of others is important to note in the context of our discussion on the root cause of the prohibition. In other words if God Himself has shown consideration for the pagans' conviction as regards their idols, then for humanity the motive force behind the prohibition of reviling the gods of others should surely be identified as an ethical parameter related to freedom of belief and human dignity. Hence, in the context of the prohibition of reviling idols, the divine usage of the relative clause *alladhīn* in respect of non-intellectual beings has clear ethical dimensions. Of course let us be clear reviling idols is one thing thing but engaging in constructive conversation about the nature of these effigies, or this form of worship is something entirely different and there should be no confusion between the two.

The next key linguistic aspect is the existence of the conjunction *fā'* attached to the verb *fayasubbū Allāh*. The English translation of this part reads "lest they out of spite revile Allah" (6:108). In fact, the existence of the letter *fā'*, meaning lest, attached to the verb *yasubbū*, revile, can be regarded as the main reason for adopting the diplomatic behavior argument in terms of the motivation behind the prohibition. This is largely due to the fact that one of the main functions of the letter *fā'* in the Arabic language is to express a cause and effect relationship, *fā' al-sababiyyah*. Actually, in the case of verse 6:108 exegetes are unanimous that *fā'* expresses a relationship of cause and effect, meaning that if Muslims revile the idols/deities of others this would lead to a reciprocal revilement of Allah by the pagans, which in turn would affect negatively the call to Islam. This being seen as the root cause of the prohibition, what is understood from it is the view (held by the latter) that the act of reviling other people's deities/idols is a legal right, a way of worshipping Allah, and morally acceptable behavior, which is not to be put into practice however, because of the harmful consequences of Allah being reviled and *daʿwah* being hindered.

This assumption and conclusion can be challenged. The conjuction *fā'*, seems to indicate the inevitability of negative ramifications emerging necessarily from the violation of freedoms of belief and human dignity. The following example gives a relevant understanding of the function of *fā'*: an imperative is directed to "Y" not to kill child "X," lest the father take revenge on "Y." It would be morally unacceptable to assume that the root cause for the prohibition of child "X's" killing is the fear of "Y" being killed in revenge. Obviously the reason for the prohibition is to maintain (and underscore) the sanctity of human life with revenge on "Y" being one of the adverse consequences emerging necessarily from the violation of the right of "X" to exist. Taking this understanding to verse 6:108, it is apparent that it is ethically more accurate to determine *fā'* as an indication of the inevitability of negative effects being caused by the violation of freedom of belief and human dignity, which should be regarded as the root motivation for the prohibition of reviling what is sacred to others.

Another argument in favor of this interpretation (that the root cause of the prohibition is freedom of belief and human dignity, is based on the second part of the verse 6:108: "Thus have We made alluring to each people its own doings" (6:108). The Arabic word *zayyannā*, which means "we made it appear alluring," reflects a certain feature of human nature to consider its own actions and beliefs as true. Commenting on this part of the verse Qutub states that "it is human nature that when a person does something, whether good or bad, he thinks that he has done well and he defends his actions."[106] Similarly, Asad points out that "Thus have We made alluring to each people its own doings" implies that:

> It is in the nature of man to regard the beliefs which have been implanted in him from childhood, and which he now shares with his social environment, as the only true and possible ones, with the result that a polemic against those beliefs often tends to provoke a hostile psychological reaction.[107]

More strikingly, al-Tabatabai observes that verse 6:108 introduces a religious ethic, through which the dignity of anything that people hold as sacred is protected from humiliation. This is because human beings defend by nature the dignity of what they hold as sacred.[108]

Therefore, providing that beliefs are related to the intellectual nature of humans, the prohibition of reviling what is sacred to others should be seen as an unchangeable ethical parameter, regardless of whether or not there is a possibility that other people could revile Allah or they would not embrace Islam. Thus, there should be a clear-cut distinction between human rights, which are based on unchangeable ethics, and any strategy of embrace or diplomacy.

The textual context in which verse 6:108 exists, serves as additional evidence for the view that freedom of belief and dignity are the root cause for the prohibition of reviling what is sacred to others. Verse 6:107 immediately preceding the prohibition verse clearly attests the right to freedom of belief:

> If it had been Allah's plan, they would not have taken false gods: but We made thee not one to watch over their doings, nor art thou set over them to dispose of their affairs. (Qur'an *al-Anʿām* 6:107)

In respect of this verse, Rida states that it "authenticates the right of freedom of belief in an unprecedented way."[109] Furthermore, he points out that the textual context of the prohibition of reviling people's beliefs pertains to the fact that humans have been created on the basis of intellectual diversity. This means that it is impossible for them to agree upon one single religion. For this reason, God sent all His prophets to guide people, but not to impose on them a certain belief. In the same way, God did not allow any of His prophets to violate humanity's freedom of belief, since humans have been endowed with this right directly by God Himself, who if He had willed would have made all people believe in one single religion.[110] Therefore, the textual context of 6:108 also does not favor the opinion which holds the revilement of people's gods an Islamic principle, a way of worship, and a Muslim's right.

The final argument supporting the thesis of the prohibition being a perpetual ethical value set by the Qur'an, emerges from the historical context of the Prophet's life which serves as the best interpretation of Qur'anic texts. In this regard, al-Bukhārī and Muslim transmit features of the Prophet's character in direct relation to the historical argument mentioned above. Al-Bukhārī narrates from Anas ibn Mālik that:

> Allah's Apostle was neither a Fahish (one who had a bad tongue) nor a Sabbaba (one who abuses others), and he used to say while admonishing somebody, "What is wrong with him? May dust be on his forehead!"[111]

In another description of the Prophet's character, Muslim narrates from Abū Hurayrah:

> It was said to Allah's Messenger (may peace be upon him): Curse the polytheists, whereupon he said: "I have not been sent as curser, but I have been sent as a mercy."[112]

These features of the Prophet's character are attested by the Qur'an in which he is described as: "a mercy for all creatures" (21:107); standing "on an exalted standard of character" (68:4); and having "a beautiful pattern (of conduct)" (33:21). The Prophet is unanimously considered the best interpreter of the

Qur'an, he lived it and gave it a living meaning. Appealing to the reality of his own behavior therefore and knowing this to be best moral example set for mankind, any claim that the revilement of what is sacred to others is an Islamic norm is simply not justified by historical facts and hence rejected.

In brief, the arguments presented throughout this section suggest that the Qur'an prohibits the revilement of what is sacred to others on the basis of an unchangeable ethical value emerging from basic human rights, namely freedom of belief and dignity. Thus, the Qur'an sets an important ethical principle aiming to secure not only the dignity of religiously different people, but also what is sacred to them. As for any act of abusive behavior towards people's beliefs and gods, it cannot, by any means, be perceived as a Muslim legal right, Islamic principle, or way of worshipping Allah. Such perceptions, found in a large number of Qur'anic exegesis sources, are more likely to have emerged from specific historical circumstances of Muslim history as well as lack of distinguishing between Qur'anic descriptive and prescriptive data in relation to non-Muslims and their beliefs.

[5]
Forgiveness

Even though previously examined Qur'anic ethical principles provide solid evidence for the Qur'an's recognition of normative religious pluralism as a value system, it is important to examine the Qur'an's stance towards forgiveness which is another ethical element. The importance of forgiveness in the process of religious pluralism arises from the fact that human relationships often suffer from levels of transgression. In situations such as these it is the ethical norm of forgiveness that reconciles otherwise broken relationships serving as a healing factor to restore things to their right path. Many Qur'anic exegetical sources however limit the scope of forgiveness only to Muslims. The main argument in defence of this interpretation is again based on either abrogation claims or the issue of specification with regards to the general sense of Qur'anic words without recourse to reason.

To analyse these claims I will examine three main Qur'anic aspects concerning the issue of forgiveness. The first is related to an exploration of those Qur'anic words expressing the meaning of the English noun forgiveness. The second is linked to the Qur'anic application of forgiveness to non-Muslim groups in society, while the third concerns elucidating the dialectical relationship between human forgiveness, God's forgiveness, and righteousness.

Qur'anic Words Expressing the Meaning of Forgiveness: *gh-f-r, ʿa-f-ā, ṣ-f-ḥ*

With regard to aspect one, the first thing to mention is that the Qur'an contains different words to convey the meaning of forgiveness. Secondly it is important to note that one of the most commonly words used to convey forgiveness (*s-m-ḥ*) in the Arabic language today exists nowhere in the entire Qur'an (which incidentally must not be taken as reason to incorrectly conclude that the Qur'an ignores the issue of forgiveness). In fact the Qur'an uses other terms which express the meaning of forgiveness in a more accurate and more sensitive way, these being: *gh-f-r, ʿa-f-ā, ṣ-f-ḥ*, and *'a-ʿ-r-ḍ*. As the latter (*'aʿraḍa*) is used figuratively as a metonymy for forgiveness in some places in the Qur'an examination of this is beyond the scope of this work.

According to Ibn Fāris the first Qur'anic linguistic root *gh-f-r*, conveys the meaning of cover, *satr*.[113] Further explanation is given by al-Aṣfahānī, who states that *gh-f-r* means to cover something in order to protect it from becoming contaminated.[114] More importantly, al-Aṣfahānī distinguishes between *gh-f-r* the doer of which is God, and *gh-f-r* the doer of which is a human being. In respect of the former, the meaning is that God protects His servants from punishment, whereas in terms of the latter, this means merely to excuse.[115]

As far as the second Qur'anic root *ʿa-f-ā* is concerned, Ibn Fāris defines it as either "to leave something or to seek it."[116] According to al-Aṣfahānī, however, it is to turn away with the aim of removing a person's guilt.[117]

With regard to the third Qur'anic word *ṣ-f-ḥ*, Ibn Fāris considers its accurate and precise meaning to be breadth, *ʿarḍ*,[118] while al-Aṣfahānī defines it as both not to cast reproach on a person and to show positive behavior in response to an offensive action. In this way, *ṣ-f-ḥ* is considered as having a higher ethical level than *ʿa-f-ā*.[119]

Therefore, semantic analysis demonstrates that Qur'anic words used to express forgiveness are not limited to the visible act of reconciliation, but rather penetrate to its inward dimensions giving the action depth of meaning. In this way, the Qur'anic concept of forgiveness is seen as directed not only towards reconciliation between conflicting parties, but also to their mutual development and improvement.

The Qur'anic Application of the Notion of Forgiveness to Non-Muslims

Examining next the Qur'anic ethical application of forgiveness to non-Muslim groups I focus on the following two main groups: the polytheists and the People of the Book. Concerning the polytheists the Qur'an states the following:

> Tell those who believe, to forgive those who do not look forward to the Days of Allah. It is for Him to recompense (for good or ill) each People according to what they have earned. (Qur'an *al-Jāthiyah* 45:14)

The verse contains an imperative command ordering believers to forgive those who do not believe in God. Its revelation in the Makkan historical context together with the content of the surah in which it occurs (*al-Jāthiyah*) would seem to provide tenable reason for limiting the scope of this forgiveness to polytheists only. However, the general description following the relative pronoun – "who do not look forward to the Days of Allah" – allows for all people identified by that description, including atheists, to be accommodated.

Therefore, the verse generally conveys that believers are ordered to forgive those who do not have a hope in God. The Qur'anic word used for forgiveness in this instance is *gh-f-r*. According to semantic analysis, it implies that believers should excuse those who do not have a hope in God and cover with patience any offensive behavior emerging from their side. In doing this, believers are promised they will be rewarded by God for their forgiveness.

Now, it is worth quoting al-Ṭabarī's comment on the verse, in which he makes the following claim: "The verse [45:14] is abrogated by God's command to believers to kill pagans. In fact, we state that the verse is abrogated, since there is a consensus among exegetes on this matter."[120] Looking at the comment, it becomes clear that al-Ṭabarī is in fact making two claims: abrogation of the verse as well as a consensus of exegetes on the abrogation. The implication of al-Ṭabarī's statement is that the ethical norm of forgiveness towards pagans has been substituted by the imperative of fighting them. In the following discussion I will, therefore, critically examine al-Ṭabarī's statement as well as the consensus claimed.

To begin with there exists no authentic occasion of revelation[121] for verse 45:14 nor an authentic comment from the first generation exegetes, in particular Ibn ʿAbbās.[122] Thus the absence of authentic evidence attributed to the Prophet makes the claim of abrogation null and void.

More particularly, al-Ṭabarī's main argument for abrogation is the following narration attributed to Ibn ʿAbbās:

> I [al-Ṭabarī] was told, *ḥaddathanī*, by Muḥammad ibn Saʿd, who said: I was told by my father, who said: I was told by my uncle, who said: I was told by my father who narrated from his father, who narrated from Ibn ʿAbbās his comment on the verse "Tell those who believe, to forgive those who do not look forward to the Days of Allah. It is for Him to recompense

> (for good or ill) each People according to what they have earned" (Qur'an *al-Jāthiyah* 45:14). [Ibn ʿAbbās] said: the Prophet – peace be upon him – was facing the pagans' offensive treatment towards him with forgiveness. Then, God commanded his Prophet to fight all pagans. In this way the verse [45:14] was abrogated.[123]

This narration serves as major evidence for the abrogation statement with regards to verse 45:14. Following expert research of the narration's chain, Ahmad Shakir however concludes:

> This is one of the most common chains of transmission found in al-Ṭabarī's *tafsīr*. This chain of transmission consists of weak and not trustworthy transmitters coming from one family. The chain is known among exegetes as *tafsīr al-ʿawfī* because the transmitter narrating from Ibn ʿAbbās is called ʿAṭiyyah al-ʿAwfī.[124]

So the abrogation claim is not justified given that the chain of transmission used in its defence is weak and identified as inauthentic. So it cannot be used as evidence for substituting the ethical norm of forgiveness with that of the imperative to fight the pagans.

Another argument against al-Ṭabarī's abrogation statement can be found in the exegetical materials succeeding his work. For example, al-Zamakhsharī states in an uncertain way that: "It was said that the verse [45:14] was revealed before the verse of combat and then was abrogated."[125] Al-Zamakhsharī's expression "it was said" does not support al-Ṭabarī's claim of consensus on the abrogation of verse 45:14. More explicitly, al-Rāzī remarks that "it is more acceptable to understand the verse [45:14] as a prescription of facing any offensive actions with forgiveness and leaving insignificant disputes."[126] It is obvious how al-Rāzī relates the verse to the issue of morality and good deeds and thus treats the abrogation claim with skepticism. In a similar way, Ibn Ashur and al-Tabatabai connect the verse to the ethical norm of forgiveness, and correspondingly do not mention anything pertaining to its abrogation.[127]

On the basis of these arguments, al-Ṭabarī's statement of abrogation, and the consensus claimed for it, appear untenable. The arguments are in fact in favor of those identifying the verse (45:14) as conveying an ethical norm of forgiveness towards non-Muslims, which cannot be subject to abrogation. Thus, the only way to reconcile al-Ṭabarī's view with the latter perspective is to consider the term abrogation as a synonym of specifying rather than substituting. In this case, al-Ṭabarī's statement would mean that the scope of forgiveness is limited to those who are peaceful among the pagans (polytheists), whereas forgiveness is excluded from those who wage war against Muslims. In fact, this understanding of the verse is the consensus opinion among exegetes. However, al-Ṭabarī's general statement, which lacks clarification, leaves ample room for confusion and speculation in terms of human relations. For this reason, there was need for a critical examination as well as clarification of al-Ṭabarī's claims, he is after all regarded as one of the most important and influential exegetes.

Another verse, revealed in the context of the polytheists at Makkah, orders the Prophet to adopt the virtue of forgiveness towards them:

> We created not the heavens, the earth, and all between them, but for just ends. And the Hour is surely coming (when this will be manifest). So overlook (*faṣfaḥ)* (any human faults) with gracious forgiveness (*al-ṣafḥ*). (Qur'an *al-Ḥijr* 15:85)

On the background of God's promise to recompense justly everyone in the hereafter, the Prophet is commanded to forgive polytheists. The Qur'anic word used for forgiveness here is *ṣ-f-ḥ*, which exists in two different grammatical forms in the verse. The first form is the imperative *faṣfaḥ*, whereas the second is the noun *al-ṣafḥ* described as beautiful, *al-jamīl*. The literal translation of the Qur'anic expression thus reads *faṣfaḥ al-ṣafḥ al-jamīl*, "so forgive with the beautiful forgiveness." Thus, the verse conveys that the Prophet was ordered to leave the offensive behavior of the polytheists to God, Who is just, and to face them with beautiful forgiveness instead.

We next examine the historical aspect of verse 15:85 to further assess the claims of those who choose to interpret its call to forgiveness in a more restricted and negative way. In this regard, al-Ṭabarī transmits from Qatādah, al-Ḍaḥḥāk, Mujāhid, and Sufyān ibn ᶜUyaynah that verse 15:85 was abrogated, meaning thus that the imperative to forgive polytheists was substituted with the imperative to fight them.[128]

Critiquing this argument the first thing to note is that the abrogation claim only emerges from the second generation of exegetes and hence is neither attributed to the Prophet nor to his Companions. This fact alone is sufficient evidence to reject assertions of abrogation since the act of determining a certain verse as abrogated cannot be based on reasoning.[129] Even so, it is not enough as Mujāhid is an important exegete who revised the entire Qur'an thirty times in front of Ibn ᶜAbbās,[130] and as such the claim attributed to him needs to be examined.

The chain of transmission through which the claim of abrogation is attributed to Mujāhid is as follows:

> [Al-Ṭabarī says:] We were told by, *ḥaddathanā*, **Ibn Wakīᶜ**,[131] who said: we were told by my father, who narrated from Isrā'īl, who narrated from Jābir, who narrated from Mujāhid, who said: "*Faṣfaḥ al-ṣafḥ al-jamīl*," "so forgive with the beautiful forgiveness," it was before the combat, *al-qitāl*.[132]

With reference to Ibn Wakīᶜ, the person from whom al-Ṭabarī receives the information concerning Mujāhid's claim of verse 15:85's abrogation, al-Dhahabī remarks in his *Mīzān al-Iᶜtidāl fī Naqd al-Rijāl*, that Sufyān ibn Wakīᶜ used to be a reliable transmitter until his clerk began intentionally to change some of his words. At this point because of the inability to distinguish between Ibn Wakīᶜ's own words and those the clerk had written, Ibn Wakīᶜ was defined as an unreliable transmitter. For this reason, al-Bukhārī was skeptical about Ibn Wakīᶜ's narration, and

Abū Zurʿah states that he was accused of lying.[133] In the same way, Ibn Ḥajar al-ʿAsqalānī states that al-Nisā'ī defined Ibn Wakīʿ as an untrustworthy transmitter, and sometimes even as "a nothing." Likewise, Abū Dāwūd refused to narrate anything from Ibn Wakīʿ.[134]

Another important fact to be taken into consideration is that al-Ṭabarī met Ibn Wakīʿ in Baghdad approximately six years before Ibn Wakīʿ's death in the year 247 AH,[135] while al-Ṭabarī's first arrival in Baghdad was approximately 241 AH.[136] This means that al-Ṭabarī heard of Mujāhid's verse 15:85 abrogation claim from Ibn Wakīʿ late in his life, when the corruption of his narrations had already occurred.

Under these circumstances the claim of abrogation attributed to Mujāhid cannot be accepted as evidence to validate the substitution of forgiveness with the imperative to fight. It also might be the reason why Abu al-Nail in his work *Tafsīr al-Imām Mujāhid Ibn Jabr* did not include the abrogation claims as Mujāhid's interpretation of the verse.

Another argument in favor of the universality of "beautiful" forgiveness is that exegetes after al-Ṭabarī did not support abrogation claims concerning it. For instance, al-Zamakhsharī states: "It was said that it [*faṣfaḥ*, forgive, 15:85] is abrogated by the verse of the sword.[137] However, it is possible that the verse is related to the pattern of good character, in this case it [the verse] cannot be defined as abrogated."[138] More explicitly, al-Rāzī states the following: "It was said that the verse [15:85] is abrogated, but it is far from being true, since the purpose of the verse is to encourage the model of good character and forgiveness. Then, how it could be abrogated?"[139]

Similarly, Ibn Ashur, al-Tabatabai, and al-Sharawi relate the verse to the achievement of good character, and consequently do not regard it as abrogated.[140]

Further arguments can be derived from the syntactic structure of the imperative *faṣfaḥ*, forgive, followed by the noun "forgiveness" described as "beautiful," *al-ṣafḥ al-jamīl*. In fact, the syntactic structure of the sentence *faṣfaḥ al-ṣafḥ al-jamīl*, "so forgive with the beautiful forgiveness," relates the act of forgiveness to three main aspects, with none of them note in favor of the abrogation claim. These three are first that forgiveness is linked to the Islamic belief system through the letter *fā'*, meaning so, which is attached to the imperative *iṣfaḥ*, forgive. The letter *fā'* here indicates *tafrīʿ*, branching. It means that the information preceding the letter *fā'* triggers the imperative succeeding it. Therefore, attached to the imperative verb *iṣfaḥ*, forgive, and succeeding God's promise of just recompense, the letter *fā'*, introduces a particular, psychological context in which the imperative of forgiveness should be conducted. In other words, *fā'* indicates that the response to any offensive behavior on the basis of forgiveness does not emerge from the inability to respond correspondingly, but it emerges from the belief in God's promise of just reward.

The second aspect determines the act of forgiveness as a virtue and ethical value through the description of forgiveness as beautiful, *jamīl*. Although, forgiveness in itself is regarded as a positive act, the Qur'an describes such an act as beautiful. The attachment of the adjective "beautiful," to the act prescribed aims to underline forgiveness as a virtue and an ethical norm, and thus to distinguish it from any type of diplomatic and pragmatic behavior.

As for the third aspect, this relates forgiveness to human nature through the usage of the definite article *al* so we have *al-ṣafḥ al-jamīl*, the beautiful forgiveness. Actually, this is the only place in the entire Qur'an, that is in verse 15:85, where such an expression exists. The function of the definite article here is to indicate identification, *ʿahd*. In a practical sense, it means that the act of beautiful forgiveness is naturally identifiable to humans by their nature.

Therefore, on the basis of the arguments presented, the imperative of forgiveness cannot be considered as abrogated. On the contrary, forgiveness is prescribed inclusively to all people as an ethical value emerging from the Islamic belief system and standing in accordance with human nature.

The Qur'anic prescription to forgive in the context of polytheists appears in a third instance which bears close affinity to the previous two cases:

> But turn away from them, and say "Peace!" But soon shall they know! (Qur'an *al-Zukhruf* 43:89)

This verse was revealed in Makkah in the context of polytheists. The Qur'anic word used is again *ṣ-f-ḥ* (analysed previously) but here it is translated as "turn away from them," and does not seem to be in accordance with the second imperative to "say peace." The question is how to implement peace when turning away from those one is to bring peace to? In this regard, al-Ṭabarī seems to provide an explanation pointing out that the meaning is to turn away from their harm, and to say "peace."[141] Al-Ṭabarī's explanation corresponds to the semantic meaning of *ṣ-f-ḥ*, since to turn away from harm means not to respond to harm by harm, but to ignore it and say "peace," instead. In this case, the difference between turning away from people and turning away from their inappropriate behavior is obvious. In this way, the general meaning of the verse should be understood as: pardon them and turn away from their polemical disputes by saying "peace."

The word "peace," *salām*, is worthy of special attention in the context of forgiveness. Grammatically speaking, the natural grammatical state of the word "peace" (*salām*), in this verse should be in the objective (*manṣūb*) case since it occurs after the imperative verb "say." However, the word exists syntactically in a nominative (*marfūʿ*) state, *salāmun*. Knowing that one of the functions of the grammatical nominative state is to indicate a constant stability,[142] the shift from the objective to the nominative state for the word "peace," (*salām*), can be regarded as a sign of a constant, interdependent relationship between forgiveness and peace.

Therefore, verse 43:89 dialectically relates the act of forgiveness to two notions: the avoidance of harm and the realisation of peace. Thus, the dialectical relationship between forgiveness, harm, and peace allows neither restricting the act of forgiveness exclusively to a certain party or determining such a value as subject to abrogation.

Turning from the homogeneous context of Makkah to the multicultural society of Madinah, we discover that despite the political power and dominance of Muslims in Madinah, forgiveness remained prescribed as a constant ethical value. In this respect, during the whole Madinan period, the Qur'an continued to emphasize the act of forgiveness towards all people, and particularly to the People of the Book. More impressively, in surah *al-Mā'idah*, the last chapter revealed in Madinah, the act of forgiveness is prescribed even towards those Children of Israel who had committed deceit and treachery. In this regard, the Qur'an states the following:

> But because of their breach of their covenant, We cursed them, and made their hearts grow hard; they change the words from their (right) places and forget a good part of the message that was sent them, nor wilt thou cease to find them – barring a few – ever bent on (new) deceits: but forgive them, and overlook (their misdeeds): for Allah loveth those who are kind. (Qur'an *al-Mā'idah* 5:13)

Revealed historically in the multicultural context of Madinah as well as in the textual context of interfaith issues, this verse orders the Prophet Muhammad to forgive even those Jews who had lost their honesty and loyalty to people and God Himself. The Qur'anic words used to express the meaning of forgiveness in the verse are *ʿa-f-ā* and *ṣ-f-ḥ*. In addition to what has already been discussed regarding the meaning of these words, the act of forgiveness in 5:13 is linked to the notion of *iḥsān*, kindness, the implementation of which leads to God's love. Thus, the verse imparts that forgiveness even towards the behavior of people of deceit and treachery is regarded by the Qur'an as *iḥsān*, kindness, and a way of gaining God's love, as long as such behavior does not turn into physical harm.

Nevertheless, there have been attempts aiming to invalidate this positive attitude to non-Muslims. For example, Qatādah states that verse 5:13 has been abrogated by verse 9:29.[143] However, al-Ṭabarī presents an argument against Qatādah's claim asserting:

> If different Qur'anic verses contradict each other in a way that they cannot be understood together, the case of abrogation is clear and obvious. But, if there is any possible way of reconciling the meaning of those verses, the claim of abrogation must be proved by evidence from God or His Prophet. This is because there is no any other way of knowing whether or not a certain verse has been abrogated. In this manner, there is neither indication nor evidence that the verse 9:29 contradicts the act of forgiveness towards Jews, since the implementation of forgiveness to Jews in their deceit and treachery is permissible except in the case of war and issues surrounding it. Thus, there is no obligation [for Qatādah] to judge that 9:29 has abrogated 5:13.[144]

Although, al-Ṭabarī himself would appear to be inconsistent in applying his conditions of abrogation, the condition of providing evidence from God or His Prophet for any claim of abrogation can be considered as a golden rule for accepting such a dangerous issue. Yet, Qatādah did not attribute his claim to the Prophet nor to any of the Companions. As for the type of abrogation to which al-Ṭabarī refers as clear and obvious due to irreconcilable contradictions in terms of the meaning, Abū Zahrah alongside experts from al-Azhar University have concluded that this type does not exist in the entire Qur'an at all.[145]

Furthermore, a number of classical and modern exegetes affirm that the meaning of verse 5:13 should be confined to the pattern of good morality towards ill-behaved people.[146] The reason for good morality is to seek God's love. In this respect, al-Bayḍāwī remarks that the ending of the verse "for Allah loves those who are kind" serves as a motive behind the imperative of forgiveness. He concludes that "forgiveness to a deceitful unbeliever is *iḥsān*, kindness, not to mention to others."[147]

Therefore, by relating dialectically the act of forgiveness to *iḥsān*, kindness, and hence to the love of God, the verse on the one hand attaches new ethico-religious dimensions to the value of forgiveness, and on the other rejects any possibility for claims of abrogation.

Another Madinan verse prescribing forgiveness towards both Jews and Christians occurs in surah *al-Baqarah*:

> Quite a number of the People of the Book wish they could turn you (people) back to infidelity after ye have believed, from selfish envy, after the Truth hath become manifest unto them: But forgive and overlook, till Allah accomplish His purpose; for Allah Hath power over all things. (Qur'an *al-Baqarah* 2:109)

The verse exists in a textual context discussing different, unsubstantiated, and hence conflicting claims made by representatives of the People of the Book. In particular, the verse imparts that there is a large number among the People of the Book wishing they could turn the followers of the Prophet Muhammad back to unbelief. Their wish is not established on the basis of compelling arguments and logical reasons, but emerges from a negative human feature, namely selfish envy. In this context, the Qur'an prescribes Muslims to face the negative mental condition of those people with forgiveness. The Qur'anic words used to convey the meaning of forgiveness are *ʿa-f-ā* and *ṣ-f-ḥ*. Al-Sharawi points out that Arabs use *ʿa-f-ā* to say: "*ʿafat al-rīḥu al-athara*," meaning "after the wind had blown, traces printed on the desert sands disappeared." As for *ṣ-f-ḥ*, he states that it means *ṭay al-ṣafaḥāt*, meaning "to turn the page."[148] Thus, according to al-Sharawi's explanation, the forgiveness prescribed here is based on both moral as well as spiritual dimensions, since to "turn the page" merely concerns the moral aspect of forgiveness, whereas to clean all traces of provoked anger from the soul is a spiritual effort.

Now, unlike his position on verse 5:13, where he rejects the claim of abrogation, al-Ṭabarī asserts here that verse 2:109 has been abrogated by God's command to Muslims to fight unbelievers, except those who embrace Islam or agree to pay the *jizyah* tax.[149] It appears that al-Ṭabarī is inconsistent when it comes to his view on abrogation. The reasons for such inconsistency are various, but in this particular instance regarding verse 2:109, al-Ṭabarī relies on a narration attributed to Ibn ʿAbbās. In fact, this is the reason why al-Ṭabarī favors abrogation here. He transmits the following narration:

> I was told by al-Muthannā, who said: We were told by Abū Ṣāliḥ, who said: I was told by Muʿāwiyah ibn Ṣāliḥ, who narrated from ʿAlī ibn Abī Ṭalḥah, who narrated from Ibn ʿAbbās that God's words – "But forgive and overlook, till Allah accomplishes His purpose: for Allah Hath power over all things" (Qur'an *al-Baqarah* 2:109) – have been abrogated by "Then fight and slay the Pagans wherever ye find them" (Qur'an *al-Tawbah* 9:5).[150]

Since this narration has been attributed to Ibn ʿAbbās, it requires careful examination. In this regard, the first point to attract attention is the terminological confusion between the verses which are claimed to have been abrogated and those they are seen to have been abrogated by. So verse 2:109 (referring to the People of the Book) is claimed to have been abrogated by verse 9:5 (referring to the pagans). Such terminological confusion contradicts the Qur'an's own terminological dictionary, which makes a clear distinction between the terms "People of the Book" (*Ahl al-Kitāb*) and "pagans" (*mushrikūn*).

Second, there is a problem with the narration's chain of transmission. This is found in the discontinuity between ʿAlī ibn Abī Ṭalḥah and Ibn ʿAbbās. In other words, there is a gap between these two persons, since ʿAlī ibn Abī Ṭalḥah never met Ibn ʿAbbās, and thus the former never heard anything from the latter. In this respect al-Khalīlī states that "it is unanimously agreed among all *Ḥuffāẓ*, the memorisers of hadith, that ʿAlī ibn Abī Ṭalḥah did not hear any *tafsīr* from Ibn ʿAbbās."[151] There is a claim, however, that ʿAlī ibn Abī Ṭalḥah heard Ibn ʿAbbās' *tafsīr* from his students like Mujāhid, Ibn Jubayr, and ʿIkrimah. Yet, no evidence exists to support such a claim. On the contrary, al-Khaṭīb al-Baghdādī narrates that "Ṣāliḥ ibn Muḥammad was asked from who ʿAlī ibn Abī Ṭalḥah had heard the *tafsīr* he narrated? Ṣāliḥ ibn Muḥammad said: from none."[152] Similarly, Ibn Manjuwayh al-Aṣbahānī in his *Rijāl Ṣaḥīḥ Muslim* asserts that "ʿAlī ibn Abī Ṭalḥah's *tafsīr* is not reliable due to discontinuity between him and Ibn ʿAbbās."[153] Furthermore, apart from the problem of discontinuity, there exist a number of doubts surrounding the name of ʿAlī ibn Abī Ṭalḥah as a transmitter. For example, Ibn Ḥajar mentions that:

> Al-Maymūnī transmitted from Aḥmad ibn Ḥanbal that: "ʿAlī ibn Abī Ṭalḥah narrates sometimes unacceptable information, *lahu ashyā' munkarāt.*" On the other hand, al-Ājurī transmitted from Abū Dāwūd that: "ʿAlī ibn Abī Ṭalḥah in terms of hadith is right and correct, but he adopted the attitude of sword." As for al-Nisā'ī, he said that: "ʿAlī ibn Abī Ṭalḥah is acceptable in hadith, *laysa bihi ba's.*" In contrast, Yaʿqūb ibn Sufyān said that: "ʿAlī ibn Abī Ṭalḥah is weak and unacceptable in terms of hadith, and some of his opinion cannot be praised." With reference to Ibn Ḥibbān, he mentions ʿAlī ibn Abī Ṭalḥah in the section of the authentic transmitters, *al-thiqāt.*[154]

Another point to mention in connection to ʿAlī ibn Abī Ṭalḥah is the fact that al-Bukhārī in his *Ṣaḥīḥ* narrates information transmitted through the above chain. However, al-Bukhārī narrates only information related to the linguistic explanation of some Qur'anic words, but not in relation to any issues concerning an Islamic ruling, or any sensitive and dangerous matters such as abrogation. Second, al-Bukhārī never mentions the name of ʿAlī ibn Abī Ṭalḥah.[155]

Therefore, the narration attributed to Ibn ʿAbbās as evidence for the abrogation of verse 2:109 cannot be accepted for the following reasons:

1. Terminological contradiction in the content.
2. Unanimous agreement among the scholars of hadith on the discontinuity between ʿAlī ibn Abī Ṭalḥah and Ibn ʿAbbās.

3. The absence of evidence proving that ʿAlī ibn Abī Ṭalḥah heard anything related to *tafsīr* from Ibn ʿAbbās' students.
4. Controversy surrounding the name of ʿAlī ibn Abī Ṭalḥah as a transmitter.

Al-Bayḍāwī also favors this conclusion stating: "There is a doubt about what is transmitted from Ibn ʿAbbās, that the verse of the sword[156] abrogated verse 2:109, since the command of the verse of the sword is not general."[157] More vividly, al-Shanqiti states that: "After investigations, it has been proved that verse 2:109 is not abrogated."[158] On the other hand, Ibn Ashur remarks that the imperative of forgiveness in this particular place aims to prevent possible inappropriate behavior from the Muslims' side as a response to the provocations of the People of the Book.[159] In this way, he relates the act of forgiveness to the ethical pattern of behavior, which cannot be subject to abrogation.

Therefore, there is no reason for determining verse 2:109 as abrogated. Instead, the act of forgiveness prescribed in the verse should be seen as emerging from the Qur'anic ethical paradigm of behavior. More particularly, by ordering Muslims to morally as well as spiritually forgive non-Muslims in the context of religious provocation, the verse introduces forgiveness as a universal value and typical feature of behavior in all situations.

The Dialectical Relationship Between Human Forgiveness, God's Forgiveness and Righteousness

Now, to further elaborate on forgiveness towards non-Muslims as a universal ethical value, which cannot be abrogated nor be based on any hidden agendas, it is important to show how the Qur'an connects dialectically human forgiveness with God's forgiveness and righteousness. In this regard, the Qur'an states the following:

> Be quick in the race for forgiveness from your Lord, and for a Garden

> whose width is that (of the whole) of the heavens and of the earth, prepared for the righteous – Those who spend (freely), whether in prosperity, or in adversity; who restrain anger, and pardon (all) men; – for Allah loves those who do good. (Qur'an *Āl ᶜImrān* 3:133-134)

These verses show clearly a multiplicity of dialectical relationships. For instance, the verses impart that to restrain anger and forgive people is a feature of righteousness, which in turn leads to God's forgiveness for forgiving people, and thus to His Paradise. On the other hand, the verses relate those people who restrain anger and forgive to the virtue of kindness, *iḥsān*, and thus to God's love. Moreover, the Qur'an's usage of the term *al-nās* which is a general word meaning people but defined by the definite article *al* in the verse indicating generalisation, shows that the act of forgiveness is not limited only to Muslims, but it is universally prescribed towards all people.

Another Qur'anic verse revealing explicitly the dialectical relationship between human forgiveness and God's forgiveness is the following:

> Let not those among you who are endued with grace and amplitude of means resolve by oath against helping their kinsmen, those in want, and those who have left their homes in Allah's cause: let them forgive and overlook, do you not wish that Allah should forgive you? For Allah is Oft-Forgiving, Most Merciful. (Qur'an *al-Nūr* 24:22)

The verse is historically related to a particular occasion. This being Abū Bakr's oath not to financially support a poor relative named Misṭaḥ who had involved himself in slandering Abū Bakr's daughter ᶜĀ'ishah who was also the wife of the Prophet. However, on hearing God's newly revealed words, "let them forgive and overlook, do you not wish that Allah should forgive you?" (24:22), Abū Bakr immediately forgave Misṭaḥ and resumed his financial support of him.[160] To reiterate because the verse conveys that human forgiveness leads to the forgiveness of God it is obvious that Abū Bakr forgave Misṭaḥ to gain God's forgiveness.

Now although the verse's revelation is linked to this particular occasion this does not mean that it is to be restricted to it. On the contrary, the dialectical relationship between human forgiveness and God's forgiveness should be understood universally. This is due to the universality of the Qur'anic message, and also due to agreement among exegetes that particular occasions of revelation do not specify the general sense of Qur'anic words.[161] In this way, the occasions, reasons and causes for revelation, in response to certain events, whilst preserving the historical context of a revealed verse and hence enriching its meanings, do not restrict them. Thus, the generally expressed imperative to "let them forgive and overlook" (24:22), should be grasped as a timeless call to Muslims to forgive all people inclusively.

In sum, as analysis in this section demonstrates, regardless of the socio-political context, the Qur'an prescribes and evaluates the act of forgiveness as a perpetual universal ethic. In this respect, the diplomatic position which attempts to relate different ethico-behavioral patterns to each of the contexts of Makkah and Madinah, seems untenable. Moreover, the Qur'anic words expressing the idea of forgiveness do not confine its meaning to the outward aspect of human behavior only, but penetrate to its inward dimensions. This is because in the Qur'an forgiveness is firmly related to belief in God and the Day of Judgment. In this way, the ethical universality of forgiveness plays an important, reconciliatory role in keeping the process of normative religious pluralism on the right track.

[6]
Conclusion

Application of the universal, ethical system introduced by the Qur'an to a particular group of people or to mere diplomacy in a number of Qur'anic exegetical sources, has made that universality appear exclusive where it should be universal and reduced its scope. Those insisting on interpretations of exclusivity base their opinions on the assumption that universal ethical obligations to non-Muslims have been abrogated, such that religiously different people and what they regard as sacred, are to be considered subjects for amoral treatment. Scattered throughout Islamic sources, opinions such as these pave the way for speculation and misleading conclusions to be presumed concerning the ethical system of Islam, thus negatively affecting the process of normative religious pluralism. However, as analysis throughout this chapter has shown, the Qur'an prescribes freedom of belief and respect for human dignity, as well as integrity and forgiveness, on a universal basis, relating this inseparably with belief in God and the Hereafter. In this way, the ethico-behavioral pattern it prescribes for Muslims with regards to non-Muslims is not limited to its outward aspect alone, but penetrates to the inner dimensions of human behavior. Thus, on one hand the Qur'an provides a feasible ethical ground on which the legitimacy of normative religious pluralism can be established, and on the other, rejects both the approach of exclusivists as well an ethico-behavioral model based on false diplomacy or any hidden strategies of embrace.

3

Structural Elements of Normative Religious Pluralism in the Qur'an

Based on its Qur'anic ethical foundations, as analysed in the previous chapter, the process of normative religious pluralism requires careful consideration for its structural elements, namely commonality, diversity, and constructive conversation. In fact, these elements constitute the dialectical structure of normative religious pluralism, since the implementation of commonality and diversity in a balanced way, despite their contradictory nature, indicates the effectiveness of religious pluralism. So, an exploration of the Qur'anic attitude towards these elements is important in order to evaluate critically both the claims of religious exclusivism and religious relativism. The former disregards religious commonalities, whereas the latter ignores religious particularities.

Obviously in the case of both, religious exclusivism and religious relativism, any constructive conversation is devoid of meaning, since one of the main functions of constructive conversation is to strike a correct balance between commonalities and particularities respectively.

[1]
Commonality

Commonality is one of the elements forming the dialectical structure of normative religious pluralism. By commonality, we mean the feeling of unity emerging from common features shared by different religious subjects taking part in the process of religious pluralism. Thus, the main function of commonality is to lay common ground upon which religious diversity and particularities can interact and flourish.

Commonality is an essential element of normative religious pluralism, for without it religious coexistence is impossible. Amarah expresses this thus: "There is neither meaning nor wisdom of diversity not based on commonality."[1] In fact, the importance of commonality can be found in Ibn Khaldūn's writings where "the concept of *ʿaṣabiyyah* seems to be the core of the Khaldunian social theory."[2] *ʿAṣabiyyah* is derived from the Arabic root *ʿa-ṣ-b* meaning to bind,[3] i.e. to bind people into a group in order to unite them. In his translation of *The Muqaddimah* Franz Rosenthal translates *ʿaṣabiyyah* as "group feeling," whereas according to Baali, among the translations of *ʿaṣabiyyah* are "feeling of unity" and "collective consciousness."[4] Considering Baali's conclusion that *ʿaṣabiyyah* is neither confined to Arab people nor necessarily based on blood relationships,[5] it would appear that Ibn Khaldūn's theory of *ʿaṣabiyyah* does not emphasise a certain type of unity, but rather emphasises the power of the collective will. Accordingly, the theory of *ʿaṣabiyyah* can be considered as one of the earliest Muslim theories emphasising the importance of the element of commonality in a constructive way.

Commonality is an important element of normative religious pluralism and the Qur'an has its own perspective concerning it. It is necessary therefore to examine the Qur'anic position as well as detail some of the methods it outlines to emphasise the feeling of unity among people. To commence we need to analyse three basic types of commonality found in the Qur'an: environmental commonality, moral commonality, and spiritual commonality.

Environmental Commonality in the Qur'an

The Qur'an creates a feeling of unity among all people on the basis of common responsibility towards the environment. Thus, the environmental sphere forms a broad common ground, where the adherents of different religions can participate and contribute together. In fact, the universality of the environment as an element of commonality in respect of normative religious pluralism emerges from a number of common features between the universe and human beings. In the case of the Qur'an, these common features can be divided into three main aspects: commonality between the universe and human beings in terms of their origin; commonality between the universe and human beings in terms of their character of obedience towards God's order; commonality between the universe and human beings in terms of their terrestrial demise.

With regard to the first aspect (environmental commonality), the commonality between the universe and human beings in terms of their origin, the Qur'an traces three major, common stages of creation. In respect of the first stage, the Qur'an states that everything in the universe was initially joined together, as one unit of creation, in a common form of gaseous mass or galactic dust:[6]

> Do not the Unbelievers see that the heavens and the earth were joined together (as one unit of creation), before we clove them asunder? We made from water every living thing. Will they not then believe? (Qur'an *al-Anbiyā'* 21:30)

According to Ibn Ashur, it is possible that the Arabic word *ratqan*, one unit of creation, means that everything in the universe existed before the creation in the form of one substance, which God divided later into countless forms having their own distinguishing characteristics.[7] Thus, the enormous environmental diversity of creation initially emerged from one common element, namely gaseous mass or galactic dust.

In the second stage concerning creation every living thing emerges again from one common substance, water. The Qur'an states: "We made from water every living thing (Qur'an *al-Anbiyā'* 21:30). Of course, the Arabic verb *jaʿalnā* in the verse means "we created."[8] Therefore, according to the verse, the creation of human beings as well as the whole environment of living diversity is based on one common element, which is water.

Finally, the third stage of creation defined by the Qur'an is the creation of man from clay: "Man We did create from a quintessence (of clay)" (Qur'an *al-Mu'minūn* 23:12).

Al-Rāghib al-Aṣfahānī is of the opinion, that "the combination of dust and water is called clay (*ṭīn*).[9] At this point, it becomes clear that the Qur'an determines the creation of man as emerging from the combination of two foundational elements, dust and water, on the basis of which the universe has been created. In this way, the Qur'anic doctrine of the common origin of the universe and man is likely to create a universal feeling of unity among people in an environmental sense.

As for the second aspect of environmental commonality, which concerns the commonality between the universe and human beings in terms of their character of obedience towards God's order, the Qur'an clearly states that:

> Do they seek for other than the Religion of Allah – while all creatures in the heavens and on earth have, willing or unwilling, bowed to His Will (accepted Islam), and to Him shall they all be brought back. (Qur'an *Āl ʿImrān* 3:83)

Both the universe and man are bound by the natural laws of creation to obey God's will. In this respect, al-Rāzī remarks that this verse indicates that everything in the universe belongs to one common source of existence and follows inescapably its order.[10] Thus, the common dependence of man and the universe on

God's order creates again a feeling of unity among people on an environmental basis.

Turning to the third aspect of environmental commonality, which pertains to the commonality between the universe and human beings in terms of their terrestrial demise (that is their ceasing to exit), the Qur'an states: "Everything (that exists) will perish except His own Face" (Qur'an *al-Qaṣaṣ* 28:88). This conveys the idea that man and the universe are mortal creatures moving towards their common end. Accordingly, the verse reveals that "the whole phenomenal world is subject to flux and change and will pass away, but He [God] will endure forever."[11] So, both the universe and human beings share the same destiny of temporary existence.

In sum, from the discussion on environmental commonality, it becomes clear that the universe and human beings are God's creatures and none of them is master of the other. Moreover, the existence of both the universe and human beings has been directed for the achievement of mutual benefit and complementarity.[12] As such this relationship (between the universe and human beings) is seen in the Qur'an as one of unity and by no means as one of enmity, which in turn provides a vast common ground for the promotion of normative religious pluralism on the basis of preserving as well as developing the environment.

Moral Commonality in the Qur'an

The Qur'an offers another broad common ground which once again gives scope for normative religious pluralism to flourish. This is moral commonality which creates a feeling of unity and brotherhood among all people. A great deal of data can be found on moral commonality in the Qur'an but following careful and accurate observation, it appears that there are two chief principles: human brotherhood and human nature.

The principle of human brotherhood is considered by some scholars to be the broadest and most central sphere of the Qur'anic concept of human relations.[13] In fact, the area of human brotherhood in the Qur'an is entirely related to the moral aspect of human life. In this regard the Qur'an remarks that:

> O mankind! Reverence your Guardian-Lord, Who created you from a single person, created, of like nature, his mate, and from them twain scattered (like seeds) countless men and women; – reverence Allah, through Whom ye demand your mutual (rights), and (reverence) the wombs (That bore you): for Allah ever watches over you. (Qur'an *al-Nisā'* 4:1)

This verse exists in the textual context of a discussion (verse 4:2 onwards) on morality towards orphans, children, and women, extremely vulnerable social groupings against whom human rights can easily be violated. It is important to note that the verse combines three key ideas with regards to morality towards vulnerable people: consciousness of God, human brotherhood, and protection of these people's rights. Actually, consciousness of God is advanced as the final goal of morality, while human brotherhood is considered an important means to realize this end. Muhammad Abdu expresses it thus in commenting on the verse:

> Knowing that you [people] are so closely related to each other because of your common descent from a single person, you should be constantly conscious of God not to transgress the boundary of morality. So you have to be compassionate towards vulnerable people, like orphans who lost their parents, and protect their rights.[14]

Therefore, in mentioning God consciousness, morality, and human brotherhood together, the verse increases one's moral responsibility towards humankind, whilst simultaneously strengthening people's feelings of compassion towards each other.[15]

The Qur'an's recognition of this broadest sphere in the field of human relations, human brotherhood, makes ample accommodation for normative religious pluralism on the basis of human moral commonalities. This is largely because the

Qur'anic concept of human brotherhood is oriented towards realizing modesty and sincere morality among people and to thereby reduce feelings of arrogance and domination.[16]

The second Qur'anic principle endorsing moral commonality is human nature. Note the Qur'an significantly states that every single human being who enters this world does so in a state of original purity and innocence:

> It is He Who brought you forth from the wombs of your mothers when ye knew nothing; and He gave you hearing and sight and intelligence and affections: that ye may give thanks (to Allah). (Qur'an *al-Naḥl* 16:78)

One reason for the original purity and innocence of human nature is largely due to humans being born in a state of complete ignorance. This full negation of human knowledge at birth implies that humanity comes into this world without any knowledge of evil, which incidentally also implies that human beings are not held accountable at this stage of their life. Of course we need to distinguish between this initial state of original purity and the concept of free will, humanity's innate ability to distinguish between good and evil and act upon this. Failure to distinguish between the two can lead to a conclusion that the Qur'an supports the Christian theory of original sin, as would appear to be the case in Lewis Scudder's study *The Qur'an's Evaluation of Human Nature*.

More strikingly, the Qur'an underlines the pure and innocent nature of a human being:

> So set thou thy face steadily and truly to the Faith: (establish) Allah's handiwork according to the pattern on which He has made mankind: no change (let there be) in the work (wrought) by Allah: that is the standard Religion: but most among mankind understand not. (Qur'an *al-Rūm* 30:30)

Ḥanīf is the key word in the verse to understanding the Qur'an's concept of the original purity and innocence of human nature. The literal meaning of the root morpheme *ḥ-n-f* is to lean or to incline (*mayl*).[17] However, "the most common use of *ḥanīf* is related to the meaning of being inclined to avoid evil."[18] Another point to be considered here is the syntactic position of the expression *fiṭratallāh* used in the verse. According to Ibn Ashur, "it is a substitute, *badal*, of *ḥanīf*."[19] In other words, it means that the original pattern on which God has made mankind, is one in which man is inclined to avoid evil.

Therefore, the Qur'anic concept of the original purity and innocence of human beings creates in man a positive outlook towards his moral world. It also shows that the original state of each and every human being pertains to the enjoinment of all that is good and the avoidance of all that is evil. This, in turn, makes it entirely possible for all mankind to be united under the auspices of a moral common ground in the process of normative religious pluralism.

Another feature of human nature or psychology, which the Qur'an constantly emphasises, is the ability of human beings to discern good from evil, right from wrong, and the useful from the harmful:

> By the Soul, and the proportion and order given to it; And its enlightenment as to its wrong and its right; – Truly he succeeds that purifies it, And he fails that corrupts it! (Qur'an *al-Shams* 91:7-10)

Commenting on these verses Ali notes:

> He [God] breathes into it [the soul of human being] an understanding of what is sin, impiety, wrongdoing and what is piety and right conduct, in the special circumstances in which it may be placed. This is the most precious gift of all to man, the faculty of distinguishing between right and wrong.[20]

It is important to clarify that man only has a potential ability to discern between good and evil, the choice of whether to live life according to a moral pattern being left to human free will. Nevertheless, regardless of the different moral senses that people possess, the idea of morality itself is common to human psychology, deeply rooted in human nature. This common moral point is universally acknowledged in different ways. Ali refers to it as "the faculty of distinguishing between right and wrong;"[21] St. Paul defines it as "a law written on the heart;"[22] Budziszewski determines it as "natural law."[23] Yet, all these expressions are confirmed in the Qur'an:

> Nay, man will be evidence against himself, even though he were to put up his excuses. (Qur'an *al-Qiyāmah* 75:14-15)

Here the Qur'an points out that despite any outward immoral behavior human beings are in fact within themselves aware of their wrongdoing. In this respect, Fakhr al-Dīn al-Rāzī states: "A person who behaves immorally and supports the wrong, and rejects the right, knows in his heart what is actually wrong and what is right."[24] So this innate human faculty to discern good from evil, right from wrong, the useful from the harmful, provides common moral ground for humanity, motivating positive moral development whilst reducing the potential influence of the very real darker side of human nature.

In sum discussion has shown that the Qur'an indicates the existence of a moral commonality within and among human beings which forms the basis of human brotherhood and human nature. Furthermore, the Qur'an's recognition of these two principles creates a universal feeling of moral unity among all people, thus forming a vast area for the promotion of normative religious pluralism as one possible solution to save the world from its moral crisis.

Spiritual Commonality in the Qur'an

Another type of commonality, which the Qur'an vividly underscores, is spiritual commonality between all human beings. This can be traced through three major doctrines in the Qur'an, those of one God, one religion, and one complete cycle of prophethood. As far as the first doctrine is concerned, the Qur'an informs us that there is only One absolute God for all human beings. This is a fundamental article of faith. The Qur'an also depicts all human souls, before their existence in the terrestrial world, as one harmonious body obeying the commands of one God:

> When thy Lord drew forth from the Children of Adam – from their loins – their descendants, and made them testify concerning themselves, (saying): "Am I not your Lord (who cherishes and sustains you)?" – They said: "Yea! We do testify!" (This), lest ye should say on the Day of Judgment: "Of this we were never mindful." (Qur'an *al-Aʿrāf* 7:172)

The verse affects human consciousness positively in respect of spiritual commonality by illustrating the whole humanity as being one spiritual unit bowing before the One God. Commenting on the verse, Henry Corbin remarkably concludes that:

> The religious consciousness of Islam is centered not on a historical fact, but on a fact which is *meta-historical*, not post-historical, but trans-historical. This primordial fact, anterior to our empirical history, is expressed in the divine question which the human Spirits were required to answer before they were placed in the terrestrial world: "Am I not your Lord?" (Quran 7:172). The shout of joy which greeted this question concluded an eternal pact of fidelity; and from epoch to epoch, all the prophets whose succession forms the "cycle of prophecy" have come to remind men of their fidelity to this pact.[25]

This trans-historical pledge given to the One God prior to their birth by all human souls to obey Him creates a universal feeling of spiritual unity among all people. Having borne witness and testified to the fact, it also puts the onus of responsibility on mankind for belief in and worship of the One God.

With regard to the second doctrine concerning spiritual commonality, the Qur'an states that God has revealed one religion to mankind throughout human history:

> The same religion has He established for you as that which He enjoined on Noah – that which We have sent by inspiration to thee – and that which We enjoined on Abraham, Moses, and Jesus: Namely, that ye should remain steadfast in religion, and make no divisions therein. (Qur'an *al-Shūrā* 42:13)

The religion that God has established for the whole of mankind is *al-Islām*. The name of *al-Islām* is related to the central idea of God's religion which means "surrender" as well as the peace that issues from our surrender to God. Therefore, the Qur'an considers all authentic religions to have been revealed on the basis of the Oneness of God. Thus, *al-Islām* refers not only to the religion revealed through the Qur'an to the Prophet Muhammad, but also to all authentic religions revealed before this specified Islam. For this reason, the Qur'an refers to the prophets Abraham and Ishmael, and the followers of the prophet Jesus, as Muslims.[26] Through such a perception of religion being one during human existence, the Qur'an lays a common spiritual ground fostering the process of normative religious pluralism.

The third Qur'anic doctrine creating a universal feeling of human spiritual unity is the integrity of the prophetic cycle. The Qur'an states:

> Not a messenger did We send before thee without this inspiration sent by Us to him: that there is no god but I; therefore worship and serve Me. (Qur'an *al-Anbiyā'* 21:25)

The meaning of this verse is confirmed by the Prophet himself who states that:

> Both in this world and in the Hereafter, I am the nearest of all people to Jesus, the son of Mary. The prophets are paternal brothers; their mothers are different, but their religion is one.[27/28]

According to this hadith, all prophets are brothers, but the

Prophet Muhammad, to whom the whole Muslim world belongs, is the nearest among people to the prophet Jesus, to whom the entire Christian world belongs. The spiritual implications of this prophetic brotherhood, and in particular the closeness of the bond between the prophets Muhammad and Jesus, provide a firm common ground for interfaith relations.

To exemplify the common spiritual feeling emerging from the atmosphere of prophetic brotherhood, it is worth quoting Nasr who states:

> Like countless Muslims, when I read the names of the prophets of old in the Qur'an or in the traditional prayers, I experience them as living realities in the Islamic universe, while being fully conscious of the fact that they are revered figures in Judaism and Christianity. I also remain fully aware that they are all speaking of the same God Who is One and not of some other deity.[29]

In the light of this analysis of spiritual commonality, it appears that the Qur'an does not aim at creating an exclusive spiritual feeling among Muslims towards others. Rather, through the doctrines discussed it leaves ample room for establishing a firm spiritual common ground for preserving the common spiritual wealth.

To summarise, an examination of the Qur'anic perspective on commonality, as an essential part of the structure of normative religious pluralism, shows that the Qur'an not only endorses the element of commonality, but more importantly, regards this element as something inherent in the universe, human nature, and the human soul. Consequently, the Qur'an goes further to recognise commonality as a perpetual divine law. Thus, the approach of the exclusivists, which refuses to acknowledge any obligations toward others, seems to be irreconcilable with the Qur'anic message of the existence of environmental, moral, and spiritual commonalities between all people.

[2] Diversity

As discussed previously, commonality is an essential element of normative religious pluralism. However, worth noting is that if the element of commonality is given considerable precedence over differences, it could lead to a religious relativism which erodes religious commitment. An outcome no person of religious commitment can allow to happen, either to themselves or their religion. Due to this fact, Altwaijri remarks that religious pluralism "does not mean at all a dilution of positions or a manipulation of ideas, or fusion of creeds into the same mould, may it even be an indubitably humanitarian mould as claimed."[30] Similarly, Jonathan Sacks argues that "the proposition of the heart of monotheism is not what it has traditionally been taken to be: one God, therefore one faith, one truth, one way. To the contrary, it is that unity creates diversity."[31] In fact, the root of this modern concept of religious pluralism embodied in the phrase "unity creates diversity" can be discovered in the works of Abū Ḥayyān al-Tawḥīdī who lived ten centuries ago. In his *Al-Muqābasāt* al-Tawḥīdī points out that: "It is a typical feature of human nature, that despite their differences humans are united, and despite their unity they are different. Moreover, people despite their differences love each other, and despite their mutual love they are different."[32] Therefore the element of commonality must also be balanced with a significant consideration for diversity. In this section I therefore discuss the Qur'anic view on diversity and its impact on the dignity of people.

Generally speaking, the Qur'an advances diversity as a natural law existing in the universe: "And of everything We have created pairs: That ye may receive instruction" (Qur'an *al-Dhāriyāt* 51:49).

According to this verse, aside from God, everything else in the universe is based on dichotomy. The dichotomic nature of the universe suggests on the one hand that "one individual is complementary to another"[33] whilst on the other that one individual is best known and understood in light of its opposite. Thus, a reciprocal relationship is set in motion (the dichotomic nature of the universe) by which we can derive the meaning that the more people know about the different other, the more they will know about themselves. In this way, in addition to being a natural law, diversity also appears as a source of knowledge, since "each of us has something someone else lacks, and we each lack something someone else has, we gain by interaction."[34]

Given the essential importance of diversity, it is vital to explore and understand the Qur'anic view on this important element of the structure of normative religious pluralism. We do so on two major levels, environmental diversity and religious diversity, going on to develop a theology of diversity. As Sacks remarks: "We need not only a theology of commonality but also a theology of difference,"[35] because the tension between religions mostly arises from differences.

Environmental Diversity in the Qur'an

The existence of countless forms having their own distinctive peculiarities in the universe is an undeniable fact. Accordingly, the Qur'an defines diversity as a fact of nature and maintains that God has created the whole universe with diversity.[36] To further explore this fact it would seem pertinent to look into three environmental spheres mentioned in the Qur'an: plants, animals, and water.

Beginning with the first environmental sphere representing the diverse world of plants, it is interesting to note that almost 22 identifiable plants belonging to 17 plant families are cited in the Qur'an.[37] They all differ from each other in shape, color, smell, and taste and in the same way, are all distinguished by their peculiarities. The Qur'an states:

> And in the earth are tracts (diverse though) neighbouring, and gardens of vines and fields sown with corn, and palm trees – growing out of single roots or otherwise: watered with the same water, yet some of them We

make more excellent than others to eat. Behold, verily in these things there are signs for those who understand! (Qur'an *al-Ra'd* 13:4)

The element of natural diversity in the verse is recognised by al-Zamakhsharī. He observes that the diversity of plants is manifested in their growing out of one earth, watered with the same water, yet having different shapes, colours, tastes, and smells. Moreover, diversity is also found in the word *ṣinwān* used in the verse, which is the plural of *ṣinwu*, meaning different palms growing out of a single common root.[38] Similarly, Ibn Ashur maintains that the main purpose of this verse is to emphasise the diversity of plants as a sign of God's great power of creation.[39]

It is important to explore at this juncture whether recognition of plant diversity as a sign of God's greatness has analogically led exegetes to view human intellectual diversity also as a sign of God's greatness. In this respect, al-Ṭabarī points out that al-Ḥasan al-Baṣrī interpreted the verse's reference to the diversity of plants as an allegory for human hearts. So, allegorically speaking, just as one substance (water) causes a diversity of plants to emerge from the earth, the same can be said for God's revelation to mankind which results in a diversity of attitudes being adopted by human hearts towards that revelation.[40] Al-Ṭabarī draws a similar allegory to al-Ḥasan al-Baṣrī's with regards to the verse, stating that the Creator of diversity among plants is the same Creator of diversity among humanity. Analogically, if God had so willed He could have created all people and plants to be the same, but He did not. Therefore, diversity as a fact of nature provides clear signs for those who understand.[41]

Further confirmation of this analogy of diversity between plants and human beings as a sign of God's greatness is expressed in other Qur'anic verses as follows:

Seest thou not that Allah sends down rain from the sky? With it We then bring out produce of various colours. And in the mountains are tracts white and red, of various shades of colour, and black intense in hue. And so amongst men and crawling creatures and cattle, are they of various

> colours. Those truly fear Allah, among His Servants, who have knowledge: for Allah is Exalted in Might, Oft-Forgiving. (Qur'an *Fāṭir* 35:27-28)

The textual context in which these verses appear concern discussion on the diversity of attitudes adopted by people towards God's revelation. The verses in their historical context address the Prophet's mental as well as spiritual suffering which emerged as a result of the polytheists' negative attitude to the Qur'an. Thus, their purpose, as Ibn Ashur observes, was to show through the visual diversity of nature's colors, that human intellectual diversity was analogously diverse. And because diversity is a natural law on the basis of which God created everything in this world, human intellectual diversity is in effect simply a reflection of this natural law.[42]

Hence, God's great creative power is revealed in the Qur'an on one level through the diversity of plants as a source of beauty, from which we analogically conclude that human intellectual diversity should also be perceived as a sign of God's greatness.

Turning to another aspect of environmental diversity, that is diversity of the animal kingdom, it can be seen again that the Qur'an recognises diversity as a natural law by drawing an analogy between the world of animals and that of humans in terms of their particularities. The Qur'an informs that:

> There is not an animal (that lives) on the earth, nor a being that flies on its wings, but (forms part of) communities like you. Nothing have we omitted from the Book, and they (all) shall be gathered to their Lord in the end. (Qur'an *al-Anʿām* 6:38)

The textual and historical contexts of this verse are similar to those previously discussed. Due to the Prophet's grief at the pagans' disbelief in the Qur'an, God revealed to him the fact that it is impossible to gather humanity to a single truth in this world. If we look at the verses which lead up to verse 38 we begin to appreciate the Qur'anic textual context for it:

> If their spurning is hard on thy mind, yet if thou wert able to seek a tunnel in the ground or a ladder to the skies and bring them a sign, – (what good?). If it were Allah's will, He could gather them together unto true guidance: so be not thou amongst those who are swayed by ignorance (and impatience)! (Qur'an *al-Anʿām* 6:35)

It is methodologically important to mention that most of the classical sources of Qur'anic exegesis failed to recognise in this verse God's law of diversity. And it was largely due to this fact, that their attention became drawn into a historical theological dispute which concerned the issue of predestination and free will. This phenomenon demonstrates, once again, the close relationship between Qur'anic texts and an interpreter's mind, influenced in turn by specific socio-political circumstances. In the 20th century Ibn Ashur moved the focus of Qur'anic exegesis regarding the verse to an important point connected to the issue of diversity. He observed that the meaning of "If it were Allah's will, He could gather them together unto true guidance" (6:35), "is related to God's will of creation not to God's will of legal obligation *taklīf*."[43] Ibn Ashur's point is crucial to understanding the nature of diversity. In other words, it is God's will to create people in a state of diversity of perceptions that makes the gathering of all people to a single truth impossible in this world.

Correspondingly, the verse representing the diversity of animals comes in the textual context of God's will of creating diversity of perceptions among humans:

> There is not an animal (that lives) on the earth, nor a being that flies on its wings, but (forms part of) communities like you. Nothing have we omitted from the Book, and they (all) shall be gathered to their Lord in the end. (Qur'an *al-Anʿām* 6:38)

The meaning of the verse, according to Ibn Ashur, is that "every group of animals has its distinguishing features and peculiarities like all human communities have their specific features and peculiarities."[44] Therefore, by applying the plural form of the Arabic word *umam*, communities, in relation to both the animal as well as human worlds, the Qur'an recognises diversity as a fact of nature. Thus, it would appear as an act of ignorance to recognise diversity as a natural law in the animal world, but to disregard or ignore it in the world of human intellectual diversity.

Evidence for diversity as a fact of nature can also be found in Qur'anic topics discussing different types of wind and rain. However, it is more relevant to end our discussion on environmental diversity in the Qur'an with the following verse:

> Nor are the two bodies of flowing water alike, – the one palatable, sweet, and pleasant to drink, and the other, salt and bitter. Yet from each (kind of water) do ye eat flesh fresh and tender, and ye extract ornaments to wear; and thou seest the ships therein that plough the waves, that ye may seek (thus) of the Bounty of Allah that ye may be grateful. (Qur'an *Fāṭir* 35:12)

Although this verse is clear in its own context as well as in its general textual context, a great Arabic linguist and exegete such as al-Zamakhsharī failed to derive from it a meaning in accordance with the overall context of the verse. Al-Zamakhsharī claims that the two different bodies of flowing water (*al-baḥrān*) are parable (*mathal*) of a believer and unbeliever, with the palatable, sweet, pleasant to drink water representing a believer, and the salt, bitter water representing an unbeliever, respectively.[45] It seems methodologically suspicious to see a scholar such as al-Zamakhsharī shifting interpretation from the literal meaning of *al-baḥrān* to a new figurative meaning, without reason. According to Qur'anic exegesis methodology, any departure from a literal to a figurative meaning being assigned to Qur'anic text must be done for a specific reason only and in accordance with the rules of the Arabic language.[46] More surprisingly, when al-Zamakhsharī came to interpret the rest of the verse, where God states that although *al-baḥrān* are different in terms of their taste, they have much in common: "Yet from each (kind of water) do ye eat flesh fresh and tender, and ye extract ornaments to wear" (35:12), at this point, al-Zamakhsharī controversially maintains that unlike the salt and bitter water, which benefits people, an unbeliever does not have any virtues in order to benefit others.[47]

Al-Zamakhsharī's statement here is an example of the fact that a wrong methodology leads to a wrong conclusion. It, in turn, proves again that although classical sources of Qur'anic exegesis are valuable materials, they should not be taken for granted particularly in respect of interfaith relations. This is because consideration should always be paid to the reality of the time in which an interpreter lives or as Nursi states "time is a great interpreter."[48]

Turning back to verse 35:12 (of the two different bodies of water), it appears that al-Rāzī was more observant than al-Zamakhsharī in respect of its textual context. Al-Rāzī points out that it is more relevant, in the light of the textual context, to interpret the verse as evidence of God's power to create two bodies of water visibly alike, but in fact different in terms of their contents. The power of God in the verse is presented in His ability to create similarities in different bodies and to create differences in similar bodies.[49] Al-Rāzī's interpretation of the verse was confirmed and developed by Ibn Ashur, who remarks that the verse reflects the divine wisdom of creating everything in accordance with the natural law of diversity, where the variety of peculiarities are based on common features and similarities.[50]

In sum discussion has shown that the Qur'an introduces environmental diversity as a natural law on the basis of which two other points analogically are emphasised; the first point pertains to God's greatness and power of creation, whereas the second proves human intellectual diversity as a fact of nature, too. The lack of recognition with regards to the analogical relationship between environmental diversity and human intellectual diversity on the part of some sources of Qur'anic exegesis should be attributed to either methodological problems or the specific historical circumstances of the exegete in question.

Religious Diversity Presented as an Earthly Fact in the Qur'an

It is important to note from the outset that although religious truth is one in God's knowledge, according to the perception of humankind it is multiple.[51] This is due to the fact that man has been given freedom of choice in this earthly life. Consequently, the Qur'an recognises this fact and clearly states that it is impossible to gather people to a single religious truth:

> If thy Lord had so willed, He could have made mankind one people: but they will not cease to dispute. Except those on whom thy Lord hath bestowed His Mercy: and for this did He create them: and the Word of thy Lord shall be fulfilled: "I will fill Hell with jinns and men all together." (Qur'an *Hūd* 11:118-119)

The sources of Qur'anic exegesis are unanimous that "one people" (*ummah wāḥidah*) in the verse, means one religious people. In fact, it is methodologically limited to such an interpretation, since the verse ending points to the eschatological consequences of that religious diversity. However, in respect of religious diversity, there is need to clarify two significant issues which the Qur'an repeatedly underscores. The first is the fact, which the Qur'an undoubtedly underlines, that humans have always been and will remain forever religiously different in their earthly life. This fact emerges from God's will to create human beings with free will, which seems to relevantly account for the meaning of God's words: "and for this did He create them" (11:119). In other words, God has created human beings with the aim of being free in terms of their will. Yet, since the natural result of this free will is diversity, the Qur'an refers to the result itself as a purpose of creation by stating that God has created people to be religiously different.[52]

The second issue which needs clarification here is that even though religious diversity is an earthly fact, in the hereafter people will be held responsible for their terrestrial beliefs and deeds.

In this regard, it is vitally important for the parties participating in the process of normative religious pluralism to know that according to the Qur'an, the only time and place where the judgment on religious differences will take place is in the hereafter, on the Day of Judgment. On the other hand, it is only the one God Who will judge people on their beliefs and deeds on that day, when those on whom God has bestowed His mercy will be known.

Failure to distinguish between these two issues could result in many negative effects on the process of religious pluralism. For instance, the confusion between the earthly dimensions of religious diversity and its eschatological ones leads very often to a perception that certain religious people are authorised to judge the beliefs of others in this world.

To further explore the Qur'anic attitude on religious diversity and thus to support the foregoing arguments, it is relevant to examine the following Qur'anic verse:

> To each among you have We prescribed a law and an open way. If Allah had so willed, He would have made you a single people, but (His plan is) to test you in what He hath given you: so strive as in a race in all virtues. The goal of you all is to Allah. It is He that will show you the truth of the matters in which ye dispute. (Qur'an *al-Mā'idah* 5:48)

The general context of surah *al-Mā'idah* is related to the People of the Book (*ahl al-kitāb*). More particularly, this verse exists in a textual context concerning the divine revelation given to three of God's prophets: Moses, Jesus, and Muhammad. For this reason, judging by the textual context of the verse, both al-Ṭabarī and al-Rāzī argue that those being addressed in the verse are Jews, Christians, and Muslims.[53] Accordingly, Qatādah suggests that in the context of Oneness (*tawḥīd*), God has created throughout history a diversity of ways leading to the Oneness of God.[54]

Seen in terms of both its own Qur'anic context and that of today's universal values, the verse recognises religious diversity as an existing fact in this world. It states that "to each among you", that is Jews, Christians, and Muslims, God has revealed a specific way leading to Him. Even though, each succeeding revelation declared abrogation of its preceding one, people in general have continued to follow the tradition they are familiar/brought up with, their religious adherence remaining unchanged. Hence, the world's major belief systems such as Judaism, Christianity, Buddhism, and Islam have always remained historically present in the world since their birth. Furthermore, they have also existed to some extent within certain geographical boundaries. The gift of free will has allowed this state of affairs to develop, for mankind is free to choose the way in which he chooses to worship and understand God, influenced by different circumstances.

Therefore, given human free will and the historical diversity of divine revelations, we are left with a number of belief systems across the world, and the verse seems to underline the existence of religious particularities in this world as an earthly fact. Formed on the basis of human free will, religious particularities are perceived by different groups as a source of their dignity. As for the eschatological ramifications of religious diversity emerging from human free will, the verse stipulates that these will be revealed by God in the hereafter. Of course, shaped by their specific historical context, many sources of Qur'anic exegesis instead of emphasising the terrestrial fact of religious diversity, as stated in the verse, emphasise the exclusive nature of Islam in terms of religious truth and salvation.

This existence of religious diversity as an unchangeable fact is more strikingly endorsed in the Qur'an when it refers to a theological issue concerning the direction of prayer, or the *Qiblah:*

> Even if thou wert to bring to the people of the Book all the Signs (together), they would not follow Thy Qiblah; nor art thou going to follow their Qiblah; nor indeed will they follow each other's Qiblah. If thou after the knowledge hath reached thee, Wert to follow their (vain) desires, – then wert thou Indeed (clearly) in the wrong. (Qur'an *al-Baqarah* 2:145)

The verse exists in a textual context discussing change in the direction faced in salah. After having prayed toward Jerusalem as the *Qiblah* for sixteen months in Madinah, Muslims were now ordered to change this direction to the Kaʿbah in Makkah.[55]

The direction faced in prayers (*Qiblah*) may sound like a minor issue, but it is in fact religiously highly symbolic for it identifies different religious groups. Moreover, Qutub states that *Qiblah* is a feature that distinguishes Islam's whole outlook on life, its concerns and aims, and its identity.[56] Therefore, it can be stated that *Qiblah* is a symbol of religious identity, independence, and particularity.

In this respect, the verse endorses religious diversity by recognising every religious community to whom God revealed a book, as having its own *Qiblah*. The verse stipulates the people of the Book and Muslims as having their own particularities in terms of the *Qiblah*, and that one religious group would never follow the *Qiblah* of the other. The reason for the existence of religious particularities embodied in the concept of the *Qiblah* is revealed in another Qur'anic verse:

> To each is a goal to which he turns;[57] then strive together (as in a race) towards all that is good. Wheresoever ye are, Allah will bring you together. For Allah hath power over all things. (Qur'an *al-Baqarah* 2:148)

Ibn Ashur claims that the meaning of the verse is that "in the process of seeking the truth, every group follows its own way of understanding."[58] Commenting more closely on the textual context of *Qiblah* in the verse, al-Rāzī remarks:

> Every religious group of people has a direction *Qiblah*, which they face in their prayers in order to get closer to God. Thus, every group is satisfied with their own direction, *Qiblah*, which they will never change. Therefore, there is no way of gathering people on one single direction, *Qiblah*.[59]

Recognising that *Qiblah* represents religious identity, independence, and particularity, it becomes clear that these verses objectively define religious diversity as an unchangeable fact of this earthly plane. They also introduce a reasonable approach for dealing with this state of affairs. The Qur'anic approach suggests that given the reality of religious diversity each group should strive to do all that is good, and that as far as matters of theological difference are concerned, only God will provide the solution in the hereafter, for "It is He that will show you the truth of the matters in which ye dispute" (Qur'an *al-Mā'idah* 5:48).

Religious particularities are therefore an immutable fact of this world, determined by the Qur'an as natural law, and therefore cannot be subject to elimination or disregard. For this reason, again in the context of Qur'anic verses discussing the *Qiblah*, the Qur'an describes those who fail to understand the reality of religious particularities as fools. Indeed, anyone who tries to disregard religious particularities in this world and fails to understand that particularities are a terrestrial feature existing in every religious group, may seem foolish to do so:

> The fools among the people will say: "What hath turned them from the Qiblah to which they were used?" Say: "To Allah belong both East and West: He guideth whom He will to a Way that is straight." (Qur'an *al-Baqarah* 2:142)

With Islam a new set of religious particularities had emerged and its followers would adhere to these, the new *Qiblah* was a sign of faith in the new religion.

> Thus, have We made of you an Ummat justly balanced, that ye might be witnesses over the nations, and the Messenger a witness over yourselves; and We appointed the Qibla to which thou wast used, only to test those who followed the Messenger from those who would turn on their heels (From the Faith). Indeed it was (A change) momentous, except to those guided by Allah. And never would Allah Make your faith of no effect. For Allah is to all people Most surely full of kindness, Most Merciful. (Qur'an *al-Baqarah* 2:143)

In fact, the element of religious diversity, represented by religious particularities, seems to be a real challenge and test for the intellectual level of human beings. On the other hand, since religious particularities form a source of dignity, the element of religious diversity becomes the genuine dimension through which the achievement of normative religious pluralism should be evaluated. Due to this importance of particularities, the Qur'an goes further to declare them as a fact inherent in all levels of human life: social, intellectual, cultural and religious:

> Say: "Everyone acts according to his own disposition: But your Lord knows best who it is that is best guided on the Way." (Qur'an *al-Isrā'* 17:84)

The Arabic word *shākilah* in the verse has been interpreted as a "side," "nature" and "religion."[60] It also has been given the meaning of a "doctrine" or a "way."[61] Furthermore, Ibn Ashur defines *shākilah* as a way and life on the basis of which a person has grown up.[62]

Considering these definitions it appears that the verse underscores a basic fact concerning particularities in respect of every single individual, which is that everyone has a particular way of acting, *shākilah*. This particular way of acting is formed in each individual due to a variety of factors which are not identical to all people. As for the question of whose acting is best guided, the verse remarks that only God is fully aware of the answer.

Therefore, our analysis of the Qur'anic view on diversity shows that the Qur'an attaches considerable importance to the issue of particularities in all aspects of life. Considered as a phenomenon inherent in the universe and human nature and thus determined as immutable terrestrial law and fact, particularities form a source of dignity and knowledge. Moreover being directly related to religious identity, religious particularities cannot become subject to disregard or elimination. Hence, any approach which seeks to undermine the existence of religious particularities in the process of normative religious pluralism or seeks to blend them into one common belief system, seems untenable in the light of Qur'anic teachings.

[3]
Constructive Conversation

The complexity of interaction between commonalities and particularities in the process of normative religious pluralism requires the existence of another element, namely constructive conversation. The importance of this third element is seen in its function to act as a mode of reconciliation between commonalities and particularities. In fact, in attempting to establish a right balance between commonalities and particularities, constructive conversation tends to prevent normative religious pluralism from going to extremes, as exclusivism and relativism have done. Due to the significant role constructive conversation plays in the process of religious pluralism, it is essential to explore the Qur'anic attitude towards it and clarify the Qur'anic position. To do this we first examine the importance of constructive conversation in the Qur'an, and second, focus on the Qur'anic principles constructing the conversation.

The Importance of Constructive Conversation in the Qur'an

It would seem relevant to initially reflect briefly on the notion of conversation. Generally speaking, conversation is normally perceived as a spoken exchange of thoughts, opinions, and feelings. Verbal communication is conducted largely by spoken words emerging from different parties taking part in a conversation. Therefore, one significant way to explore the importance of constructive conversation in the Qur'an is to observe linguistically the Arabic root *q-w-l*,[63] which means "to utter words" and which thus indicates the dynamics of conversation.

According to al-Idrisi, the root morpheme *q-w-l* is repeated in the Qur'an 1722 times, appearing in 49 different morphological forms.[64] The morphological diversity of *q-w-l* referring to the variety of physically as well as ideologically different persons, suggests that the Qur'an leaves ample room for thoughts, opinions, and feelings to be presented, listened to, discussed, and critically evaluated. In addition, the multiple distribution of the root morpheme *q-w-l* in the Qur'an, on the one hand emphasises the value of constructive conversation, whilst on the other poses a great challenge to those who assume that it is God who has allowed such vast space for discussing different opinions in the Qur'an.

Another way of exploring the importance of constructive conversation is to look into the Qur'anic method of employing words as a powerful tool for communication. In fact, although it is not clear for some scholars as to what exactly makes the text of the Qur'an superhuman or miraculous, the traditionally held Islamic view assumes that the miracle exists in the Qur'anic words themselves.[65] Thus, the scriptural text often advances the idea that words have the ability and power to change. For instance, the Qur'an states that God ordered Moses and Aaron to initiate a polite conversation with Pharaoh with the aim of discussing the release of the Israelites who were suffering terribly under his yoke:

> "...Go, both of you, to Pharaoh, for he has indeed transgressed all bounds; But speak to him mildly; perchance he may take warning or fear (Allah)." (Qur'an *Ṭā Hā* 20:43-44)

Note, even to a tyrant of such magnitude who had "transgressed all bounds" both are astonishingly told to speak mildly. This fact did not escape Muslim scholars of course, but how they chose to understand the order to do so is interesting. Methodologically speaking, it is fact that classical sources of Qur'anic exegesis did not formulate any theories on constructive conversation derived from this verse. Even a rationalist like al-Rāzī did not recognise in the instruction to converse mildly the existence of a powerful ethico-humanistic approach and its potential. Al-

Rāzī asks: "Why did God command Moses to be polite and mild with an ungrateful unbeliever?"[66] The first answer he gives is that Pharaoh used to look after Moses when he was a little child and therefore was like a father to him. For this reason Moses was ordered to speak mildly to him.[67] The second answer he gives is that the nature of titans (*jabābirah*) is such that they must be spoken to mildly, with politeness, otherwise their arrogance surfaces and the objectives desired are unlikely to be gained.[68]

Now the fact that al-Rāzī even chooses to pose the question as to why God commanded Moses to address this ungrateful unbeliever with politeness raises ethico-humanistic concerns. Similarly the limited reasons al-Rāzī gives for this as being mere parental respect on the one hand or insincere diplomacy on the other is indicative, for it suggests that the possibility of it being a humanistic approach with a view to reconciliation was not entirely present in his mind. Note, al-Rāzī calls Pharaoh an "ungrateful unbeliever," whereas God Himself mentions him merely by his political title "Pharaoh." This difference in discourse, between the pure text of the Qur'an and that of an interpreter, could occur under pressure of negative socio-political circumstances. For instance, al-Rāzī's entire life was spent under the shadow of the Crusades which would explain his own line of reasoning. In other words he was unlikely to have witnessed any practical constructive conversations taking place with regard to interfaith relations, with a humanistic interpretation of the verse for him therefore, in all likelihood, becoming lost in the context of interfaith conflict.

To determine whether verses 20:43-44 serve as evidence for the importance of constructive conversation, a number of different contexts need to be outlined. The first is textual context. The verses appear in surah *Ṭā Hā*, the content of which is linked to a variety of different types of conversation. The second is the context of revelation. In this respect, the verses were revealed in Makkah when the Muslims were suffering under pagan oppression.[69] The role of the Prophet during the Makkan phase was to act as warner and to call to Islam, in other words conversation.

As for the context of real historical action, this concerns God's command to Moses and Aaron to face Pharaoh. In fact, one of the aims was to warn Pharaoh against committing transgression. The sentence "for he has indeed transgressed all bounds" (Qur'an *Ṭā Hā* 20:43), functions as a reason for God's command to send Moses and Aaron to Pharaoh.[70] However, realisation of this purpose was to be conducted through words, note not mere words, but polite and mild words. To reiterate, God orders Moses and Aaron to speak to one of the most evil people mentioned in the Qur'an, mildly. To speak mildly (*qawlan layyinan*) to someone means to show respect for their opinions, neither to disregard them nor to make a mockery of them.[71] It is vital to understand that even though God knew that Pharaoh was never going to change, nevertheless He still orders a speech based on *qawlan layyinan*. Moreover, by using the word *laʿall*, which indicates possibility, God gives Moses and Aaron the hope of Pharaoh perhaps changing. The question is why? One answer is that a principle is elucidated, not confined to its own historical setting, but rather established for future application. The principle holds that we must engage in constructive communication, or constructive conversation, the underlying implication being that words have the power to change.

In sum all three contexts outlined above support the argument that verses 20:43-44 advance the issue of constructive conversation as an ethico-humanistic principle and means of communication and reconciliation.

The Qur'anic emphasis on the importance of constructive conversation can also be seen in other verses:

> When it is said to them: "Come to what Allah hath revealed, and to the Messenger": Thou seest the Hypocrites avert their faces from thee in disgust. How then, when they are seized by misfortune, because of the deeds which their hands have sent forth? Then they come to thee, swearing by Allah. "We meant no more than good-will and conciliation!" Those men, – (Allah) knows what is in their hearts; so keep clear of them,[72] but admonish[73] them, and speak to them a word to reach their very souls. (Qur'an *al-Nisā'* 4:61-63)

The Qur'anic textual context in which these verses occur, underlines the importance of referring to God's as well as the Prophet's judgement in the case of unmanageable disputes, *tanāzu*ᶜ. In particular, the verses exemplify the negative attitude of the hypocrites towards referring to God's and the Prophet's judgement in the case of unmanageable disputes. Furthermore, the verses reveal that when hypocrites are seized by misfortune because of their refusal to accept just judgement, they do not draw useful lessons from the situation, but try instead to clarify their acceptance of wrong judgement by telling lies. In this context and under these circumstances, the Qur'an provides guidance on how Muslims should communicate with such people in such a situation.

The first guidance provided is the need to realise that God knows what is in people's hearts: "those men, – (Allah) knows what is in their hearts" (4:63). Consequently, the guidance implies that human interrelationships should be observed on the level of their actions and statements not intentions. Accordingly, Izutsu remarks that there are two kinds of relationships: horizontal relationships, which occur between humans; and vertical relationships which take place between God and human beings.[74] Therefore, in terms of horizontal relationships it is human statements that are taken into account. In contrast, with vertical relationships it is human intentions that will be judged by God in the hereafter. The lack of distinguishing between these relationships leads inevitably to tension among people.

The second Qur'anic guidance is derived from the words "*fa'a*ᶜ*riḍ* ᶜ*anhum*" (4:63). Now, according to al-Rāzī the meaning of "*fa'a*ᶜ*riḍ* ᶜ*anhum*" is either to turn away from these people without accepting their excuses or to turn away from them without disclosing their lies.[75] Both meanings given by al-Rāzī are built on the literal meaning of "*fa'a*ᶜ*riḍ*," which simply means turning a face away from something or somebody. However, Ibn Ashur argues that "*fa'a*ᶜ*riḍ* ᶜ*anhum*" is used figuratively as a simile for forgiveness.[76]

The factor judging between al-Rāzī's and Ibn Ashur's opinions is the textual context. It is important to observe here that the textual context of "*fa'aʿriḍ ʿanhum*" provides an adequate reason for departing from the literal to the figurative meaning. This is because immediately following the command "*fa'aʿriḍ ʿanhum*" comes another command "*wa ʿiẓhum,*" that is, advise them (4:63). Naturally, it is forgiveness that creates a pathway for advice to enter human hearts. Otherwise, by turning away from those one is addressing it becomes impossible to advise them. For this reason, interpreting "*fa'aʿriḍ ʿanhum*" as being to forgive them is more appropriate, since it corresponds to the textual context, human nature, and God's description of the Prophet as a mercy to the worlds.

The third guidance the Qur'an provides concerning communication with the hypocrites is to offer advice with words conveying deep meaning touching their very hearts: "advise them, and speak to them a word to reach their very souls" (4:63). Classical interpretation of this however, once again seems to have been the product of socio-political pressure. For example, al-Zamakhsharī gives it a meaning as follows: "Speak to their evil souls a word threatening them to be destroyed and killed if their hypocrisy appears again. So, if it happens there will be no other solution except a sword."[77] Exactly the same meaning copied from al-Zamakhsharī, but not acknowledged, exists in al-Rāzī's *tafsīr*.[78] It is obvious how the interpretation of both scholars differs from the original Qur'anic discourse, which does not mention any such notions as "evil souls," intimidation, killing or swords.

What is the Qur'anic import? We see that constructive conversation appears in the verses in the context of reference to the hypocrites. We are informed that their intentions are only known to God. The role of Muslims is to forgive, advise, and speak meaningful words to them. The point being that the verses clearly indicate that conversation, in words communication, is the preferred Qur'anic means to effect reconciliation between people.

The Qur'an's emphasis on the power of words to change can also be seen in surah *Ibrāhīm*:

> Art thou not aware how God sets forth the parable of a good word? [It is] like a good tree, firmly rooted, [reaching out] with its branches towards the sky, yielding its fruit at all times by its Sustainer's leave. And [thus it is that] God propounds parables unto men, so that they might bethink themselves [of the truth]. (Qur'an *Ibrāhīm* 14:24-25)

Classical sources of Qur'anic exegesis have held long discussion with extensive research on a) the kind of tree the good word parable refers to and b) the wider meaning of the term "good word"[79] burdening the purity of the verses with unnecessary polemics.

In fact leaving the words in their general sense leads the beauty of their meaning to emerge. Note both expressions, "good word" and "good tree" are a form of indefinite noun, *nakirah*, which indicates unspecified meaning. For this reason, the term "a good word" should be understood to mean in its broadest sense inclusively.

Keeping this view, the main focus of the verses would appear to be on the power, impact, and positive consequences of applying the principle of "a good word." The allegory to the "good tree" (the firm root, the branches reaching to the sky, the never ending fruit), denotes the enduring nature and benefit of this, leaving us with a clear picture that "a good word" is a firm means of communication, with lasting impact on human hearts and lives, always leading to positive results.

Brought together, these three elements demonstrate the power of "a good word" to change. As such in surah *Ibrāhīm*, (in which the verses occur), we see prophets applying this principle, engaged in conversation employing good constructive words as a means of communication.

In sum it has been shown that the Qur'an stresses the importance of constructive conversation as a means of communication and reconciliation between human beings. This is largely due to constructive words having the power to resolve problems and effect positive change. Moreover, the Qur'an prescribes that constructive conversation be implemented inclusively, that is with all members of society, the examples of Pharaoh and the hypocrites being a case in point. Similarly implementation of constructive conversation is prescribed for every stage of a society's socio-political development, since the Qur'an's emphasis on conversation is presented in both the Makkan and Madinan surahs, as shown in the case of surahs *Ṭā Hā* and *al-Nisā'*, respectively.

Qur'anic Principles of Constructing Conversation

Constructive communication is a two-way street. It requires the art of both communicating and listening. Mere conversation is not what is required in religious pluralism. Exchanging words with the aim of getting one's view across, or complaining without listening to the other side, achieves little or nothing, especially when it comes to religious pluralism. The religious conversation as it were is a delicate and nuanced affair, a vital function of which is to balance between commonalities and particularities. What is the best way to conduct it?

The Qur'an appears to delineate four principles to construct conversation and these are directly related to religious pluralism: a) purposeful conversation, b) objective conversation, c) non-judgmental conversation, and the principle of d) non-manipulative conversation.

Purposeful Conversation

The Qur'an states:

> Say: "O People of the Book! Come to common terms[80] as between us and you: That we worship none but Allah; that we associate no partners with Him; that we erect not, from among ourselves, lords and patrons other than Allah." If then they turn back, say ye: "Bear witness that we (at least) are Muslims (bowing to Allah's Will)". (Qur'an *Āl ʿImrān* 3:64)

The verse represents an invitation to the People of the Book to meet with Muslims and engage in conversation. Note, the nature of this conversation is not aimless but has clear purpose. To express this purpose, and the meaningful nature of the encounter, the Qur'an uses the singular form of the word *kalimah* (a word) while referring to the conversation.[81] Moreover, this conversation is described as equitable, *kalimah sawā'*. This means that it should have a clear purpose likely to be achieved equally by people. In this respect, Ibn ᶜAṭiyyah remarks that *kalimah sawā'* means a conversation based on themes equally accepted by all people.[82] The Oneness of God is determined by the verse therefore as a clear purpose of the conversation.

Objective Conversation

The Qur'an states:

> And they say: "None shall enter Paradise unless he be a Jew or a Christian." Those are their (vain) desires. Say: "Produce your proof if ye are truthful." (Qur'an *al-Baqarah* 2:111)

The verse demonstrates certain religious groups confidently discussing their entry into Paradise without any evidence to support their opinion. For this reason, the Qur'an defines these opinions and statements as "vain desires," *amānī*. It also requires those making these statements to produce proof of their veracity. Note in this context of speech the Qur'an links truth directly to evidence. So in the case of religious pluralism, conversation is to be based on real facts and evidence, not on bias and partiality, otherwise this could lead to what Hassan Hanafi calls "clerical diplomacy and brotherly hypocrisy."[83]

The principle of objectivity for the construction of conversation is also stressed in the Qur'an through the personality of the prophet Abraham. The Qur'anic Abraham represents objectivity in seeking the truth. Triggered by this Abrahamic model of objectivity, Hanafi attempts to establish a framework of objective conversation. He suggests that religions should be examined through a hermeneutical process which includes three major sections: criticism, interpretation and realisation. The first is historical criticism of the text. This aims to determine the authenticity of Scripture in history. The second defines the meaning of the text and mainly deals with the language and historical circumstances from which the text originated. The third applies to the realisation of the meaning of the text in human life, which is the final goal of the Divine Word.[84] This suggested framework could be of great importance for religious pluralism in terms of its epistemological dimensions.

Non-judgmental Conversation

The third Qur'anic principle to develop constructive conversation is the principle of *non-judgmental conversation*. In fact, this principle distinguishes constructive conversation from mere debate, in which the purpose of criticism is to achieve victory or domination. In this regard, the Qur'an mentions how Jews and Christians were judgemental of each other, with each accusing the other of unbelief:

> The Jews say: "The Christians have naught (to stand) upon"; and the Christians say: "The Jews have naught (To stand) upon." Yet they (Profess to) study the (same) Book. Like unto their word is what those say who know not; but Allah will judge between them in their quarrel on the Day of Judgment. (Qur'an *al-Baqarah* 2:113)

Al-Wāḥidī mentions the occasion of this revelation. The occasion is transmitted by Ibn ᶜAbbās and defined as authentic by al-Humaidan, who states that "its chain of transmission is authentic."[85] Al-Wāḥidī states with regards to the verse:

> This was revealed about the Jews of Madinah and the Christians of Najran. When the delegation of Najran came to the Messenger of Allah, Allah bless him and give him peace, the Jewish rabbis came to see them. They had a debate with each other and the debate got so heated that they shouted at

> each other. The Jews said: "You are not following the true religion," and declared their disbelief in Jesus and the Gospel. In response, the Christians said: "You are not following the true religion," and declared their disbelief in Moses and the Torah. Allah therefore revealed this verse.[86]

It is obvious from the historical context expressed by the occasion of the revelation as well as from its textual context that the verse disapproves of judgemental behavior during conversation. Moreover, it shows that when such judgemental behavior emerges from people who are heirs of a divine guidance, it is a clear sign that they have lost that guidance,[87] becoming equal to those who are ignorant. It is important to understand that even though Muslims are not directly mentioned in the verse they are nevertheless not immune from its description or application to them. For this reason using applicability al-Rāzī comments on the verse:

> Know that exactly the same manifestation happened among the community of Muhammad – Allah bless him and give him peace – where each group is judgemental about the other by accusations of unbelief, while they all still read the same Qur'an.[88]

Therefore, judgemental behavior during conversation prevents that conversation from achieving its real purpose. For this reason, when it comes to the issue of judgement with regards to people's beliefs, the Qur'an repeatedly states that this is the right of God only, for only God can judge people and decide their place in Heaven or Hell. Of course, the Qur'an clearly describes the features of those belonging to the truth and likely to enter Paradise, as it clearly describes the features of those belonging to evil and likely to enter Hell. However, such descriptions serve as guidance for human beings, not as authorisation from God for people to judge each other.

Non-manipulative Conversation

As far as the fourth Qur'anic principle of constructive conversation is concerned, this is the principle of *non-manipulative conversation.* Constructive conversation should not be based on a hidden agenda, to drag people into one's beliefs and convictions. In fact, this is one of the most problematic issues if not dilemmas religious people struggle with. Very often, conversation is not used as a means to present compelling argument, listen to others, or understand their viewpoint, but rather as a medium for conversion to certain beliefs. For instance, Carl Rahner's theory of "*Anonymous Christians*" (1966) is an example of what a constructive conversation in the case of religious pluralism should not be. This is largely because Rahner's theory is based on a hidden agenda to convert people. And this understanding of inter-faith communication is not confined to Christianity but applicable to all religions.

The principle of non-manipulative conversation can be derived from the following Qur'anic verse:

> They say: "Become Jews or Christians if ye would be guided (to salvation)." Say thou: "Nay! (I would rather) the Religion of Abraham the True and he joined not gods with Allah." (*al-Baqarah* 2:135)

Al-Ṭabarī mentions the occasion for this revelation as narrated by Ibn ʿAbbās:

> ʿAbdullāh ibn Ṣūryā al-Aʿwar [a Jew] said to the Prophet Muhammad, may Allah bless him and give him peace: "There is no truth except ours, so if you [Muhammad] want to be guided you should follow us." And Christians said the same. Then, Allah revealed the verse.[89]

As this shows both groups established an approach to communication based on religious exclusivism, which naturally leads to the idea of conversion. In contrast, verse 2:135 moves the discussion to the personality of prophet Abraham, who is presented in the Qur'an as a sign of objectivity in seeking the truth. Thus, the Qur'an disapproves adoption of any manipulative approach with respect to interfaith dialogue (conversation) prescribing instead an approach based on compelling evidence.

In sum as analysis in this section has shown the Qur'an attaches great importance to constructive conversation as a means of communication between all people at every level of the socio-political stages of society. According to the Qur'an, constructive conversation or communication must be a meaningful act whereby different views are intelligibly presented on the basis of compelling argument and evidence, and where each side makes an attempt to understand the other. Thus, the function of constructive conversation is to broaden the range of opinions and arguments and hence to attain a reasonable balance between differences and similarities.

[4]
Conclusion

The dialectical elements of commonality and diversity are presented in the Qur'an as a fact of nature and unchangeable law inherent in the universe and human nature. Thus, the process of normative religious pluralism cannot be regarded in the Qur'an as mere theory or idea. Rather it is advanced as a divine law emerging from the gift of free will given by God to humanity, the natural result of which is diversity. Consequently, both the exclusivist approach, which refuses to accept the different other, as well as the relativist approach, which disregards particularities, contradict Qur'anic guidance in this regard. This is because religious commonalties and particularities should not be employed as a means of religious dilution or seclusion, respectively. Rather, they should be balanced by way of a constructive conversation, which is endorsed by the Qur'an as an essential vehicle for communication between all people at every stage of the socio-political development of society.

4

The Main Objectives of Normative Religious Pluralism in the Qur'an

In the Qur'an (and as shown in the previous chapter), normative religious pluralism is not regarded as mere toleration of other faiths, but rather a divine law, or *sunnah ilāhiyyah*. Thus, according to the Qur'an, implementation of normative religious pluralism is a necessary process for human peace and prosperity. Conversely, transgression of its requirements inevitably leads to tension and hate. This transgression can take many forms, one of the most critical pertaining to objectives. So, for instance, by moving objectives of religious pluralism away from their universal terrestrial basis to exclusive eschatological polemics and accusation, transgression results. Objectives can also be manipulated to serve interests contradicting humanitarian aims. Thus, according to Amarah, certain participants in the religious pluralism process tend to use it as a political tool to gain influence and power in the Muslim world.[1] In similar fashion, the objectives of religious pluralism can also be directed toward realizing certain ends, in this case religious dilution in order to underpin modern liberalist theory (as would seem to be the case with John Hick, whose classic theory of religious pluralism focuses on epistemological principles rather than religious tenets[2]). On the other hand, the objectives of normative religious pluralism can be reduced from their universal nature to an exclusive interpretation of principles focusing on one particular religious group, as in the case of some Qur'anic exegetical sources. These problematic areas pose a potential threat to the whole process of interfaith relations. As Altwaijri rightly remarks:

> If inter-religious coexistence, which is at the same time coexistence among cultures and civilizations, is not geared to the service of lofty humanitarian goals, it will lose its fine edge. It will become more akin to propagandist moves and empty slogans than sincere actions aimed to better the life of modern man.[3]

This chapter will therefore explore the main objectives of normative religious pluralism in the Qur'an to hence shed light on whether these objectives are exclusively limited to a certain religious group or are inclusively humanitarian. Of course we can derive many secondary objectives of religious pluralism from the Qur'anic text, since religious commonality is a vast field for the promotion of valuable goals in interfaith relations. However, closely scrutinising the Qur'an, it would appear that four main objectives of normative religious pluralism are essential to the peacebuilding process:

1. **Knowledge of the other.** This objective signifies the need for mutual understanding mentioned in the Qur'an under the notion of *taᶜāruf.*
2. **Cooperation with the other.** This objective signifies the need for mutual engagement, *taᶜāwun*, in the process of religious pluralism.
3. **Competing with the other in good works.** This objective signifies the need for mutual contribution mentioned in the Qur'an by the phrase *Fastabiqū al-khayrāt.*
4. **Mutual support.** This is mentioned in the Qur'an as *tadāfuᶜ*,

and mainly signifies the need for mutual support against oppression.

[1]
Knowledge of the Other: Mutual Understanding – *Taʿāruf*

The significance of knowing the other emerges largely from human nature being relaxed in the company of what is known and familiar, and fearing and keeping distant from what is unknown and unfamiliar. Accordingly, Asani concludes that the reason for religious conflict and transgression of religious pluralism "is not so much a clash of civilizations as it is a clash of ignorances."[4] In fact, ignorance of the other seems to pose a threat not only to religious coexistence, but also to the coexistence of cultures and civilisations alike. For this reason, the Qur'an defines knowledge of the other as the purpose of creation, both in terms of biological and social diversity. In this respect the Qur'an states the following:

> O mankind! We created you from a single (pair) of a male and a female, and made you into nations and tribes, that ye may know each other (not that ye may despise (each other). Verily the most honoured of you in the sight of Allah is (he who is) the most righteous of you. And Allah has full knowledge and is well acquainted (with all things). (Qur'an *al-Ḥujurāt* 49:13)

What is the historical context of this verse and how is it linked to the objective of knowing the other? As no authentic occasion exists for its revelation, we need to examine the place of its revelation to thus understand the circumstances in which it was revealed and so understand its meaning. Commentators on the Qur'an regard all the surah to have been revealed in Madinah. However, some scholars maintain the revelation to have been Makkan, since the verse starts with the phrase "O mankind!" a recognisable sign of Makkan chapters. Nevertheless, al-Zarkashī classifies the whole of surah *al-Ḥujurāt* as being Madinan.[5]

There is also an opinion from Ibn ʿAbbas of this thirteenth verse of the Madinan surah as having been revealed in Makkah. Methodologically speaking, it is unfeasible to assume that Makkan verses could exist in Madinan chapters. This is because during the revelation, Qur'anic verses were arranged in special units called chapters or surahs (*suwar*). Assuming a Makkan verse to exist in a Madinan surah, would imply that the verse had been revealed in Makkah and not arranged in any surahs, remaining in isolation pending revelation of its future surah in Madinah. The most dangerous implication of this notion is that the arrangement of a certain Makkan verse into its proper place in a Makkan surah would have had to have been forgotten thus requiring its insertion later in Madinah into a relevant Madinan surah. In contrast, however, we are very likely to come across Madinan verses existing in Makkan origin surahs as a result of the *hijrah* (migration to Madinah). Meaning that a surah is said to be of Makkan origin when its beginning was revealed in the Makkan phase, even if it contains verses from Madinah where it was completed during the Madinan phase following the migration.[6] In addition, it is inaccurate to regard a verse commencing with the phrase "O mankind!" as always signifying a surah to be Makkan in origin, since the same phrase also exists in surahs unanimously accepted as Madinan (i.e. *al-Baqarah* and *al-Nisā'*).

Given these arguments the clear conclusion is that the entire surah is a Madinan one. Also untenable is the statement that verse 49:13 originated in Makkah and was later arranged into a Madinan surah.

In point of fact, the verse is entirely conducive to a Madinan environment in terms of the objective of knowing the other. Unlike the homogeneous nature of Makkan society, Madinah was multicultural, with *ahl al-kitāb* coexisting alongside the local groups. For this reason, the migration from Makkah to Madinah is very often illustrated as being a migration from a tribal mentality to one of multiculturalism. However, there seems to have been a gap between the existence of diversity as a fact in Madinan society and human perception towards such a phenomenon.

Historically speaking, the consensus among pre-Islamic Arabs was that differences among people lead to a hierarchical social order based on those differences. In this respect, commenting on the above verse, Ibn Ashur remarks that:

> It was common among Arab tribes, before Islam, to claim superiority and domination over the other. It was to the extent that a Bedouin was asked whether he would agree to become a *Bāhilī*[7] and as a reward he would enter Paradise. The Bedouin remained thinking and then answered: "I would agree providing that the inhabitants of Paradise would never know I was a *Bāhilī*." Such wrong perception of diversity had led to animosity and continuous wars between those people.[8]

Therefore, clear misconception prevailed with regards to the purpose of diversity. Built on the assumption that differences constructed social hierarchy, the phenomenon of diversity was perceived as a reason for social inequalities. This was the historical condition in which verse 40:13 was revealed. Although a multicultural society, the approach followed was still exclusive. The revelation of verse 49:13 in this historical context, changed the mindset instilling a new perception of diversity and its purpose. In fact, the Qur'an advanced the idea that the objective of co-existence is not to seek superiority and domination over different people, but to reach mutual understanding by knowing each other.

Having established a correlation between the objective of knowing the other and the historical circumstances of the verse's revelation, we next examine the textual context in which the verse occurs to investigate relevant thematic relationships between the objective of knowing the other and the textual context of the verse. In order to do so, it is important to define first the topical unity of surah *al-Ḥujurāt*.

The definition of topical unity in Qur'anic exegesis is a process based on reasoning. Because of this, different definitions and opinions may exist with regard to the topical unity of a certain Qur'anic surah. However, as long as these definitions and opinions are in accordance with the whole textual context of the surah in question, they are likely to be accepted despite their multiplicity.

In the case of *al-Ḥujurāt*, Qutub defines its topical unity as follows: "It [*al-Ḥujurāt*] lays down, almost independently, a complete sketch of a noble world, free of anything that may be described as unbecoming."[9] In a similar way, Hijazi states that the surah revolves around the idea of achieving a high standard of morality.[10] Therefore, the surah's topical unity can be summarised as the achievement of a noble world based on a high standard of purity, purity of conscience as well as purity of behavior.

The second thematic step is to explore the relationship between the topical unity of achieving a noble world and the objective of knowing the other. In this respect, the textual context of the surah criticises and disapproves of behavior adopted on the basis of ignorance and suspicion towards others. According to surah *al-Ḥujurāt*, there is a possibility that people can be harmed out of ignorance. Thus, in order to avoid such damage, the Qur'an orders believers to investigate any given information as well as to determine the accuracy of that information before adopting a negative attitude towards others. The Qur'an states:

> O ye who believe! If a wicked person comes to you with any news, ascertain the truth, lest ye harm people unwittingly and afterwards become full of repentance for what ye have done. (Qur'an *al-Ḥujurāt* 49:6)

Verification of the truth of what people may say or do requires accurate knowledge of those people, otherwise wrong and harmful accusations might occur. Consequently, lack of knowledge might lead to the adoption of negative attitudes towards the other. Such attitudes might manifest themselves in the form of ridicule, defamation, negative assumption, spying and backbiting. In fact, all these forms of communication are prohibited in the following verses of *al-Ḥujurāt*:

> O ye who believe! Let not some men among you laugh at others: It may be that the (latter) are better than the (former): Nor let some women laugh at others: It may be that the (latter are better than the (former): Nor defame nor be sarcastic to each other, nor call each other by (offensive) nicknames: Ill-seeming is a name connoting wickedness, (to be used of one) after he has believed: And those who do not desist are (indeed) doing wrong.

> O ye who believe! Avoid suspicion as much (as possible): for suspicion in some cases is a sin: And spy not on each other behind their backs. Would any of you like to eat the flesh of his dead brother? Nay, ye would abhor it...But fear Allah. For Allah is Oft-Returning, Most Merciful. (Qur'an *al-Ḥujurāt* 49:11-12)

According to al-Biqāʿī, there exists a relationship between God's command to verify information given concerning people and the avoidance of all negative attitudes mentioned above.[11] In the same way, Ibn Ashur argues that it was the lack of realisation that the purpose of diversity was to learn to know one another, that led pre-Islamic Arabs to live in a state of animosity, warfare, ridicule, defamation, negative assumption, spying, and backbiting.[12]

Therefore, the achievement of a noble world (the topical unity of *al-Ḥujurāt*), seems to be directly related to the objective of knowing the other. Thus, there appears to be thematic relevance between the textual context of the surah and the objective of mutual acquaintance (*taʿāruf*). This thematic relevance is found in the negative consequences which emerge as a result of a wrong perception of diversity and ignorance of the other.

Another context which plays a significant role in understanding verse 49:13 is the current civilisational condition. In this age of globalisation, the question of the objectives of religious pluralism takes central position while reflecting on verse 49:13. So, it is methodologically important, in the case of Qur'anic exegesis, to take into consideration the context of the reality in which a certain Qur'anic verse is interpreted.[13]

To demonstrate the importance of the civilisational context for understanding the objective of knowing the other, it seems relevant to present both the classical and modern interpretations of the verse:

> O mankind! We created you from a single (pair) of a male and a female, and made you into nations and tribes [*shuʿūb* and *qabā'il*], that ye may know each other (not that ye may despise (each other). Verily the most honoured of you in the sight of Allah is (he who is) the most righteous of you. And Allah has full knowledge and is well acquainted (with all things). (Qur'an *al-Ḥujurāt* 49:13)

Studying Ibn ʿAbbās' commentary on the verse we find only three words explaing the words *shuʿūb* and *qabā'il*. Al-Bukhārī narrates that Ibn ʿAbbās explained the meaning of *shuʿūb* as *qabā'il ʿiẓām*, the broadest category of lineage, as he explained the meaning of *qabā'il* as *buṭūn*, tribal sub-districts.[14] Mujāhid in his commentary on the verse, adds only one sentence to Ibn ʿAbbās' statement, this being that the goal of human division into *shuʿūb* and *qabā'il* is to know people's line of descent.[15] Al-Ṭabarī and al-Zamakhsharī also provide very limited commentary on the verse restricting the meaning of *taʿāruf* to people's descent.[16] A close scrutiny of al-Rāzī's commentary on the verse reveals that he limits the meaning and implications of it only to believers and excludes "unbelievers." Al-Rāzī claims that "the verse comes as an explanation and confirmation of the previous verses [prohibiting ridicule and backbiting]". However, in the case of "unbelievers," "it is permissible to treat them with ridicule and backbite due to their [wrong] religion and faith."[17] Another reason for al-Rāzī's exclusive view on the verse is that the verse addresses the issue of social equality. Yet, according to him, unbelievers cannot be categorised as equal to believers, since "an unbeliever and a believer are two incompatible sorts; an unbeliever is inanimate lower than animals, whereas a believer is what is meant by being human."[18] Finally, al-Rāzī mentions that the verse contains the phrase "the most honored of you" (49:13), but "there is not any honor for an unbeliever since he/she is lower than animals and more humiliated than vermin."[19]

Thus in the classical sources of Qur'anic exegesis we find limited and exclusive interpretations of the verse such that deriving from it a humanistic approach in terms of knowing the other in a process of religious pluralism is not recognised. But these interpretations are largely the product of their time, the historical context and circumstances being such that societies were predominantly homogeneous, divided by cultural boundaries, and surrounded by religious wars. As was the case in al-Rāzī's lifetime.

Turning to some modern sources of Qur'anic exegesis with regards to verse 49:13, it becomes apparent that the current civilisational context has played an important role in underlining the objective of knowing the different other. By adopting a humanistic approach, some modern exegetes have demonstrated a new understanding of the verse. For instance, Qutub remarks that the purpose of making people into nations and tribes is not so that they "stir up conflict and enmity. It is rather for the purpose of getting to know one another and living peacefully together."[20] Moreover, Qutub states that through such a purpose "Islam establishes its human global system under God's banner alone."[21] Even though this statement appears controversial in terms of its meaning, it is a fact that Qutub, unlike classical sources, defines knowledge of the other and thus realization of a peaceful life as a purpose of diversity. Another striking expression in Qutub's comment is the phrase "human global system" which according to him, must rest on the Oneness of God.

Similarly, Ibn Ashur states that the wisdom of diversity is people knowing one another at different social levels starting from the level of the family and reaching to that of civilisations.[22] However, what is more significant to note is that Ibn Ashur relates the purpose of knowing the other to human nature. He observes that perceived as a reason for a mutual understanding, diversity comes in accordance with human nature, whereas perceived as a reason for conflict and enmity, it goes against human nature.[23] Thus, by relating the purpose of diversity to human nature, Ibn Ashur seems to suggest that striving for mutual understanding is a universal human objective. Going further, al-Tabatabai states that in addition to being a purpose of diversity, knowledge of the other is the backbone of society. Consequently, the absence of this objective (knowing the other), according to al-Tabatabai, leads to the decline of society and the destruction of humanity.[24]

Due to the fundamental importance of knowing the other, Ramadan considers knowledge of the other at the level of specialists alone as inadequate, pointing to, and perhaps more importantly, the need to know one another at the grassroots level.[25] Correspondingly, in his comment on verse 49:13, Najar suggests that mutual knowledge, *taʿāruf*, should be understood as a whole process focusing mainly on three aspects, namely solidarity, consultation, and the commandment of what is good.[26] In this way, Najar's interpretation of *taʿāruf* seems to clarify Ramadan's thesis. In other words, knowledge of the other taken as solidarity emphasises a grassroots understanding, whereas seen as consultation, it focuses particularly on specialists. As for the commandment of what is good, it could underline the importance of knowing the other at all levels.

Therefore, interpreted in the light of the current civilisational context, the verse reveals new geographical, social as well as psychological dimensions to the objective of knowing the other, *taʿāruf*. In fact, diversity expressed by the verse is seen as a universal source of knowledge psychologically related to human nature and hence to the process of self-understanding in the light of the other.

Overall, analysis of the historical, textual, and current civilisational context of verse 49:13 has shown that the knowledge of the different other is a universal Qur'anic objective. Moreover, in addition to being universal and in accordance with human nature, such an objective constructs the axis of the peacebuilding process. For this reason, striving for mutual understanding can be accommodated by the Qur'an as one of the main objectives of normative religious pluralism. Thus, the objective of knowing the other will dispel prejudice, stereotypes, and the desire for superiority and domination, which constitute major barriers to normative religious pluralism, or as Henzell-Thomas advises:

> We must purge the mind of prejudice, conditioning, false notions, and unanalysed authority – "Idols of the human mind" which distort and discolour the true nature of things – and rely instead on direct experience, perception, observation, and "true induction" as methods of gaining sound knowledge.[27]

[2]
Cooperation With the Other in Righteousness and Piety: Mutual Engagement – *Taʿāwun*

In this section another Qur'anic imperative concerning interfaith relations will be examined as an objective of normative religious pluralism. This is the imperative of cooperation with the other in righteousness and piety. In fact, analysis in the previous section led to the conclusion, that knowledge of the other and hence the realisation of mutual understanding can be regarded as one of the main objectives of religious pluralism in the Qur'an. However, according to the Qur'an, fostering knowledge and mutual understanding among adherents of different religious affiliations should lead to a higher level objective, namely cooperation. The move from knowing the other to cooperation with the other means a move from mere coexistence or interaction to mutual engagement in the process of religious pluralism. Actually, it is the element of engagement that promotes the objective of cooperation to a higher level than mere knowledge of the other.

Yet, an analysis of classical Qur'anic exegesis reveals a number of classical sources to view, it would appear, the issue of mutual engagement and cooperation as controversial and problematic. These sources claim cooperation with the other to have been abrogated thus leaving cooperation as exclusively restricted to Muslims alone. This being the case, a careful exploration of the Qur'anic text is essential with regards to the issue of cooperation. The most central Qur'anic verse related to this is:

> O ye who believe! Violate not the sanctity of the symbols of Allah, nor of the Sacred Month, nor of the animals brought for sacrifice, nor the garlands that mark out such animals, nor the people resorting to the Sacred House, seeking of the bounty and good pleasure of their Lord. But when ye are clear of the Sacred Precincts and of pilgrim garb, ye may hunt and let not the hatred of some people in (once) shutting you out of the Sacred Mosque lead you to transgression (and hostility on your part). Help ye one another in righteousness and piety, but help ye not one another in sin and rancour: fear Allah, for Allah is strict in punishment. (Qur'an *al-Mā'idah* 5:2)

In general, the verse regulates some aspects of the relationship between Muslims and God as well as between Muslims and other people. After being ordered not to violate the commands of God, believers have been obliged to guarantee the inviolability of animals brought for sacrifice as well as the inviolability of those people peacefully resorting to the Sacred House. In the same way, Muslims have been ordered to cooperate in righteousness and piety with those polytheists who shut them out of the Sacred Mosque during the treaty of *Ḥudaybiyyah*, instead of taking revenge on them.

Turning next to the issue of abrogation, there exists a claim which asserts verse 5:2 to have been abrogated and substituted by other verses ordering Muslims to fight and slay the polytheists. It would appear that, according to the abrogation claim, the relationship between Muslims and polytheists, is one confined to fighting and mutual destruction only.

To examine this assertion, we need to start with its historical aspect. In this respect, al-Ṭabarī mentions scholars as being unanimous in the verse having been abrogated. However, there has been disagreement on whether the whole or only a part of the verse was abrogated.[28] For instance, al-Ḍaḥḥāk claims the entire verse to have been abrogated,[29] whereas al-Mujāhid asserts that only the garlands made from the Makkan bark part was abrogated for environmental reasons.[30] As far as al-Ṭabarī himself is concerned, the part which was abrogated is "nor of the Sacred Month, nor of the animals brought for sacrifice, nor the garlands that mark out such animals, nor the people resorting to the Sacred House" (Qur'an *al-Mā'idah* 5:2).[31] Regardless of the disagreements, all scholars claiming abrogation agree that the verse was abrogated by the following Qur'anic text:

> ...fight and slay the Pagans wherever ye find them, and seize them, beleaguer them, and lie in wait for them in every stratagem (of war);... (Qur'an *al-Tawbah* 9:5)

Although al-Ḍaḥḥāk claims verse 5:2 to have been abrogated by 9:5, it appears that he also contradicts this by stating 9:5 to have been abrogated by the following verse: "...thereafter (is the time for) either generosity or ransom..." (Qur'an *Muḥammad* 47:4).[32]

The problem with al-Ḍaḥḥāk is that firstly, the chronological order of surahs, *Muḥammad*-47, *al-Tawbah*-9, and *al-Mā'idah*-5, (as mentioned by al-Zarkashī),[33] does not favor his abrogation claims. Secondly, his assertion that the whole of verse 5:2 had been abrogated would imply, if accepted, that the sanctity of God's commands can be violated. Of course, not one Muslim scholar in history has claimed such a thing.

As for Mujāhid's assertion referring to the garlands made from Makkan bark part having been prohibited on environmental grounds, this also cannot be accepted, because the Qur'anic text does not stipulate that Makkan bark should be used. In fact, garlands would be perceived as recognisable signs emphasising the inviolability of people as well as the animals wearing them. In fact, there is no evidence to support Mujāhid's abrogation claim.

Al-Ṭabarī states that according to most exegetes, God's commandment to the believers not to violate the sanctity of "the people resorting to the Sacred House, seeking of the bounty and good pleasure of their Lord" (5:2), applied to the polytheists only. However, he further remarks:

> There is no doubt that it ["the people resorting to the Sacred House, seeking of the bounty and good pleasure of their Lord"] was abrogated by the verse "fight and slay the Pagans wherever ye find them, and seize them, beleaguer them, and lie in wait for them in every stratagem (of war)" (9:5), since it would be contradictory to simultaneously command inviolability of the pagans whilst also to fight them.There is a consensus among scholars, that **the people of war among the pagans must be fought and slain.** Providing that **by pagans is meant those of them who are people of war,**[34] there is no doubt that it [5:2] is abrogated.[35]

Al-Ṭabarī's statement explicitly shows that his abrogatio conclusion is made with reference to those pagans who are people of war. Thus, it becomes clear that by abrogation, al-Ṭabarī means the act of specifying the general ruling of the verse, but not its substitution. However, such a conclusion failed to calculate the existence of peaceful pagans to whom verse 5:2 refers. Actually, the ambiguous nature of the term abrogation and al-Ṭabarī's own lack in distinguishing between warmongering and peaceful polytheists open the way for speculation and misleading conclusions.

More importantly, there are other scholars who conclude verse 5:2 to be *muḥkam*, that is not subject to abrogation. For instance, al-Zamakhsharī mentions al-Ḥasan al-Baṣrī as stating: "There is nothing abrogated in surah *al-Mā'idah*."[36] In the same vein, Abū Maysarah states: "There are eighteen obligations, *farīḍah*, in surah *al-Mā'idah*, and nothing is abrogated in it."[37] Furthermore, al-Zamakhsharī ascribes a hadith to the Prophet, wherein he states:

> Surah *al-Mā'idah* is from the last Qur'anic chapters revealed; therefore treat all lawful issues in it as lawful, and all unlawful as unlawful.[38]

The content of this particular hadith is narrated by al-Qāsim ibn Salām in his book *Faḍā'il al-Qur'ān*, through the following chain of transmission: "We were told by Abū al-Iamān from Abū Bakr ibn ᶜAbdullah ibn Abū Maryam from Ḍumrah ibn Ḥabīb and ᶜAṭiyyah ibn Qays, who said: the Prophet – peace be upon him – said..." and then mentions the above hadith.[39]

However, the chain of transmission contains a gap between Ḍumrah ibn Ḥabīb, ᶜAṭiyyah ibn Qays and the Prophet. In other words, there is ommission in the chain in terms of the name of a Companion, since both Ḍumrah ibn Ḥabīb[40] and ᶜAṭiyyah ibn Qays[41] were Successors (*tābiᶜūn*). Because of this discontinuity, the hadith is defined as *Mursal* (a hadith where the chain only goes up to a Successor) and classified as weak (*ḍaᶜīf*). Moreover, one of the narrators, Abū Bakr ibn ᶜAbd Allāh ibn Abū Maryam, has been subject to criticism with scholars in the field of hadith unanimous on his weakness as a narrator of *aḥādīth*.[42] Although this particular hadith is cited by al-Zamakhsharī as evidence for negating abrogation in surah *al-Mā'idah*, it is weak and therefore cannot be accepted. Nevertheless there exists another hadith in which the same meaning is transmitted through another chain of transmitters and which is classified as authentic. Aḥmad ibn Ḥanbal narrates it as follows:

> We were told by ᶜAbd al-Raḥmān ibn Mahdī, who said: We were told by Muᶜāwiyah from Abū al-Ẓāhiriyyah, from Jubayr ibn Nufayr who said: "I visited ᶜĀ'ishah and she asked me: 'Do you read surah *al-Mā'idah*?'" He said: "I answered: 'Yes, I do.' She said: 'It was the last surah revealed, therefore whatever lawful matters you find in it, consider them as lawful, and whatever unlawful matters you find in it, consider them as unlawful.' I also, asked her about the Prophet's character and she said: 'His character was the Qur'an.'"[43]

After careful examination Shuaib al-Arnaut concludes the hadith's chain of transmission to be authentic and all transmitters trustworthy (*thiqāt*).[44] The same hadith is also narrated by al-Ḥākim in his *Al-Mustadrak*, wherein he concludes that "the hadith is authentic and in accordance with the conditions of the Two Shaykhs,[45] but they did not record it."[46] Therefore, taken together, both hadith constitute reliable evidence proving *al-Mā'idah* to have been the last surah revealed. Accordingly, al-Zarkashī's chronological order of Qur'anic chapters, defines *al-Mā'idah* as the last surah revealed. He also remarks that in his Farewell Sermon (during his final Hajj) the Prophet recited from *al-Mā'idah*. After Prophet Muhammad delivered the sermon, the following verses of the Qur'an were revealed:

> This day I have perfected your religion for you, completed My Favor upon you, and have chosen for you Islam as your religion. (*Al-Mā'idah*, 5:3)[47]

Al-Zarkashī's claim is supported by ʿUmar ibn al-Khaṭṭāb, who narrates that once a Jew said to him:

> "O the chief of believers! There is a verse in your Holy Book which is read by all of you (Muslims), and had it been revealed to us, we would have taken that day (on which it was revealed as a day of celebration." ʿUmar ibn al-Khaṭṭāb asked: "Which is that verse?" The Jew replied: "This day I have perfected your religion for you, completed My favor upon you, and have chosen for you Islam as your religion" (5:3). ʿUmar replied: "No doubt, we know when and where this verse was revealed to the Prophet. It was Friday and the Prophet was standing at ʿArafah" (i.e. the Day of Hajj).[48]

Under these circumstances, and given that *al-Mā'idah* was the last surah to have been revealed to the Prophet, any claims of abrogation whether for the surah in general, or more specifically in relation to verse 5:2, are deemed illogical. This conclusion is underscored by the opinions of Abū Muslim al-Isfahānī,[49] Muhammad Abu Zahrah,[50] the late Muhammad al-Ghazali[51] and other scholars who see absolutely no case for abrogation in the entire Qur'an.

In sum, as historical analysis has revealed, no authentic evidence exists to support the claim of abrogation for verse 5:2. Furthermore, both the chronological order of surah *al-Mā'idah* as well as an authentic hadith concerning it, constitute decisive evidence that the entire content of the surah is not subject to abrogation.

The sentence "Help (*taʿāwanū)* ye one another in righteousness and piety" pertaining to the objective of cooperation is another case in point. This concerns an exclusive restriction in meaning of the scope of the imperative *taʿāwanū*, or cooperate (translated as help by Yusuf Ali). For example, al-Ṭabarī seems to confine this cooperation to believers, stating: "The meaning of 'and cooperate in righteousness and piety,' (5:2), is to help – O, believers – each other in righteousness."[52] To refute this exclusive meaning we need to examine the textual context and implications of verse 5:2.

In terms of the textual context of the verse, the first thing to note is that from its very beginning the surah inclusively commands the fulfilment of all contracts and obligations: "O ye who believe! Fulfil (all) obligations" (Qur'an *al-Mā'idah* 5:1).

The purpose of the Arabic definite article *al* attached to the word obligations, ***al-ʿuqūd***, is to show the inclusivity of all obligations, *istighrāq al-jins.*[53] In other words, the grammatical function of the definite article indicates that believers are obliged to fulfil all their contracts and obligations equally with all people. In fact, this is a kind of inclusive cooperation in righteousness.

Note also the textual context of verse 5:5 which mentions the food and chaste women of the People of the Book as being lawful for Muslims. Now, if cooperation had meant an exclusive collaboration between Muslims only, then surely such legislation would have been highly controversial? In fact surah *al-Mā'idah* deals extensively with topics related to the People of the Book, and this together with the title of the surah itself, emphasise the need for an inclusive cooperation based on righteousness and piety.

And in this we cannot, in addition, ignore the overall context of the Qur'an, which also does not support exclusivity of cooperation. This is largely because the Qur'an in many places encourages inclusive cooperation with the other in righteousness. So, for instance, we read in surah *al-Tawbah*:

> If one amongst the Pagans asks thee for asylum, grant it to him, so that he may hear the Word of Allah; and then escort him to where he can be secure. That is because they are men without knowledge. (Qur'an *al-Tawbah* 9:6)

This verse (revealed in one of the latest Madinan surahs) clearly encourages cooperation with the polytheists in goodness. Therefore, as long as the Islamic concept of cooperation with the other is regulated by righteousness and piety, it seems at the very least, unreasonable to presume that it is limited exclusively to Muslims. Even, according to the Qur'an, the potential result of inclusive cooperation is mutual love:

> It may be that Allah will grant love (and friendship) between you and those whom ye (now) hold as enemies. For Allah has power (over all things); And Allah is Oft-Forgiving, Most Merciful. (Qur'an *al-Mumtaḥinah* 60:7)

Turning next to the textual implications of verse 5:2, we focus on the part directly related to the imperative of cooperation:

> ...and let not the hatred of some people in (once) shutting you out of the Sacred Mosque lead you to transgression (and hostility on your part). Help ye one another in righteousness and piety, but help ye not one another in sin and rancour: fear Allah: for Allah is strict in punishment. (Qur'an *al-Mā'idah* 5:2)

The verse refers to a historical conflict which occurred between the polytheists and Muslims in *Ḥudaybiyyah* when the former prevented the latter, including the Prophet, from visiting the Kaʿbah. More particularly, with the aim of preventing Muslims from committing possible transgressions, the verse on the one hand prescribes detachment from the historical context of the conflict, and on the other commands cooperation in righteousness and piety. The two imperatives are joined together through a conjunction known in Arabic grammar as *wāw al-ʿaṭf* (a particular type of "and") which indicates a relationship between the two orders. In other words, the verse establishes cooperation in an inclusive sense, on an honorable ground detached from the historical conflict. Thus, through the function of the *wāw al-ʿaṭf* the past is reconciled with the present.[54]

The idea of reconciliation between the past and the present through the channel of inclusive cooperation in righteousness and piety can be deduced from al-Zamakhsharī's comment on the verse. He remarks that to cooperate in righteousness and piety means to forgive, whereas the prohibition of cooperation in sin and rancour means not to take revenge.[55] It is clear that those who should be forgiven with no revenge taken on them are the polytheists. This in turn implies that cooperation in righteousness and piety, according to the Qur'an, has humanistic dimensions. Furthermore, Ibn Ashur defines the command to cooperate in righteousness and piety as reason (*taʿlīl*) for the prohibition on taking revenge.[56] We are to bring the good out in each other as human beings. Overall, this means that cooperation in righteousness and piety in itself is a course of ethical action advanced by the Qur'an as a main objective of human relations.

The humanistic dimensions of cooperation in goodness are presented more vividly in al-Qurṭubī's comment on the verse. He points out that "God's prescription of cooperation in righteousness and piety concerns all human beings."[57] More significantly, in his comment on verse 5:2, Ibn al-Qayim al-Jawziyyah concludes that "the purpose of human relations is cooperation in righteousness and piety... such a purpose comes in accordance with the divine wisdom of creating humans on the basis of perpetual need for mutual help and cooperation."[58] Hence, in addition to being inclusive, al-Jawziyyah's conclusion also defines the objective of cooperation in righteousness and piety as an unchangeable divine law in this world.

Therefore, both the textual context as well as the textual implications of verse 5:2 prove the scope of the imperative of positive cooperation to be universal, ruling out any exclusive interpretation in this regard.

As far as the civilisational context of today's world is concerned, we have unprecedented proof of the significance of this concept for the peaceful existence of mankind. Universal human cooperation in good works resonates perhaps more deeply than any time before, in an era which is witnessing increasing global integration and need for global sustained peace. So, it might have been one of the reasons why a number of modern exegetes have emphasised the objective of cooperation in righteousness and piety as an irreplaceable principle of society. For example, Rida states that "cooperation is one of the pillars of social guidance in the Qur'an."[59] Of course, it is a fact that human beings are naturally social creatures, but what Rida may have intended is that humans are naturally oriented towards cooperation in whatever sense, but the Qur'an has guided them to that kind of cooperation which is related to righteousness and piety, and prohibited cooperation in sin and rancour. In this way, righteousness (*birr*), in verse 5:2 is understood in its broadest sense to mean morality towards human beings, including human rights.[60] On the other hand rancour, or rather aggression (*ʿudwān*), is understood in its broadest sense as meaning immorality towards humans, i.e. aggression against human life, property, and dignity.[61]

Another modern exegete, al-Tabatabai, defines cooperation in righteousness and piety, and non-cooperation in sin and rancour, respectively as "a principle of Islamic religion."[62] More strikingly, al-Sharawi asserts that: "It is the cooperation in righteousness and piety that makes the faith a universal issue."[63] Al-Sharawi's statement is of paramount importance to the process of normative religious pluralism, since it (the statement) establishes the universality of Islam on the basis of inclusive cooperation in righteousness and piety. It is worth noting here the paradox which abrogationists face, that of requiring restriction of cooperation with the "other" whilst simultaneously earnestly calling that "other" to the universality of Islam.

In summary, some classical sources of Qur'anic exegesis regard verse 5:2 as abrogated, whereas others restrict the imperative of righteous cooperation as applicable only to Muslims.

Such interpretations, on the one hand, have given the impression that Islam is an entirely exclusive religion, whilst on the other have opened ample room for speculation and misleading conclusions. However, as analysis of verse 5:2 has shown, the imperative to cooperate in righteousness and piety is neither subject to abrogation nor to restriction. Thus, the universality of the Qur'anic prescription of cooperating in righteousness and piety can serve as a main objective of normative religious pluralism in terms of mutual engagement in the field of religious commonalities.

[3]
Competing With the Other in Good Works: Mutual Contribution – *Tasābuq*

Previous sections have thus far discussed two main objectives of normative religious pluralism in the Qur'an: knowledge of, and cooperation with, the other. As explained, the former signifies the need for mutual understanding, whereas the latter indicates mutual engagement in the process of religious pluralism.

This section examines a third Qur'anic imperative which is to compete with the other in good works. Constituting an important objective of normative religious pluralism, unlike the previous two, it emphasises the importance of active contribution. Taken as a whole we see in the three objectives a movement of ascent from mere understanding to engagement to active contribution, transforming religious pluralism into a dynamic process.

The objective of competing in good works is derived mainly from two Qur'anic verses:

> To each is a goal to which he turns;[64] then strive together (as in a race) towards all that is good. Wheresoever ye are, Allah will bring you together. For Allah hath power over all things. (Qur'an *al-Baqarah* 2:148)

> To each among you have We prescribed a law and an open way. If Allah had so willed, He would have made you a single People, but (His

> plan is) to test you in what He hath given you: so strive as in a race in all virtues. The goal of you all is to Allah. It is He that will show you the truth of the matters in which ye dispute. (Qur'an *al-Mā'idah* 5:48)

Generally speaking, the meaning of both verses is directed towards the idea that despite the existence of diversity, efforts should be concentrated on vying with one another in good works. In this way, the prescription of competing with the other in the context of diversity can be considered as a significant objective of normative religious pluralism.

However, certain classical Qur'anic exegetes have once again limited the scope of the verse, applying an exclusive meaning to the idea of competing with one another in good works, limiting this understanding to Muslims rather than the whole of humanity. In fact, the exclusive approach predominates in respect of these sources. For example, al-Ṭabarī comments on 2:148:

> What God means by His words "then strive together (as in a race) towards all that is good" (2:148) is that: [here al-Ṭabarī speaks directly on behalf of God] I explained the truth to you O believers and guided you to the *Qiblah* which Jews and Christians, and all other communities have gone astray from. Therefore, as a token of gratitude to your God, embark on doing righteous deeds...And in order not to go astray as previous communities did, keep your *Qiblah* and do not lose it like they did.[65]

Al-Ṭabarī supports this statement by citing Qatādah according to whom the meaning of "then strive together (as in a race) towards all that is good" (2:148), is not to be defeated in respect of your *Qiblah*.[66]

Yet at the same time some of these classical assumptions are shown to be inconsistent with regards to claims for exclusivity. For instance, while in 2:148 al-Ṭabarī confines competing in good works to Muslims only, in 5:48 he apparently lifts the restriction to include all people. This is understood from the context of his comment on 5:48, and more clearly from the usage of the general word *nās* (people). According to al-Ṭabarī the meaning of "so strive as in a race in all virtues" (5:48), is to be understood as "embark – **O people**[67] – on doing righteous deeds and seeking closeness to your God."[68]

Inconsistency again appears in Ibn Ashur's comments on the two verses. In relation to 2:148 he appears to take a highly exclusive position stating the imperative of competing in good works to be directed to Muslims only. This in order not to involve them in any debate with the People of the Book over the *Qiblah*, but rather to concentrate their efforts on resolving the problems of Muslim society.[69] In contrast he suddenly becomes inclusive when it comes to 5:48, regarding the statement of diversity and endorsement to compete in all virtues stipulated in the verse as applicable to all humanity. He explains that diversity is the result of man's freedom of choice endowed by God to all humanity. Thus the wisdom in man's competing with one another in good works is to realise truth in knowledge, morals, and belief.[70]

Therefore, what we have in these explanations of the two verses from the exegetical sources is absolute exclusivism or unsystematic inclusivism, which fail to emphasise the Qur'an's prescription to compete in good works as being a universal objective of human relations. To prove this latter point we need to first examine the textual context in which the verses exist. In this respect, it should be noted that both surahs *al-Baqarah* and *al-Mā'idah* are Madinan, meaning that the verses were revealed in a diverse society. This makes it more likely that the purpose of the verses was to recognise diversity as a matter of earthly fact and to construct out of it a universal objective, rather than create a homogeneous society.

In fact, the textual context of both verses appears to favor the universality of the objective to compete in good works. Looking at verse 2:148, we see how diversity as a matter of earthly fact is confirmed through the discussion on the *Qiblah*. The Qur'an states that no one religious community will ever follow the *Qiblah* of the other. This is because, "to each is a goal, *wijhah*, to which he turns" (2:148). According to Ibn Ashur, *wijhah* means "a way of thinking,"[71] while al-Sharawi clarifies that the meaning of *wijhah* is based on the freedom of choice.[72] Therefore, in this textual context, the verse implies that human cognitive systems are different, but regardless of the fact, there should be a common objective of competing in good works (*fastabiqū al-khayrāt*).

With regard to verse 5:48, there is no disagreement on its occurring in the textual context of discussion on the three divine revelations of the Torah, Gospel, and the Qur'an. For this reason al-Rāzī states that "to each among you have we prescribed a law and an open way", addresses the Jews, Christians, and the Muslims.[73] Moreover, the verse explicitly points to diversity as an undeniable fact of this life: "If Allah had so willed, He would have made you a single People, but (His plan is) to test you in what He hath given you: so strive as in a race in all virtues" (5:48). Therefore, the historical as well as textual context of both verses serves to justify the argument that the verses construct out of diversity an inclusive objective to compete in good works.

The sentence "so strive together as in a race in all virtues (*fastabiqū al-khayrāt*)" (2:148, 5:48) is an imperative with the Arabic verb *fastabiqū* being mainly translated into English as "strive together as in a race" and also "vie with one another, or simply race." Yet what is the precise meaning of *fastabiqū*? It is important to look into the Qur'anic usage of the word, the most relevant being traced in surah *Yūsuf*: "So they both raced each other to the door" (Qur'an *Yūsuf* 12:25)

The verse illustrates a dynamic incident in which Joseph and the ʿAzīz's[74] wife race to reach a door which the wife had locked. Each had a different reason to get there first. Hers was an attempt to seduce him, whilst his was to escape the room. The race therefore was not based on a common purpose.

In another part of surah *Yūsuf*, the word *istabaq* is mentioned: "We went racing with one another" (Qur'an *Yūsuf* 12:17). But here, instead of dynamic action as in 12:25, the word *nastabiq* in the verse is understood to mean proof of excellence among people in a certain activity.[75]

Therefore, the Qur'anic usage of the word *istabaq* shows it to have connotations of dynamic action (whose aim can be positive or negative) as well as meaning proof of excellence among a group of people in a certain activity.

Under these circumstances, the imperative "*fastabiqū al-khayrāt,*" "so strive together as in a race in all virtues" (2:148, 5:48) can be understood to mean both realising the objective of active and dynamic contribution and also excelling in our action to achieve our objectives to the best of our ability (note so long as this competition is towards virtuous goals). And this applies to the process of normative religious pluralism. Since a race can be used for achieving positive and negative purposes, the Qur'an limits the act of competing only to noble and righteous goals whilst it disapproves of any kind of competing in sin, transgression, or any evil purpose:

> Many of them dost thou see, racing each other in sin and transgression, and their eating of things forbidden. Evil indeed are the things that they do. (Qur'an *al-Mā'idah* 5:62)

In fact, this combining of notions of competition with goodness in the Qur'an gears the process of normative religious pluralism towards servicing a noble and humanitarian objective whilst preventing it from serving nefarious ends. In this respect, reflecting on verse 5:48, the Christian theologian Grodz remarks critically that:

> The notion of vying or competing combined with goodness is inappropriate in the contemporary Western world where these terms have recently become more often associated with a ruthless way of attaining one's own goals. In an approach like that, other people are basically treated as objects-rivals, opponents or, at worst, enemies. Thus, they become an obstacle rather than a source of inspiration.[76]

Another meaning which can be derived from "*fastabiqū al-khayrāt*" is to strive with one another for moral and spiritual development, which in turn positively affects all other aspects of daily life. Needless to say, in the context of today's world so vital is the need for moral and spiritual growth that all religions are in agreement as to its urgent development and advancement. Once again, it is worth quoting a Christian viewpoint on this meaning of "*fastabiqū al-khayrāt*". Thus according to Grodz:

> In my understanding, 'vying in good works' implies some sort of noble competition that inspires and encourages people to do what is good. There is space for sincerity and authenticity, but not for pretence. 'Vying in good works' also means striving for spiritual development in a way that does not apply any pressure on others to accept someone else's point of view and convictions, but at the same time gives an opportunity to present unobtrusively the spiritual wealth of one's religion to followers of other religions, and to draw creatively on the wealth of other traditions.[77]

In summary, the Qur'anic prescription of competing in good works is limited exclusively to, in most exegetical sources, Muslims or at least not systematically emphasised as a universal objective of human relations. However, examination of the Qur'anic textual as well as overall context, as well as today's civilisational context, reveals the imperative to compete in good works to be a universal Qur'anic order. Thus, emerging from a textual context discussing religious particularities, the Qur'anic imperative to compete positively in all virtues in actual fact encourages humanity to energise and make a healthy and active contribution leading to the emergence of excellence and development in society. In this sense, the Qur'anic universal prescription of competing in good works forms one of the main objectives of normative religious pluralism.

[4]
Mutual Support – *Tadāfuʿ*

Another main objective of normative religious pluralism that the Qur'an recognises is a mutual support between religions. Compared to the previous three objectives of religious pluralism, that is, mutual understanding, cooperation, and contribution, the objective of mutual support creates a real test for religious co-existence. How can religiously committed people express support for religions different from theirs? In this respect, the Qur'an points out that the objective of mutual support between religions concerns mainly the protection of religious freedom, which is the most important foundation of religious pluralism. Secondly, it concerns the issue of repelling any oppression and aggression on earth.

To further elaborate on this statement regarding the objective of mutual support, we need to explore Qur'anic verses relevant to the issue of interfaith support. In this regard, the most central verses discussing the issue occur in surah *al-Ḥajj*:

> To those against whom war is made, permission is given (to fight), because they are wronged; – and verily, Allah is most powerful for their aid; – (They are) those who have been expelled from their homes in defiance of right, – (for no cause) except that they say, "our Lord is Allah". Did not Allah check one set of people by means of another, there would surely have been pulled down monasteries, churches, synagogues, and mosques, in which the name of Allah is commemorated in abundant measure. Allah will certainly aid those who aid his (cause); – for verily Allah is full of Strength, Exalted in Might, (able to enforce His Will). (Qur'an *al-Ḥajj* 22:39-40)

Generally speaking, the verses define oppression and especially the restriction of religious freedom as the main reason for permission to use physical self-defence. The verses also point out that lack of self-defence against oppression inescapably leads to overwhelming corruption destroying religions.[78]

Yet, restriction of the scope of these two verses as well as the cause (oppression and restriction of religious freedom) of the implied mutual support has led a number of Qur'anic exegesis sources to once again interpret them exclusively. For example, in his interpretation of "Did not Allah check one set of people by means of another", al-Zamakhsharī divides the set of people into Muslims and unbelievers, and states that if God had not repelled unbelievers with Muslims, the polytheists would have destroyed the holy places of all religions.[79] Similarly, al-Rāzī comments on this part of the verse that "God gives permission for the followers of His religion to fight unbelievers."[80] Even

Tantawi with respect to the verse goes on to confine the law of mutual support (*tadāfuʿ*) to the issue of belief and unbelief.[81]

It seems that a large number of Qur'anic exegetes, influenced by certain methodological perceptions and particular historical events, have limited the scope of mutual support to certain ideological boundaries and thus reduced the universality of the Qur'anic objective to an exclusive aim pertaining to one particular group of people. Given this, we need to explore the historical, textual, and thematic implications of the verses in order to challenge this exclusive claim.

With regards to historical context no authentic occasion of revelation has been narrated in relation to the verses. However, what is explicitly clear from the content of *al-Ḥajj* is that the surah is a Madinan one. Correspondingly, in the chronological order of the revelation of the surahs set by al-Zarkashī, he recognizes *al-Ḥajj* to be a Madinan surah.[82] Another point to historically consider is that, according to al-Ṭabarī, those who were expelled from their homes without any rights were Muslims suffering religious persecution at the hands of the Makkan polytheists. Consequently, it was religious persecution which led to the *Hijrah* (Muslim migration from Makkah to Madinah).[83]

Putting these two points together (*al-Ḥajj* being a Madinan surah and the issue of religious persecution in Makkah), what we can deduce is that verses 22:39-40 were revealed at the very early stage of Madinan society, or shortly after the migration (*Hijrah*). In other words the permission to fight in self-defence (revealed in the passive voice "*yuqātalūn,*") against the religious persecution of the Makkans, was revealed in the multicultural society of Madinah which had offered asylum to the Muslims. An important implication of this revelation in the multicultural setting of Madinah – and the absence of such revelation in the homogeneous society of Makkah – is that to repel oppression requires a united front, that is inclusive mutual support between religions. So, this might have been the reason for the Prophet's establishment of the Constitution of Madinah shortly after his arrival in the city, through which he realized in actuality and thereby practically the objective of mutual support by uniting all religious groups on the basis of protecting human rights and repelling oppression.

In fact, implications for the inclusivity of mutual support between religions can be traced back even earlier to Makkah. It is a well-known fact that the Prophet sought support from the Christians in Abyssinia, and also historical fact that he turned to the Christian scholar Waraqah for advice as well as support as explicitly underlined in Waraqah's answer offering the Prophet support:

> Anyone who came with something similar to what you [Muhammad] have brought was treated with hostility; if I should remain alive till the day when you will be turned out [by your people] then I would support you strongly.[84]

Turning to the textual meaning of verses 22:39-40, we try to uncover the real reason for the permission given to fight oppression and religious persecution. This was not an ideological point of view. For this reason, al-Ṭabarī states that the meaning of "Did not Allah check one set of people by means of another", should be understood in its broadest sense to include all people, since God has not provided any indication for the restriction of the meaning.[85] Furthermore, al-Sharawi makes it clear that the verse concerns all of humanity, and cannot be restricted to the classification of believers and unbelievers. More explicitly, he states that the verse is related to the issue of oppression at every time and every place.[86] Therefore, with the purpose of protecting religious freedom and repelling oppression, God has enabled people to unite themselves in order to protect their rights. For this reason, the Qur'an stipulates that "if God had not enabled people to defend themselves against one another" (Asad, Qur'an 22:40), there would have been destruction in terms of religion.

Actually, by mentioning the threat of monasteries, churches, synagogues, and mosques being destroyed together in the context of religious persecution, the Qur'an underlines the importance of mutual support among religions against oppression. Moreover, according to al-Tabatabai, this threat of destruction is not restricted to the physical aspects of the places of worship, but also to the entire religion.[87] Thus increasing the responsibility of faiths to act inclusively, working on a united front to support one another in repelling oppression and protecting religious freedom.

So, protection of religious freedom requires religiously inclusive support. If religions fail to do this they jeopardise not only their own existence, but also the meaningful existence of all humanity. This fact is stressed by the Qur'an in the context of the Children of Israel and their oppression and fight to gain their religious freedom.[88] After the oppression is successfully repelled, the Qur'an concludes that "...And if God had not enabled people to defend themselves against one another, corruption would surely overwhelm the earth" (Asad, Qur'an 2:251).

The objective of mutual support between religions, therefore, concerns the protection of religion and thus the protection of human life from any kind of corruption. According to Abu Zahrah, the protection of religion in the context of Islam means protection of any religion, even the religion of Zoroastrianism, since religiosity is what distinguishes human beings from other creatures. In this respect, the protection of religion is perceived as the protection of the holiest meaning of human life.[89]

The inclusivity of the objective of mutual support is also underscored by the textual context of the surah *al-Ḥajj*, where the humanistic approach seems to be the main feature of the surah. Surah *al-Ḥajj* consists of 78 verses in which the general word "people" (*nās*) is mentioned fifteen times. More strikingly, the surah begins by addressing all people "O Mankind" and ends (with regards to the last part of the content, i.e. the last page) by addressing all people.

In the context of today's world, mutual support between differing faiths has become without doubt one of the main objectives of a large number of international events and organisations.

And this development is vital given an increasingly volatile climate in which initiatives for burning and bombing religious temples, attempts to burn religious scripture, and easy insulting of holy prophets, has put faiths and those who profess them in danger. It is of paramount importance therefore that all religions work together in a climate of mutual support not competition against such aggression.

In sum analysis has shown that the claim of limiting mutual support exclusively to Muslims is based on classical opinion only and not underpinned by any compelling argument. What we do discover through an exegetical examination of verses 22:39-49 (using a systematic methodology) however, is that implementation of this mutual support does not depend on a specific belief system or ideology. In fact, the scope of the Qur'anic objective covers universally all parties protecting religious freedom and repelling any kind of oppression. For this reason, the universality of mutual support between religions in the context of diversity can be accommodated by the Qur'an as one of the main objectives of normative religious pluralism.

[5]
Conclusion

Some sources of Qur'anic exegesis have limited the universal objectives of the human relationship exclusively to Muslims, whereas other sources have been inconsistent in this regard. In addition to the specific historical circumstances in which they wrote and which could have influenced their interpretation, the failure of these sources to recognise systematically the universality of a number of common human objectives seems also to have emerged largely from an absence of a holistic thematic approach to the Qur'an. Having applied the holistic thematic approach in this chapter, we discover that the Qur'an universally endorses four main objectives of the human relationship, which in ascending order are:

a) Mutual understanding – *taʿāruf*
b) Mutual engagement – *taʿāwun*
c) Mutual contribution – *istibāq al-khayrāt*
d) Mutual support – *tadāfuʿ*

Note all four objectives are mentioned in Madinan surahs. In other words in a multicultural society. They are also mentioned in the textual context of religious diversity making them serve as main targets of normative religious pluralism. This wider more inclusive understanding immediately forms the basis, or axis, for a peacebuilding process, wherein achieving universal righteousness and excellence in the context of diversity is seen as the final goal of normative religious pluralism.

5

Qur'anic Prescriptions Seemingly Contradictory to Normative Religious Pluralism

Having explored exegetically the Qur'anic conception of normative religious pluralism in terms of its ethical foundations, structural elements and main objectives, it is important next to analyse another factor. This is certain Qur'anic prescriptions, or concepts, which seemingly contradict the concept of religious pluralism as elaborated. The verses concerning these prescriptions can be grouped into two categories: those related to the issue of warfare and fighting; and those imperatives related to alliance with non-Muslims.

It is important to examine the verses in question because alongside their supposed contradiction of religious pluralism, they are also historically underpinned by scholarly opinions not in favor of the peacebuilding process – a stance which needless to say affects negatively interfaith relations. Moreover, historically grasped as contradictory to normative religious pluralism, these groups of verses are often quoted as evidence to support an exclusivist view of interfaith relations. There is also the issue of Islamic concepts of warfare and alliance. These present a difficult area in terms of being accurately understood by non-

Muslims in the Western context, thus leading to speculation, misleading statements and conclusions often being made in regard to these two notions. For instance, in his work *God, Muhammad and the Unbelievers*, David Marshall attempts to make the case that it is instinctive to the sincere worshipper of God to seek to emulate, in attitude and in action, the divine mind, which in the case of Islam, according to Marshall, declares war on unbelievers. The author's perception of Muslims as God's weapon for punishing unbelievers, thus leads him to draw the conclusion that for Muslims their relationship with non-Muslims is always based on war.[1] This conclusion is likely if, like the author, one ignores essential rules and conditions regulating the hermeneutical process of Qur'anic exegesis.

Given problematic areas such as these, this chapter analyses and elucidates the meaning as well as root cause of the Qur'anic prescriptions to fight and those which prohibit taking non-Muslims as allies. In doing so, it aims to advance a progressive understanding of these ideas in the light of normative religious pluralism. In fact, the chapter seeks to answer the question of whether Qur'anic normative teachings, from this particular angle related to the issues of warfare and alliance, contradict religious pluralism.

[1]
An Analysis of the Qur'anic View on Warfare Contextualised to Normative Religious Pluralism

The issue of warfare in the Qur'an will be studied within the context of normative religious pluralism. This means it will only be analysed in terms of whether the Qur'an's prescription to fight contradicts the principles of religious pluralism. The key to understanding this lies in establishing the root cause for Muslims to fight (*qitāl)* in the Qur'an. *Qitāl* and its derivatives (from the linguistic root *q-t-l*) are specifically used in the Qur'an for military fighting and war. Note the term jihad falls beyond the scope of this study and will not be examined. Its meaning is far more general and also concerns inner struggle as well as human effort to the utmost of one's ability in the way of God, and in every aspect of life.

Analysis will focus on three main aspects: the historical background of warfare at the time of the Qur'anic revelation; a morphological analysis of *q-t-l*, and some of its derivatives; a textual and contextual study of some Qur'anic verses containing the command to fight.

Historical Background of Warfare At the Time of the Qur'anic Revelation

Methodologically speaking, historical context is important for the hermeneutical interpretation of Qur'anic verses, in other words the latter should not be detached from their historical context. Accordingly, to viably understand the Qur'an's concept of warfare, we need to create a virtual historic climate similar to that in which the verses referring to war were revealed.

To begin with the essential thing to note is that the Qur'an was first revealed in a harsh and intolerant nomadic environment which failed to recognise peaceful co-existence among difference. The Revelation began in Makkah, which was a part of *Arabia Ferox*, or Wild Arabia in which ʿAdnānī Arabs lived. Ibn Khaldūn describes their nature as: "The Arabs are a savage nation, fully accustomed to savagery and the things that cause it. Savagery has become their character and nature."[2] Tribal despotism, oppression, and injustice were features of their society, and their life was far removed from any democratic values. Ibn Khaldūn states: "Under the rule of Bedouins, their subjects live as in a state of anarchy, without law. Anarchy destroys mankind and ruins civilisation."[3] ʿAdnānī Arabs lived in an environment, where "blood relationship alone traces the orbit of their lives."[4] Raised in these conditions their way of thinking was "purely egotistic,"[5] intolerant, and violent. For this reason, in the centuries preceding the Qur'an as well as during the Revelation, much warfare too place between the Arabs. These wars are known as *Ayyām al-ʿArab*, literally Days of the Arabs, wherein day refers to battles. These early Arabian epics chronicled the wars among and within the tribes. According to Ḥājjī Khalīfah, there have been two compilations of *Ayyām al-ʿArab*. The first, known to have been written by Abū ʿUbaydah Muʿammar ibn al-Muthannā, mentions 1200 Days, or battles, The second, attributed to Abū al-Faraj al-Aṣbahānī, mentions 1700 battles.[6] Some of these battles lasted decades. For example, the war of Basūs between Taghlib and Bakr, two ʿAdnānī tribes, lasted for 40 years (495-535), and all because (such was his despotic nature) Kulayb, the leader of Taghlib, could not bear to hear his wife Jalīlah, originally from Bakr, claim her brother Jassās to be the greatest man ever.[7]

Therefore, the environment in which the Qur'anic revelation began was inherently marked by severe war and entrenched in violence. Pre-Islamic Arabia was not therefore an environment that was prepared to co-exist with Qur'anic teachings, since "the gulf between the moral views of the Arabs [Makkans] and the prophet's ethical teachings [was] deep and unbridgeable."[8] This gulf generated widespread tension, which later turned into all out war against Muslims on three fronts. As a result, Muslims in Madinah were facing attack on three fronts and had to somehow face this multi-level onslaught:

> The first [front] was against the polytheists of Mecca who initially oppressed [Muslims] and expelled them out of their homes. The second front was against the Jews in Medina who were hostile to the Prophet and sided with the Meccan polytheists, in spite of all the Prophet's efforts to remind them of the monotheistic and Abrahamic bonds that related them to the Muslims and to secure their rights in his document following his immigration to Medina. The third front was against the Bedouins, possibly the worst of all enemies since they were scattered across Arabia, were known to be mercurial and opportunistic, and were open to being used by the enemies of Islam in Mecca and the Jews in Medina against Muslims.[9]

Under these circumstances and threat, Muslims were permitted to defend themselves:

> To those against whom war is made, permission is given (to fight), because they are wronged; – and verily, Allah is Most Powerful for their aid; – (They are) those who have been expelled from their homes in defiance of right, – (for no cause) except that they say, "our Lord is Allah". Did not Allah check one set of people by means of another, there would surely have been pulled down monasteries, churches, synagogues, and mosques, in which the name of Allah is commemorated in abundant measure. Allah will certainly aid those who aid his (cause); – for verily Allah is full of Strength, Exalted in Might, (able to enforce His Will). (Qur'an *al-Ḥajj* 22:39-40)

Generally speaking, the verses define oppression and especially the restriction of religious freedom, as the main reasons for the permission to physical self-defence. The verses also point out that a lack of self-defence against oppression inescapably leads to overwhelming corruption destroying religions.[10] More particularly, the verb given in the passive voice *yuqātalūn*, "those against whom war is made", indicates that the real reason for the permission to fight was oppression and religious persecution, and not due to any belief system different to Islam. For this reason, al-Sharawi states that the verses are related to the issue of oppression at every time and every place.[11]

In sum historical examination reveals warfare to have been an inherent feature and historical characteristic of pre-Islamic society. And it was in this toxic climate that the Qur'an was revealed. It naturally followed that the newly revealed divine message would be fought oppressively without reason. Given these circumstances and resultant persecution, that is against an oppressively initiated war against Muslims, the Qur'an legitimised the right to fight in self-defence. Therefore, the root cause of the Qur'anic imperative to fight lay not historically in the different belief system of the other, but in the oppression and persecution of Muslims leading to war being waged against them.

A Morphological Analysis of the Root *q-t-l*

The triliteral linguistic root *q-t-l* means to cause somebody humiliation and fatality,[12] or the removal of the soul from the body.[13] In this respect, the literal meaning of *q-t-l* is to kill. However, its range of meaning also includes to fight because fighting is associated with causing humiliation and death. Thus, a cause-and-effect relationship exists between the meaning of *q-t-l* and that of to fight.

The root *q-t-l* and its derivatives in the Qur'an exist mostly in the form of descriptive text conveying information on historical events related to the meaning of *q-t-l*. And events are mentioned for moral lessons to be drawn, in this instance from human experience associated with issues relating to *q-t-l*. Nevertheless, *q-t-l* and its derivatives do exist in the Qur'an in the imperative (or command) form, in other words prescribing Muslims to fight. Note however, this imperative form of *q-t-l* constitutes less than one percent of the entire Qur'anic content, which fact is essential to grasp in terms of the peaceful nature of its message. For it should be borne in mind that the Qur'an was revealed in a climate of intense violence and constant warfare, in which its verses and message of peace, invoking human dignity, stood out all the more starkly against a backdrop of fierce tribal aggression and hostile mindsets. Note also that the Qur'an contains imperatives to peace (i.e. *al-Baqarah*, 224).

The *q-t-l* linguistic root and its derivatives occur in the Qur'an mainly in forms I and III of the Arabic morphological forms. Forms II and VIII also exist, but as they are very restricted and do not play any role in deriving principles of warfare, they will not be analysed.

The first morphological form is *qatala* which equates to the basic form, or verb pattern, of *faʿala*. The source noun, *al-maṣdar*, of *qatala* is *qatl*. This morphological form shows that the action of killing or fighting is initiated from one side without a tendency of the other side to retaliate. For this reason, lexicographers explain the meaning of the first form of *q-t-l* by the

Arabic word *imātah*, which means to cause initially death.[14] Because of this, Baalbaki in his *Mawrid* translates the first morphological form *qatala* as "to kill, slay, murder, assassinate."[15]

The third morphological form of *q-t-l*, is *qātala* which equates to the standard form of *fāʿala*. The source noun, *al-maṣdar*, of *qātala* is either *qitāl* or *muqātalah*. The third morphological form indicates a consequence of an action and thus adds to the first form an associated meaning.[16] In other words, the act in the third form is conducted in response to another act. In that case, *qātala*, *qitāl*, or *muqātalah* means that the act of killing or fighting is done in response to another initially started act of killing or fighting. Accordingly, Baalbaki translates the third morphological form *qātala* as "to fight, combat, battle (against),"[17] but not as to kill, slay, murder, assassinate, though these occur within the process of fighting.

The difference in the meaning then between the first and the third morphological forms of *q-t-l* is that the first form *qatala*, *qatl*, is associated with oppressive as well as aggressive initiation of war on others without reasonable reasons for such an action, whereas the third form *qātala*, *qitāl*, or *muqātalah*, is associated with the right to self-defence against unjustly initiated war.

For this reason, when the Qur'an applies the first morphological form of *q-t-l* and not in a textual context of the third form *qātala*, *qitāl*, or *muqātalah*, it always refers to aggression and oppressive fighting and killing of innocent people. For example, the Qur'an uses the first morphological form *qatala*, *qatl*, with reference to Pharaoh's killing of Bani Israel's baby boys, the killing of prophets by some of the People of the Book, the plot hatched by the sons of prophet Jacob to kill Joseph, the pre-Islamic tradition of some Arabs to kill their daughters, the killing of one of Adam's sons by the other. All these actions of killing were committed oppressively against innocent people reluctant to fight or kill. Accordingly, the Qur'an refers to all these cases, none of which exists in the textual context of self-defence, by using the first morphological form of *qatala*, *qatl*.

As far as the third morphological form *qātala* or *qitāl*[18] is concerned, the Qur'an always uses this in the context of the right to self-defence against unjustly initiated war. In other words to resist aggression and thus restore peace and justice.

So, an accurate understanding of the Qur'anic verses relating to the issue of fighting requires distinguishing verb forms in order to understand correctly the message being conveyed. We must not project our own meaning simplistic fashion, but elucidate the meaning being conveyed to us. And we must not take verses out of context to suit our own interpretations.

Keeping this in mind it is important to note that in the following verse in which Muslims are commanded to fight, God's prescription to fight is expressed in the third morphological form (*qitāl*):

> Fighting is prescribed for you, and ye dislike it. But it is possible that ye dislike a thing which is good for you, and that ye love a thing which is bad for you. But Allah knoweth, and ye know not. (Qur'an *al-Baqarah* 2:216)

So *qitāl*, not *qatl*, is used in the verse to express the word translated as "fighting". This is a point of huge significance for being in the third morphological form it indicates the right to self-defence against aggressive oppression. In fact in the entire Qur'an nowhere does the word *qatala*, *qatl* appear in Form I, that is the first morphological form, with reference to the People of the Book.[19] What does exist in this regard is only the imperative of the third morphological form *qātala*, *qitāl*, indicating that fighting People of the Book is prescribed only in the case of their unjustly waging war on Muslims, and not due to their beliefs or way of thinking.

Now, the imperative to fight using the verb *qatala* in its first morphological form occurs in four verses of the Qur'an only, and in all four occurrences it is with reference to the polytheists as well as hypocrites, who are people of war against Muslims. With regard to polytheists, the direct imperative occurs in verse 2:191 (surah *al-Baqarah*) and verse 9:5 (surah *al-Tawbah*) whereas with regard to the hypocrites, it occurs in verses 89 and

91 of surah *al-Nisā'* (4:89-91). Note, all four verses exist in the textual context of the third morphological form, that is *qātala, qitāl*. In other words, the order given to Muslims to kill in these four verses, is related to those polytheists and hypocrites who are people of war against Muslims. The context of war in the four verses is expressed by the contextual indications (morphological and thematic) showing that the Form I imperative to fight (*qatala*) was prescribed within the context of a war initially waged on Muslims.

In sum, analysis of the linguistic root *q-t-l* (to fight/kill), reveals that the Qur'anic concept of warfare related to the issue of fighting is expressed using the third morphological form of Arabic verb morphology, that is *qātala*, *qitāl*, or in its textual context. And because Form III is used this signifies that the act of killing or fighting is done in response to another initially started act of killing or fighting, and thus associated with the right to self-defence. This proves morphologically, that the root cause of the Qur'an's imperative to fight is in response to the initiation of oppression expressed by war on Muslims, and is not based on any different belief system.

Textual and Contextual Study of Some Qur'anic Verses Connected to the Imperative of Fighting Against Others

In this section, two key Qur'anic verses are examined with reference to the issue of warfare. Both occur in surah *al-Tawbah*: verse 9:5 (which prescribes fighting against the polytheists) and verse 9:29 (which concerns the issue of warfare in relation to the People of the Book). The rationale behind the selection of these two particular verses is rooted in the hugely significant controversy surrounding their understanding. Note, since both verses were revealed in the one of the latest revealed surahs and address groups religiously different to the Muslims, it is likely that their exploration will satisfactorily answer the question of whether the Qur'anic prescription to fight contradicts the conception of normative religious pluralism.

An Analysis of the Imperative to Fight and Slay the Polytheists in Verse 9:5

The Qur'an stipulates the following:

> But when the forbidden months are past, then fight and slay the Pagans wherever ye find them, and seize them, beleaguer them, and lie in wait for them in every stratagem (of war); but if they repent, and establish regular prayers and practise regular charity, then open the way for them: for Allah is Oft-forgiving, Most Merciful. (Qur'an *al-Tawbah* 9:5)

Critics of Islam often cite this verse quoting it out of context to promote the idea of Islam being a religion of violence. There are two main problematic areas which need examination: first, the claim of abrogation, and second the root cause for the imperative to fight and slay the polytheists.

Claim of Abrogation: The first thing to note is that the verse is known as "the verse of the sword,"[20] which many exegetes define as a verse abrogating all virtues and ethics towards non-Muslims. To examine this serious claim we need to trace its origins and analyse the argument.

In this respect, no evidence from the time of the Prophet and his Companions exists to support abrogation. The earliest exegetical work in which abrogation is mentioned, seems to be Ibn Abū Ḥatim al-Rāzī's *Al-Tafsīr bi al-Ma'thūr* written at the end of the ninth and beginning of the tenth centuries. Ibn Abū Ḥatim writes in the work:

> We were told by my father, [who said]: We were told by al-Suḥayn ibn ʿĪsā ibn Maysarah, [who said]: We were told by Muḥammad ibn al-Muʿallā al-Iāmī, [who said]: We were told by Juwaybir who narrated from al-Ḍaḥḥāk that: "Every verse in the book of Allah which refers to any obligations or covenant between the Prophet – peace be upon him – and any one of the pagans was abrogated by surah *al-Tawbah* "and seize them, beleaguer them, and lie in wait for them in every stratagem (of war)"[9:5].[21]

This narration from Ibn Abī Ḥātim has also been transmitted

by al-Suyūṭī in his *Al-Dur al-Manthūr fī al-Tafsīr bi al-Ma'thūr.*[22] The narration clearly states verse 9:5 to have abrogated every other verse in the Qur'an prescribing certain obligations towards polytheists. From here, it came to be understood that any good moral behavior, as well as ethics such as forgiveness, compassion, mercy, etc. towards non-Muslims, were no longer to be considered valid. So much so that Ibn ʿAṭiyyah asserts, without any evidence, that "this verse [9:5] did abrogate every obligation and covenants contained reportedly in 114 Qur'anic verses."[23] Hence, it was through this channel that the view came to be widely disseminated that Muslim moral obligation towards others was abrogated with the verse of the sword.

However, this huge and sweeping statement cannot be accepted simply on the basis of al-Ḍaḥḥāk's narration. Firstly, it is attributed neither to the Prophet nor to any of the Companions. Secondly, the hadith is not authentic at all due to the weakness and unreliability of Juwaybir ibn Saʿīd al-Azdī (one of the transmitters in its chain).[24] All scholars of Hadith unanimously agree on Juwaybir being a weak and unreliable transmitter. For instance, according to Ibn Ḥibbān, Juwaybir narrated from al-Ḍaḥḥāk things upside down,[25] whilst Ibn Ḥajar in his *Taqrīb* concludes Juwaybir to be a very weak transmitter, "*ḍaʿīf jiddan.*"[26] Therefore, Juwaybir's narration attributed to al-Ḍaḥḥāk corroborates nothing, is unauthentic and thus cannot be accepted as evidence to establish verse 9:5 as having abrogated every obligation in respect of non-Muslims.

Examining the arguments of those scholars who nevertheless maintain the validity of abrogation we note that their views are unreliable in themselves and that they advance no credible evidence to support their theory. For example, al-Samarqandī claims without mentioning any supporting evidence that: "*it is said*[27] that this verse [9:5] abrogated 70 Qur'anic verses related to obligations and covenants"[28] (italics mine). Similarly, al-Bagawī claims, without providing any chain of transmission, that al-Ḥusayn ibn al-Faḍl[29] stated: "This verse [9:5] abrogated every Qur'anic verse referring to forgiveness and patience towards the offences of enemies."[30] Equally, al-Qurṭubī transmits the same narration attributed to al-Ḥusayn ibn al-Faḍl ᶜAbbās without any chain of transmission.[31] Similarly, Ibn Kathīr provides three narrations in support of the abrogation claim,[32] without any of them being authentic. The first narration is that of al-Ḍaḥḥāk, as already analysed. The second is ascribed to Ibn ᶜAbbās through al-ᶜAwfī's chain of transmission, about which Ahmad Shakir concludes that: "This chain of transmission consists of weak and not trustworthy transmitters coming from one family. This chain is known among exegetes as *tafsīr al-ᶜawfī* because the transmitter narrating from Ibn ᶜAbbās is called ᶜAṭiyyah al-ᶜAwfī."[33] The third narration provided by Ibn Kathīr in favor of abrogation is attributed again to Ibn ᶜAbbās, but this time through ᶜAlī ibn Abī Ṭalḥah's chain of transmission. Yet, "Alī ibn Abī Ṭalḥah's *tafsīr* is not reliable due to the break in the chain between him and Ibn ᶜAbbās."[34/35]

Therefore, it is unquestionably clear from the analysis that the widely spread claim of the so called "verse of the sword" as abrogating all moral obligations towards others, is not supported by the Prophet or any of his Companions, and neither is it supported by any authentic hadith or plausible argument.

Moreover, what cannot be ignored is that this supposed abrogation of 9:5 contradicts basic fundamental principles of the Qur'an. These include: the inviolability of human life, freedom of belief, human brotherhood etc. For this reason, in one of the earliest and most reliable sources of abrogative and abrogated verses in the Qur'an, *Kitāb al-Nāsikh wa al-Mansūkh* written by Abū Jaᶜfar al-Nuḥās, verse 9:5 is not defined as an abrogative to any other verses.[36] In the same way, exegetes such as al-Ṭabarī, al-Zamakhsharī, al-Rāzī, al-Bayḍāwī and others do not mention anything with regard to verse 9:5 being abrogative to the moral obligations of Muslims towards non-Muslims.

As for the second problematic area with regard to verse 9:5 this concerns the root cause for the imperative to fight and slay polytheists. In general, there has been disagreement among exegetes over the root cause. Some exegetes such as al-Rāzī and Ibn Ashur infer the imperative to have general meaning, thus concerning all polytheists until they embrace Islam. Thus, al-Rāzī asserts the imperative "slay the Pagans" to be a general command, going on to surmise that the blood of unbelievers is permitted until they realise three conditions, these being to repent from unbelief, establish prayer, and give in charity.[37] Similarly according to Ibn Ashur "in verse 9:5 there is legality and permission for jihad [against pagans], and an indication that nothing else can be accepted from them except Islam."[38] In a more restricted interpretation, al-Sharawi confines the slaying of polytheists geographically to the Arabian Peninsula, claiming that "the punishment of the pagan is murder, *ʿiqāb al-mushrik huwa al-qatl*. Why? Because in this place [the Arabian Peninsula] two religions cannot exist."[39] To support this claim al-Sharawi presents the argument that the Arab polytheists were fully aware of the Prophet's honesty, as they were also aware of the authenticity of the Qur'anic Revelation due to their knowledge of the Arabic language. Hence, because of these two facts, they could not be excused from accepting Islam, in other words the obligation to embrace Islam in their case was binding.[40]

Another group of exegetes point to the constant warmongering of the polytheists against the Muslims, together with their transgression of covenants, as the reason for the imperative to slay them. In favor of this opinion are exegetes such as al-Ṭabarī, al-Zamakhsharī, Abū Zahrah and others. Their main argument concerns the overall Qur'anic context, and more importantly the textual context in which verse 9:5 exists.

Examining al-Rāzī, Ibn Ashur, and al-Sharawi's reasoning it is clear that the central point of their argument is the question of belief. In other words the polytheists' belief system is the root cause for the imperative to slay them. For all three scholars therefore acceptance of Islam is the only avenue for the cessation of fighting and slaying. For instance, al-Rāzī bases his opinion on the literal meaning of "but if they repent, and establish regular prayers and practise regular charity, then open the way for them" (9:5). Note, for al-Sharawi the Qur'anic principle of freedom of belief does not apply to the pagans of the Arabian Peninsula.

So, according to al-Rāzī every polytheist must be killed until he/she repents, establishes regular prayer, and practises charity. However, this argument clearly contradicts the textual context in which the imperative to slay polytheists appears:

> (But the treaties are) not dissolved with those Pagans with whom ye have entered into alliance and who have not subsequently failed you in aught, nor aided any one against you. So fulfil your engagements with them to the end of their term: for Allah loveth the righteous. (Qur'an *al-Tawbah* 9:4)

Al-Ṭabarī employs this verse as a contextual argument to maintain that it is only people of war to whom the imperative of slaying in 9:5 refers. He remarks that the imperative to fight and slay the polytheists applied only to those who had transgressed the covenant and involved themselves in enmity and war against the Prophet. For those who remained loyal to the covenant and did not wage war against the Prophet, God ordered the Prophet to remain loyal to them.[41] More explicitly, al-Ṭabarī also argues against perceiving the imperative in its general sense, because the verse following the imperative does not allow for such a general perception:

> How can there be a league, before Allah and His Messenger, with the Pagans, except those with whom ye made a treaty near the sacred Mosque? As long as these stand true to you, stand ye true to them: for Allah doth love the righteous. (Qur'an *al-Tawbah* 9:7)[42]

Al-Ṭabarī states that this verse: "Supports our argument, and goes against the statement that it is permitted to kill every pagan after the forbidden months are past, for God commanded His Prophet and the believers to stand true to those pagans who stand true to them."[43]

Following al-Ṭabarī's approach of employing textual context[44] as counter-argument to challenge the view of belief motivating the imperative to slay polytheists, we have other clear-cut evidence, in terms of textual context, which points to the root cause as being polytheist aggression, transgression of oaths, and declaration of war against the Prophet and his followers, necessitating a response:

> But if they violate their oaths after their covenant, and taunt you for your Faith – fight ye the chiefs of Unfaith: for their oaths are nothing to them: that thus they may be restrained.
>
> Will ye not fight people who violated their oaths, plotted to expel the Messenger, and took the aggressive by being the first (to assault) you? Do ye fear them? Nay, it is Allah Whom ye should more justly fear, if ye believe! (Qur'an *al-Tawbah* 9:12-13)

As is clear from the verses, it is not the belief system of others that is defined as a necessary condition for fighting, but their aggression, transgression, and initiation of war. This meaning is supported by an authentic interpretation of 9:5 by Qatādah. Al-Ṭabarī transmits:

> We were told by Bishr ibn Muʿādh, who said: We were told by Yazīd, who said: We were told by Saʿīd, who narrated from Qatādah a narration related to the words of God: "But when the forbidden months are past, then fight and slay the Pagans wherever ye find them," to the end of the verse 9:5. In this regard, Qatādah used to say: "Open the way for those who God commanded you to open their way. People are three groups: Muslims obliged to give regular charity, zakah; people associating partners with God, this kind of people are obliged to pay tax, *jizyah*; and people of war, who if they pay one tenth of their capital, their safety as well as the safety of their trade with Muslims is guaranteed."[45/46]

So, Qatādah's *tafsīr* of verse 9:5 clearly shows that it is not a choice of embrace Islam or death that is offered to polytheists, but rather, there is an option to fulfill obligations and co-exist peacefully.

Ibn Taymiyyah also supports the position that it is not the polytheist's belief system that underlies the imperative to fight and kill them, but rather their persecution of Muslims. He dedicated a whole work entitled *Qāʿidah Mukhtaṣarah fī Qitāl al-Kuffār wa Muhādanatihim wa Taḥrīm Qatlihim li Mujarrad Kufrihim* to the issue of warfare. In this work, he concludes that it is not permissible for a Muslim to kill a person because of his/her beliefs whatever they might be. He attributes his conclusion to the opinion of the majority of Islamic scholars. As for his comment on verse 9:5, he states that: "It is not permissible to kill a pagan given that he/she is subject to an agreed covenant or asylum, or providing that he/she does not belong to the people of war."[47] In other words, Ibn Taymiyyah's words imply that it is only those polytheists who are people of war who can be fought against.

Another modern response to an exclusive view of 9:5 is Asad's interpretation of the verse. He points out that:

> Now the enemy's conversion to Islam – expressed in the words, "if they repent, and take to prayer [lit., "establish prayer"] and render the purifying dues (zakah)" – is no more than one, and by no means the only, way of their "desisting from hostility"; and the reference to it in verses 5 and 11 of this surah certainly does not imply an alternative of "conversion or death..."[48]

Therefore, the "conversion or death" attitude adopted by al-Rāzī and Ibn Ashur contradicts the textual context of verse 9:5 as well as many scholarly opinions in this regard. Moreover, this attitude also contradicts the Qur'an's universal principle of freedom of belief as expressed in the verse "Let there be no compulsion in religion" (2:256), which clearly states that conversion to Islam by force is not permissible.[49]

Turning to al-Sharawi, regardless of freedom of belief being a universal principle, it seems that he would qualify "universal" to exclude Arab pagans from it. As mentioned earlier, in his opinion pagan Arabs can only be offered two options: "Islam or death." And he supports this argument with two observations:

that Arab pagans were well aware of the honesty of the Prophet, and also aware of the authenticity of the Qur'an given their strength in the Arabic language. Putting these two facts together, he concludes freedom of belief as being inapplicable to the Arab polytheists.[50]

Yet if this is the case then how should the verse following 9:5 be understood:

> If one amongst the Pagans asks thee for asylum, grant it to him, so that he may hear the word of Allah; and then escort him to where he can be secure. That is because they are men without knowledge. (Qur'an *al-Tawbah* 9:6)

This verse seems to directly contradict al-Sharawi because it includes the exact group of people he chooses to exclude from the right to freedom of belief. In contrast, the verse proves freedom of belief and dignity to be inclusive values encompassing Arab pagans too. In this respect, attention is captured syntactically from the very beginning of the verse by way of a conditional sentence introduced by the Arabic conditional particle *in*, translated into English as "if." The function of the conditional particle *in* indicates unlikeness, meaning that the condition introduced in the sentence by *in* (if) is unlikely to happen.[51/52] Thus in this instance the conditional particle *in* is used in the verse to indicate that it is very unlikely that anyone from among the pagans would come and ask the Prophet for asylum, but should they happen to do so then to "grant it to him, so that he may hear the word of Allah; and then escort him to where he can be secure" (9:6). This syntactic point shows that despite the pagans' reluctance and unwillingness to interact peacefully with Muslims, the Qur'an orders Muslims to guarantee asylum and safety to them if they ask for this.

Another important syntactic point to emphasize in verse 9:6 is the existence of inversion. According to the Arabic syntactic structure of the conditional sentence, the verb should follow the conditional particle *in*.[53] However, in verse 9:6 it is followed by a noun (*aḥadun*, anyone) which refers to any pagans, while the verb *istajāra* (ask) is postponed in the sentence. This linguistic approach is referred to as inversion.[54] The function of the inversion in 9:6 is to place particular emphasis on the person asking for asylum, and not so much on the asylum itself. Thus, the aim of the inversion is directed towards preserving human dignity from any possible violation.

Furthermore, the conditional sentence presented in verse 9:6 prescribes two actions in response to anyone from the pagans asking for asylum. The first action requires Muslims to grant asylum to the pagan, where he/she can hear the Qur'an, whereas the second pertains to the issue of escorting the pagan, when the asylum is over, to a place where he/she can be secure. Reflecting on these two actions it becomes clear that polytheists in general and Arab polytheists particularly have been inclusively considered to enjoy the right to freedom of belief.

Al-Sharawi's statement also contradicts the teachings of the Prophet, who forbade Muslims during war to kill children, women, worshippers, and elderly people. This negates al-Sharawi's "Islam or death" option, for if it were valid then the Prophet would not have forbidden Muslims to kill this group of people. In addition, there is no single authentic evidence proving that the Prophet killed or ordered to be killed any person because of his/her belief.

Finally, al-Sharawi deprives Arab polytheists of the right to freedom of belief with the justification that knowing the profound honesty of the Prophet, and the authenticity of the Qur'an based on knowledge of the Arabic language, they should have accepted his message. However, this argument could just as well be applied to humanity today. For there are those who study the biography of the Prophet and so are well aware of his honesty, and who study the Arabic language and have great linguistic knowledge of it. Are we to infer that as a result of this they are to be deprived of the right to freedom of belief and consequently killed if rejecting Islam? Logically, this line of reasoning is unacceptable for belief is determined by a host of other factors.

As this brief analysis has shown verse 9:5 does not therefore abrogate any moral obligation towards non-Muslims. To repeat this is because the verb used in the imperative to "fight and slay the Pagans" is in the third morphological form *qitāl*, which indicates the right to self-defence against a previously waged war. As such, the object of the imperative ("Pagans") must be given a literal not a metaphorical meaning and understood as a synecdoche, *majāz mursal*. A synecdoche is a figure of speech in which a term for a part of something refers to the whole of something, or vice-versa. In other words, the word "Pagans" in the verse pertains to only to people of war and hence relates the root cause of the imperative to the pagans' aggression, and not their belief system.

This being the case (that the verse does not abrogate moral obligation towards non-Muslims, and was not motivated by the belief system of others), it is apparent that verse 9:5 and its imperative to fight and slay the polytheists does not contradict the process of normative religious pluralism.

An Analysis of Verse 9:29's Imperative to Fight the People of the Book

This section focuses on one of the most central Qur'anic verses concerning the issue of warfare in respect of the People of the Book:

> Fight those who believe not in Allah nor the Last Day, nor hold that forbidden which hath been forbidden by Allah and His Messenger, nor acknowledge the religion of Truth, from among the People of the Book, until they pay the *jizyah* with willing submission, and feel themselves subdued. (Qur'an *al-Tawbah* 9:29)

From the outset, it is worth mentioning that no authentic comments or explanations directly relating to this verse exist either from the Prophet or his Companions. However, much discussion and controversy surrounding the verse can be found in the succeeding generations. Some of the issues debated have concerned the motive for the imperative to fight as well as its scope.

Some sources of Qur'anic exegesis have linked the root cause for the command to fight (*qātilū*) to the four characteristics mentioned in the verse: unbelief in God, unbelief in the hereafter, lack of prohibiting what God and His Messenger have prohibited, and lack of acknowledging the religion of truth. Yet, the larger part of the disagreement has related to the command's scope which for some exegetes has been left vague. For example, al-Ṭabarī and al-Zamakhsharī briefly outline the general meaning of the verse without clear focus either on its scope or underlying cause for the command to fight.[55] Al-Rāzī on the other hand, states explicitly that all People of the Book come within its purview, most of them because of their unbelief, but even if some Jews still remain true to the Oneness of God, they are also to be fought unless they pay the *jizyah* (tax).[56] Thus, for al-Rāzī the root cause underlying the command to fight People of the Book lies either in their unbelief or refusal to pay the *jizyah*. Rida however, argues that all four characteristics are necessary conditions to initiate fighting against the People of the Book. Accordingly, those of them who believe in God and the hereafter, and prohibit what God and their prophets had prohibited, and acknowledge truly their religion, should not be fought.[57] However, for Ibn Ashur even if the People of the Book believe in God and the hereafter and prohibit what God has prohibited in their scriptures, they still nevertheless should be fought for failure to acknowledge the true faith of Islam.[58]

What is clear from these opinions is that although they disagree as to the scope of the command, they are in consensus as to its motivation which is belief. Furthermore, note all these scholars base their argument, in different ways, on the four characteristics existing in the relative pronoun.

However, the implications of these views, and initiation of aggression against the People of the Book in the light of universal human values, not only historically but also, and even more sharply, in today's global world, is unacceptable. Even Rida's opinion, which seems to be the most liberal, cannot be accepted since the classification "People of the Book" today is a largely cultural construct with most people defining themselves as agnostics. Indeed, today's global context only serves to highlight more starkly the failure of these opinions to diagnose the real cause of the command to fight. However, this aside, the main reason for rejecting opinions such as these is their contradiction of central Qur'anic principles including freedom of belief, human free will, human dignity etc.

In contrast are scholarly opinions which state that the command to fight is to be applied only to those who initiate hostilities against Muslims, that is, Muslims are to fight those who wage war on them. This is self-defence. Thus, the scope of the command falls on those of the Book who are people of war. As for the four characteristics following the imperative to fight, they should be understood not as conditions which permit the declaration of war, but as informative descriptions characterizing those who stoke oppressively the fires of war against peaceful people. To support this view, we examine next the historical, textual, and intertextual contexts of verse 9:29.

As mentioned earlier, it is important to examine as much as possible the historical context of the verse being interpreted. In terms of the historical context of verse 9:29 we know that it exists in surah *al-Tawbah* which contains information about the battle of *Tabūk* in 630 C.E./9 AH – it can be estimated that the verse was revealed around this year. Generally, the years preceding 630 C.E./9 AH witnessed a deterioration in interfaith relations, especially between the Muslims and the Jews, mainly due to the latter's constant transgression of the mutually signed pact of Madinah.[59] More particularly, in 628 C.E./7 AH one of the Prophet's emissaries (carefully selected people sent to rulers of the surrounding kingdoms to invite them to Islam) was aggressively killed. In this respect al-Wāqidī narrates:

> I was told by Rabīʿah ibn ʿUthmān, who transmitted from ʿUmar ibn al-Ḥakam, who said: The Prophet – peace be upon him – sent al-Ḥārith ibn

> ᶜUmayr al-Azdī with a message to the governor of Bostra, *Buṣrā*. When the Prophet's messenger arrived at Mu'tah,[60] he was stopped by Shuraḥbīl ibn ᶜAmrū al-Ghassānī, [a Christian, one of the representatives of the Byzantine emperor], who asked him: "Where are you heading towards?" He responded: "Towards Sham." [Shuraḥbīl ibn ᶜAmrū al-Ghassānī] said: "You might be one of Muhammad's messengers?" [Al-Ḥārith ibn ᶜUmayr al-Azdī] answered: "Yes, I am a messenger of the messenger of God." Then, [Shuraḥbīl ibn ᶜAmrū al-Ghassānī] ordered his men to capture and bind him. Then, he approached al-Ḥārith ibn ᶜUmayr al-Azdī and slew him without any resistance from al-Ḥārith's side. This was the only case when a messenger sent by the Prophet was killed.[61]

Evaluating the narration's chain of transmission we note its source as ᶜUmar ibn al-Ḥakam ibn Thawbān al-Madanī (657 C.E./37 AH–735 C.E./117 AH), who lived most of his life in the first century of Muslim history. He is classified as an authentic transmitter,[62] along with the second transmitter Rabīᶜah ibn ᶜUthmān al-Hudayr al-Tīmī al-Madanī also classified as an authentic transmitter.[63] With regard to the author of *al-Maghāzī*, Muḥammad al-Wāqidī, al-Baghdādī confirms his having heard the narration from Rabīᶜah ibn ᶜUthmān.[64] However, there has been controversy regarding his reliability as a transmitter of hadith. Some scholars have praised him, but most of them have criticised him. Thus, according to one of the rules of the *Jarḥ wa Taᶜdīl* discipline (a systematic approach to critiquing a narrator's position as a narrator) the critics of a narrator are to be considered over praises for him,[65] meaning that Muḥammad al-Wāqidī should be considered a weak transmitter. In fact, this is Ibn Ḥajar's conclusion with regards to al-Wāqidī's status as a transmitter of hadith. Ibn Ḥajar states: "Muḥammad ibn ᶜUmar al-Wāqidī was abandoned, *matrūk*, despite his immense capacity of knowledge."[66]

However, it seems that the reasons for accepting the narration outweigh those for its rejection. First of all, it should be underlined that the methodology of evaluating the narrations related to Muslim history cannot be equated with the methodology of evaluating the Prophetic Hadith, since the latter pertains directly to Islamic law, whereas the former is mostly informative. If the same rules and conditions of evaluating Prophetic hadith are applied to Muslim history, this will lead to loss of a great deal of the Muslim historical heritage. The point being that there is a necessity to differentiate between Hadith methodology and the historical methodology of evaluating the reliability of events. In this respect, it is important to note that after examining *al-Maghāzī*, al-Salūmī concludes that al-Wāqidī had a specific methodology in narrating historical events, different from the methodology of the scholars of Hadith. For example, it was acceptable for al-Wāqidī to narrate from a person a certain historical event which had occurred in his tribe or in his close circle of family members without examining his trustworthiness or memorising capability, as is the case among scholars of Hadith. Thus, it is al-Wāqidī's different methodology which seems to have been the reason for Hadith scholars to classify him as a weak transmitter.[67]

The second reason for accepting the narration is the fact that it is inherently not related to issues of the Islamic belief system or any aspect of Islamic legislation. The narration simply suggests that a Muslim was killed unfairly by a Christian in a Christian land. Now, it needs to be stressed that the information narrated corresponds exactly to al-Wāqidī's area of interest and expertise. Al-Baghdādī and Ibn ʿAsākir write that al-Wāqidī informed about himself the following:

> Whoever I managed to trace from the children of the Companions of the Prophet, the children of the martyrs, or their servants, I asked them: "Have you heard any of your relatives telling you about cases and places of killed people?" When they informed me about any case of killing and its place, I went to identify that place. I did go to the area of *Al-Muraysīʿ*,[68] where I stayed until I identified the exact place of the battle.[69]

There is much other evidence witnessing that al-Wāqidī was a distinguished expert in the field of *al-maghāzī*, identifying the battles. For this reason, al-Salūmī remarks that there is a unanimous consensus among biographers on al-Wāqidī being one of the most important sources of the historical aspect of Muslim battles.[70]

The third reason for accepting al-Wāqidī's account of the information relayed to him by Rabīʿah ibn ʿUthmān with regards to the aggressive killing of al-Ḥārith ibn ʿUmayr al-Azdī by Shuraḥbīl ibn ʿAmrū al-Ghassānī, is the fact that prominent scholars of Hadith have transmitted as well as relied on this narration. For example, Ibn Saʿd transmits the narration in his *Al-Ṭabqāt al-Kubrā*.[71] In the same way, Ibn ʿAbd al-Barr transmits it in *Al-Istīʿāb fī Maʿrifah al-Aṣḥāb*[72], and Ibn al-Athīr in *'Usud al-Ghābah fī Maʿrifah al-Ṣaḥābah*.[73] More importantly, Ibn Ḥajar al-ʿAsqalānī who is unanimously regarded as the most reliable source of knowledge in the field of Hadith, transmits al-Wāqidī's narration in his *Al-Iṣābah fī Tamyīz al- Ṣaḥābah*,[74] and also mentions it in *Fatḥ al-Bārī* to explain the reason for the battle of Mu'tah.[75]

The fourth reason for relying on al-Wāqidī's narration is Ḥārith ibn ʿUmayr al-Azdī's tomb existing in the small village of Liwa' Busayra in southern Jordan. This is clear archaeological evidence witnessing to the authenticity of Ḥārith ibn ʿUmayr al-Azdī's death in southern Jordan, far from his homeland.

In sum, all four reasons form compelling evidence to prove that in 628 C.E./7 AH an aggressive killing of a Muslim by a Christian took place.

As far as the content of the narration is concerned, it conveys three important points. First that the Muslim killed was no mere Muslim, but the messenger of the Prophet no less. Second that the Christian who killed him was not just any Christian, but the governor of Bostra (today Busra), and representative of the Byzantine Emperor at the time. Third that the act was not an accident but a premeditated crime which failed to recognise freedom of expression, and without any justification violated the right to life of an unresisting person. In fact, these three points sent a clear message to the Muslims, that the Northern Arab Christians announced war on the Prophet and his followers. Consequently, it triggered the first brutal war – known as the battle of Mu'tah – which took place between the Christians and Muslims in the year 629 C.E./8 A.H.[76] This time, the Byzantine Emperor Heraclius supported the Northern Arab Christians and sent his army to fight alongside Shuraḥbīl ibn ʿAmrū al-Ghassānī against the Muslims.[77] Thus, both Byzantine and Northern Arab Christians allied themselves against the Muslims.

Tension and conflict between the Christians in the North and Muslims continued to increase, and such was the extent that Muslims in Madinah lived under constant fear of imminent invasion from Ghassānī Christians. In this respect, al-Bukhārī narrates that ʿUmar ibn al-Khaṭṭāb said:

> ...At that time I had a friend from the Anṣār who used to bring news (from the Prophet, peace be upon him) in case of my absence, and I used to bring him the news if he was absent. In those days we were afraid of one of the kings of Ghassān tribe. We heard that he intended to move and attack us, so fear filled our hearts because of that. (One day) my Anṣārī friend unexpectedly knocked at my door, and said, "Open, Open!" I said, "Has the king of Ghassān come?" He said, "No, but something worse; Allah's Apostle (peace be upon him) has isolated himself from his wives."[78]

In another place in his *Ṣaḥīḥ*, al-Bukhārī transmits that ʿUmar ibn al-Khaṭṭāb said: "In those days it was rumoured[79] that Ghassān (a tribe living in Sham) were getting their horses ready to invade us."[80]

At the same time, certain leaders of the Byzantine Christians refused to tolerate those of their people who had embraced Islam on the basis of religious conviction, persecuting and killing them. Ibn Taymiyyah reports that "when a number of Christians, in the region of Maan,[81] embraced Islam, their Christian leaders in Sham went to kill those of them who were prominent."[82] More particularly, Ibn Ḥajar al-ʿAsqalānī transmits from Ibn Isḥāq that when Farwah ibn ʿAmrū al-Jadhdhāmī – a Christian working for the Byzantine Emperor in Maan – embraced Islam, the Byzantines on learning of this, tracked him down and killed him.[83]

Tension and conflict between the Northern Christians and Muslims peaked when the former learned of Islam's victory in the Arabian Peninsula. For Northern Christians the polytheist Arabs' embrace of Islam following the battles of Makkah and Ḥunayn, was perceived as a direct threat to their power and identity.[84] Accordingly, they gathered their troops and stationed them along the borders between Sham and Hijaz[85] with the purpose of obstructing the expansion of Islam into their lands.[86] This aggressive warlike stance was witnessed by traders travelling between Sham and Hijaz, and relayed to the Prophet and Muslims in Madinah. In fact, it was for this reason, and to prevent a surprise attack, that the Prophet mobilised the Muslims in 630 C.E./9 AH, and went north as a response to the military challenge.[87] Ibn Ḥajar al-ᶜAsqalānī also relied upon this reason to explain what triggered the battle of Tabūk, or what is known as the great expedition to Tabūk.[88]

It was under these particular circumstances outlining the clear historical context of war, that verse 9:29 was revealed. In this respect, al-Ṭabarī transmits the following:

> I was told by Muḥammad ibn ᶜAmrū, who said: We were told by Abū ᶜĀṣim, who said: We were told by ᶜĪsā, who narrated from Ibn Abī Najīḥ, who narrated from Mujāhid that the verse, "Fight those who believe not in Allah nor the Last Day, nor hold that forbidden which hath been forbidden by Allah and His Messenger, nor acknowledge the religion of Truth, from among the People of the Book, until they pay the *Jizya* with willing submission, and feel themselves subdued" (Qur'an *al-Tawbah* 9:29), was revealed when the Prophet and his Companions were ordered to face the battle of *Tabūk*.[89]

The chain of transmission is authentic because Muḥammad ibn ᶜAmrū ibn al-ᶜAbbās, known as Abū Bakr al-Bāhilī al-Baṣrī, "was a reliable transmitter."[90] Equally, "Abū ᶜĀṣim al-Nabīl al-Baṣrī, the name of whom is al-Ḍaḥḥāk ibn Makhlad, was also a firm reliable transmitter, *thiqah thabat*."[91] Likewise "ᶜĪsā ibn Maymūn al-Jurashī, known as Ibn Dāyah, was a reliable transmitter,"[92] along with "Ibn Abī Najīḥ, whose name is ᶜAbdullah."[93] As for Mujāhid, he is the well known successor, "the Imam of Qur'anic exegesis and knowledge, and a reliable transmitter."[94]

However, there has been a claim that Ibn Abī Najīḥ did not hear any *tafsīr* directly from Mujāhid, but that the former narrated Mujāhid's *tafsīr* from the Book of al-Qāsim ibn Abī Bazzah.[95] Although, Ibn Ḥibbān attributes this claim to Yaḥyā al-Quṭṭān, it seems that the originator of the claim is actually his teacher, Sufyān ibn ᶜUyaynah, as is narrated by al-ᶜAlā'ī in his *Jāmiᶜ al-Taḥṣīl fī Aḥkām al-Marāsīl.*[96] Thus, it is likely Sufyān ibn ᶜUyaynah's claim could be true, since he was born in al-Kūfah in 725 C.E./107 AH, but then moved to Makkah in 737 C.E.C/120 AH[97] and lived there until his death in 813 C.E./198 AH,[98] while Ibn Abī Najīḥ died in 749 C.E./132 AH in Makkah, too.[99] Moreover, it appears that Sufyān ibn ᶜUyaynah knew ᶜAbdullah ibn Abī Najīḥ well, since the former transmitted directly *aḥādīth* from the latter, and informs that ᶜAbdullah ibn Abī Najīḥ was appointed as a mufti of Makkah after the death of ᶜAmrū ibn Dīnār.[100]

Yet, the existence of counter-arguments against Sufyān ibn ᶜUyaynah 's claim makes the investigation more complex. In this regard, al-Bukhārī reports that "ᶜAbdullah ibn Abī Najīḥ al-Makkī did hear [*tafsīr*] from Ṭāwūs, ᶜAṭā', and *Mujāhid*[101] ...."[102] Similarly, al-Dhahabī states the following: "Some people say that Ibn Abī Najīḥ did not hear the whole *tafsīr* from Mujāhid. I say: He [Ibn Abī Najīḥ] was one of the most special people of Mujāhid."[103]

It seems very difficult to conclude with explicit certainty that Ibn Abī Najīḥ did or did not hear directly *tafsīr* from Mujāhid. For this reason, when Ibrāhīm ibn al-Junayd asked Yaḥyah ibn Maᶜīn – an expert, and one of the founders of the discipline of *Jarḥ wa Taᶜdīl* – whether it was true that Ibn Abī Najīḥ did not hear *tafsīr* from Mujāhid. He [Ibn Maᶜīn] said: "I do not know whether or not it is true."[104] The real difficulty for determining whether or not Ibn Abī Najīḥ did hear *tafsīr* from Mujāhid emerges from the fact that no chronicle records have been made of Ibn Abī Najīḥ's date of birth. Thus, even though it is logically sound to assume that Ibn Abī Najīḥ received his knowledge of *tafsīr* directly from Mujāhid, since both were in Makkah and participated in the same area of knowledge, this could not be the case because Ibn Abī Najīḥ might have started seeking knowledge after the death of Mujāhid.

Nevertheless, all those scholars of the opinion that Ibn Abī Najīḥ did not hear *tafsīr* directly from Mujāhid, unanimously agree that Ibn Abī Najīḥ did transmit Mujāhid's *tafsīr* directly from al-Qāsim ibn Abī Bazzah.[105] In this case, knowing that the intermediary between ʿAbdullah ibn Abī Najīḥ and Mujāhid is al-Qāsim ibn Abī Bazzah, and knowing that al-Qāsim ibn Abī Bazzah himself is a reliable transmitter, *thiqah*,[106] we have adequate proof of the authenticity of Mujāhid's *tafsīr*, when received through the chain of transmission analysed.

To summarise, it appears that the Jewish-Muslim conflicts of Madinah triggered off a wave of conflicts between the Northern Christians and Muslims. The first occurred in 628 C.E./7 AH when an envoy of the Prophet was aggressively killed by a Christian governor, causing the first fierce war between the Christians and Muslims to take place in 629 C.E./8 AH known as the Battle of Mu'tah. Then, as a result of this battle, and also due to the Muslim's rapid expansion and victory over the idolatrous Arabs in the Arabian Peninsula, the Northern Christians mobilised troops against them, stationing them in the region of *Tabūk* in 630 C.E./9 A.H. to obstruct the expansion of Islam into their lands. It is in this historical context of war, Mujāhid (who had read the entire Qur'an 30 times in front of Ibn ʿAbbās, and who had also revised the explanation of the whole Qur'an 3 times with him)[107] informs us that verse 9:29 was revealed.[108] Thus as analysis of the historical context of verse 9:29 reveals, the command to fight in the verse relates to the aggression of the People of the Book (as expressed in their challenge to war) and not their belief system. In light of this, it is clear that the scope of the prescription to fight is based exclusively on those of the People of the Book committed to agrestic and warfare, and not those who wish to live in peace.

Turning next to the textual context of verse 9:29, we note the Arabic morphological form used for the imperative to fight which first draws our attention. Form III of the root *q-t-l* is used giving us *qātala*, which indicates that the act of fighting must be performed in response to another initially started act of killing or fighting. In this respect, the prescription to fight is related to the right to self-defence against an unjustly initiated war, not to the belief system of those who are the object of the imperative. Note, for the command to be related to the People of the Book's belief system it would have to appear in the verse as Form I, that is *uqtulū* (slay or kill them).[109] For example, see verse 40:25 wherein Pharaoh commands all Israelite male children to be killed using Form I of the root *q-t-l*:

> Now, when he [Moses] came to them in Truth, from Us, they said, "Slay the sons of those who believe with him, and keep alive their females," but the plots of Unbelievers (end) in nothing but errors (and delusions)!...(Qur'an *Ghāfir* 40:25)

As is clear, the first morphological form of *q-t-l* is applied, since the command is not related to the right to self-defence, but Pharaoh's act of killing unjustly innocent children.

Another textual indication is the word *ḥattā*, until: "fight... until they pay the *Jizyah*" (9:29). Sources of Arabic grammar define mainly three functions for *ḥattā*: "the end of a purpose, motivation, and exception."[110] The first function, "end of a purpose" (*intihā' al-ghāyah*), means that what is after *ḥattā*, represents the point where the action of what is before *ḥattā*, must end. For example, if a person says: "I will walk until I reach the library", it means that the action of the intended walk will end when the person reaches the library, because the library is the purpose of the person's walking, but not its motivation. In fact, a person's motivation for walking to the library is to gain knowledge. The second function of *ḥattā* is known as motivation. Unlike the previous function, the second shows that what is after *ḥattā* serves as a motivation for the action before *ḥattā*. At this point, it should be noted that in respect of the second function, it is more accurate to translate *ḥattā* into English as "in order to." For example, in terms of the second function of *ḥattā*, it is more accurate to say in English: "I will read the newspaper in order to know what happened in Egypt yesterday"; instead of saying: "I will read the newspaper until I know what did happen in Egypt yesterday." For this reason, Sībawayh points out that with regard to the second function of *ḥattā*, it appears as a synonym of the Arabic word *kai*,[111] which equates to "in order to" in English. Thus, as can be seen in this second example, the information provided after the word *ḥattā*, "in order to," serves as a motivation for the action mentioned before *ḥattā*, "in order to." In other words, the motivation for reading the newspaper is to learn about recent events in Egypt. As for the third function of *ḥattā*, this is defined as an exception, meaning that the action before *ḥattā*, is done as an exception to what is after *ḥattā*. For example, if a person addresses another person by saying: "I will not enter the room until you enter it first," this means that the action of entering the room by the first person is refused, but exception is made only if the second person enters the room first. It is obvious, that in this case *ḥattā*, works as a condition.

Now, what is the function of *ḥattā*, in verse 9:29?

> Fight those who believe not in Allah nor the Last Day, nor hold that forbidden which hath been forbidden by Allah and His Messenger, nor acknowledge the religion of Truth, from among the People of the Book, ***until***[112] they pay the *Jizyah* with willing submission, and feel themselves subdued. (Qur'an *al-Tawbah* 9:29)

Taking all three functions of *ḥattā* into consideration (reverse order) we come up with the following:

1) *Exception*: This appears unlikely given the context. Largely because *ḥattā* as exception would mean to fight the People of the Book as a permanent and inclusive act up to the point at which (or except in the circumstance that) they pay the *jizyah*. However, this view contradicts many other Qur'anic

texts which exclude from the scope of war and do not permit to be attacked children, women, the elderly, priests, those embracing Islam, and peaceful people in general.

2) *Motivation*: If applied to the verse this would mean fighting People of the Book in order to obtain *jizyah* from them. In other words the root cause of fighting would be payment (of *jizyah*). This assumption is false and contradicts teachings of the Qur'an, the historical context of the verse as analysed, and does not correspond to the morphological form of the imperative *qātilū*. Furthermore, interpreting *ḥattā* as motivation, would imply killing all non-Muslims living in Islamic countries today, if they refuse to pay their taxes. Of course everyone suffers a penalty of some sort for tax evasion, across the world, but they are not put to death for this.

3) *End of a purpose* (*intihā' al-ghāyah*): If applied to the verse, this interpretation would mean fighting must end at the point at which non-Muslims agree to pay the *jizyah*. In other words, the action of fighting here, which is not motivated by *jizyah* but by the right to self defence against an initially initiated war declared on Muslims, ends at the point in which agreement is reached by the People of the Book agreeing to pay the *jizyah*. This agreement signifies that they agree to observe the general system of the state as well as the social order. In fact, the psychological condition of the latter whilst accepting the *jizyah*-based agreement is described as "subdued" (*ṣāghirūn*) where once it had been rebellious bent on war. However, some Muslim scholars have erroneously drawn the conclusion from this that humiliation is a requirement from the People of the Book (necessary condition) when accepting to pay the *jizyah*.[113] This view is implausible because "the payment of *Jizyah* cannot be considered a penalty, for Islamic law does not punish any non-Muslim for his/her faith."[114] In this regard, Thomas Arnold remarks:

> This tax [*Jizyah*] was not imposed on the Christians, as some would have us think, as a penalty for their refusal to accept the Muslim faith, but was paid by them in common with the other dhimmīs or non-Muslim subjects of the

> state whose religion precluded them from serving in the army, in return for the protection secured for them by the arms of the Muslims. When the people of Ḥīrah contributed the sum agreed upon, they expressly mentioned that they paid this jizyah on condition that "the Muslims and their leader protect us from those who would oppress us, whether they be Muslims or others."[115]

So this third function of *ḥattā* (the end of a purpose) is the correct interpretation for it corresponds to the historical context of the verse, linguistic rules, and the main objectives of the Qur'an. In other words *ḥattā* as used in the verse denotes the end of the action of fighting. This provides clear evidence that the root cause of the command to fight is not the belief system of the People of the Book for were it so then fighting would not cease with the payment of the *jizyah*, rather it could only end when Islam had been accepted and the beliefs changed.

As far as the intertextual context of verse 9:29 is concerned, in the first place it should be stressed that the overall Qur'anic context rejects the claim that the root cause of the imperative to fight lies in the People of the Book's beliefs. This denies and contradicts the universal Qur'anic principles of freedom of belief, human dignity, and diversity, which emerge as a natural result of mankind's creation as creatures of free will.

Secondly and more particularly, the theme of surah *al-Tawbah*, as well as its preceding surah *al-Anfāl*, is entirely geared to the context of war as a result of (provoked by) aggression and oppression. It is methodologically unacceptable therefore to selectively take out of their proper context certain prescriptions mentioned in these surahs, and then graft onto them a generalised interpretation to sanction a policy announcing war on those of different faiths, contradicting the Qur'an and Islamic teaching! For instance, Watt would appear to be doing just this in his *Muhammad at Medina*, wherein he makes the following comment on verses 9:29-32:

> The passage as a whole marks the transition to a policy of hostility to the Christians. This policy found its expression in the great expedition to

> Tabūk in 630/9, and was continued not merely for the rest of Muḥammad's lifetime but also afterwards, at least until Syria had been completely subjugated. In so far as the passage prescribes hostility to the Byzantine Empire and to Christians in general, it long continued to influence the Muslim attitude to the Christian church.[116]

Watt's statement is generalisation based on a selective disregard of the historical, textual, and intertextual context of the Qur'an's verses. Whilst pointing to verses 9:29-32 as evidence for the Qur'an's hostile attitude towards Christians in general, Watt suggests the root cause of this supposed hostility as being the Christian belief system. This is false association. In reality, the block of verses referred to by Watt is not in favor of this generalised claim, because the verses (9:29-34) themselves go beyond the scope of differing belief and explain metaphorically that a circle of priests among the People of the Book had waged war on God Himself, hindered/turned people away from the path of/worshipping God, and devoured unjustly the wealth and possessions of mankind hoarding up gold and silver and not spending it in the way of God. In other words the verses speak for themselves and intrinsically do not support any attempt at generalisation. What we are being told in no uncertain terms is that aggression and oppression is to be challenged. It is this which is being addressed necessitating response in the interests of justice and peace, not people's belief systems.

Finally, God's rhetorical question in a verse preceding 9:29 provides explicit intertextual evidence of the Qur'anic root cause for the prescription to fight being not people's beliefs and religions, but their aggression:

> Would you, perchance, fail to fight against people who have broken their solemn pledges, and have done all that they could to drive the Apostle away, and have been first to attack you? Do you hold them in awe? Nay, it is God alone of whom you ought to stand in awe, if you are [truly] believers! (Qur'an 9:13)

Obviously, the violation of covenants, the hatching of plots to assassinate or expel the Prophet, the initiating of oppressive wars on others, all these actions contradict any belief system, not to mention the belief systems of what is referred to as the monotheistic religions.

Therefore, examination of the historical, textual, and intertextual context of verse 9:29, has shown that the root cause for the Qur'an's command to fight the People of the Book is their aggression expressed in the act of waging of war against the Muslims. Accordingly, the scope of the command to fight falls only on those People of the Book who are people of war. As for the four characteristics succeeding the imperative to fight, they should be understood not as conditions permitting the declaration of war, but as informative descriptions of those who oppressively kindle the fires of war against peaceful people.

In summary, analysis reveals that Qur'anic exegesis sources do not systematically present the Qur'an's concept of warfare contextualised to interfaith relations. Misinterpretation and confusion characterise understanding of the prescription to fight as reflected in the inconsistency of statements and conclusions scattered throughout the sources. This in turn affects detrimentally, and needlessly, elucidation of the meaning and root cause of the command to fight as well as its scope, opening the doors vastly to speculation and misleading conclusions.

In actual fact, there is no real complexity in the verses in question. In the Arabic at least the position is clear if one were to look a little closely. Although various reasons can perhaps be cited for the inconsistency, it would seem that in addition to the specific historical circumstances of the exegetes interpreting the verses, a major role has been played via the employment of an atomistic methodology to Qur'anic exegesis. This approach prevents crystallisation of the thematic coherence of the topic in question. Versus the atomistic approach is the more superior thematic, holistic one. Applying the latter, that is systematically examining the historical, linguistic, and contextual aspects of, in this case the prescription to fight, we discover no contradiction to exist between the Qur'anic conception of normative religious pluralism and the command to fight. This is because the root cause for this command is not the belief system of others, but their initiation of war on peaceful people. Thus, the scope of the Qur'anic imperative to fight refers only to people of war.

[2] An Analysis of the Prescription to Not Take Jews and Christians as *Awliyā'*, Patrons: A Case Study of Qur'anic Verse 5:51

This final section of the chapter analyses the Qur'anic prescription to not take Jews and Christians as *awliyā'* or patrons. This is one of the most controversial Qur'anic verses with regards to normative religious pluralism:

> O ye who believe! Take not the Jews and the Christians for your allies and protectors;[117] they are but allies and protectors to each other. And he amongst you that turns to them [for protection] is of them. Verily Allah guideth not a people unjust. (Qur'an *al-Mā'idah* 5:51)

This command not to take the Jews and Christians as allies/protectors and generally friends has caused much controversy and speculation. Aside from the issue of translation, this has largely been due to the fact that the textual implication of the prescription is speculative, *ẓannī*, and not definitive, *qaṭʿī*, respectively. Furthermore and in particular, inaccurate translation of the word *awliyā'* has triggered and exacerbated controversy surrounding the verse. *Awliyā'* has a very complex meaning as well as sense and connotation. To simply translate it as friends is to do it a disservice.

Because of this exegetes such as al-Zamakhsharī and al-Rāzī misconstrue *awliyā'* to derive an understanding requiring Muslims to isolate themselves from religiously different people and ignore them, making of this a normative obligation.[118] In fact most exegetes interpret *awliyā'* and the command this way, concluding that Muslims are not permitted to show any affection towards religiously different people.[119] As a result, this perception has led to double standards developing amongst certain Muslims with regards to how they behave towards the religious other.

It is extremely unfortunate, yet not surprising, that all these interpretations of verse 5:51 have been noted in the West and construed as a hostile attitude on the part of Muslims towards Jews and Christians. As mentioned earlier this has been nurtured and exacerbated by most western translations of the Qur'an rendering the term *awliyā'* as friends, allies etc. Consequently, the verse has been employed as evidence to support the view that the Qur'an does not leave enough room for accommodating normative religious pluralism.

To derive a correct understanding of the issue this section examines verse 5:51 in the light of three major aspects: a semantic analysis of the term *awliyā'*, the historical context of the revelation of the verse, and a textual and intertextual study of the verse. In fact, by examining the verse from these three particular angles, we reach a coherent understanding of what is being in reality commanded, enabling us to answer the question of whether the prescription forbidding taking Jews and Christians as *awliyā'* contradicts the conception of normative religious pluralism.

A Semantic Analysis of the Word *Awliyā'*

As mentioned *awliyā'* is a complex and ambiguous term. The word appears in the verse as an accusative masculine plural noun in an indefinite grammatical form, and this latter not being limited to any indicative description, increases its complexity and ambiguity. To establish its sense and implications as well as precise and accurate meaning, we need to examine *awliyā'* semantically.

One of the earliest semantic accounts of the root morpheme *wāw-lām-yā'*, from which the word *awliyā'* is derived, is given by Ibn Fāris, who explains that this linguistic root, in itself and in respect of all its derivatives, signifies "closeness."[120] However, with direct connection to the word *awliyā'*, Ibn Fāris states that "a person in charge of other person/s is referred to as his/her or their *walī*,"[121] the singular of *awliyā'*. Of course, Ibn Fāris' definition "a person in charge of other person/s" means a person who is in charge of managing other person/s' life affairs. In this respect, the English translation of *awliyā'* would be more accurate if rendered as "guardians." At this point, it is important to note that Ibn Fāris mentions another derivative of the root *wāw-lām-yā'*, which is *mawlā*, and states that it conveys the following meanings: a slave who was set free, a person who freed a slave, a friend, an ally, a cousin, protector, and neighbor.[122]

After Ibn Fāris, another scholar in the field of semantics, al-Rāghib al-Aṣfahānī, explains the meaning of *walā'*, the source noun of *wāw-lām-yā'*, as follows: "Two or more subjects united together, in a way that there is nothing between them that is not part of them."[123] It seems that al-Aṣfahānī's definition of *walā'* is more akin to the notion of fusion than to Ibn Fāris' "closeness." More importantly, al-Aṣfahānī distinguishes different areas to which the notion of *walā'* is related, such as: a place, affiliation, religion, friendship, protection, and belief.[124]

Two centuries after al-Aṣfahānī, Ibn Manẓūr transmitted many different meanings of the root *wāw-lām-yā'*. In addition to Ibn Fāris' observations on the meanings of *mawlā*, Ibn Manẓūr remarks that *mawlā* also means: a lord, a possessor, a master.[125] With regard to ally, *ḥalīf*, as one possible meaning derived from the root *wāw-lām-yā'*, Ibn Manẓūr states that this is a person or group of people with whom another person or group of people is/are united, and the latter draw their comfort and dignity from the former, and fulfil their orders too.[126] Moreover, Ibn Manẓūr attributes to Ibn Isḥāq the statement that one of the meanings of the expression "God is their *walī*" is that God supports them against their enemies, and He also supports them in making their religion prevail over the religion of others.[127]

Chronologically succeeding Ibn Manẓūr, Sharīf al-Jurjānī had a greater opportunity to acquaint himself with written works in the field of semantics prior to his time, and thus managed to compile his famous compilation *Al-Taʿrīfāt*. In this work, al-Jurjānī adopts a laconic style that is defining terms and notions related to Islamic knowledge concisely. In this respect, he provides a concise, but meaning-saturated definition of *walī*. Al-Jurjānī writes: "*Walī* is whoever you take as a subject to unconditional obedience."[128] Al-Jurjāni's definition of *walī* in itself, seen from the religious aspect, provides a firm ground for grasping the essential meaning of the command in verse 5:51.

As opposed to the terse, succinct style of al-Jurjānī it seems that contemporary semantic discourse on the concept of *walī, awliyā'* and its definition is more complicated and verbose. For example, Baalbaki applies more than 35 different English words to explain the meaning of *walī*.[129] However, all those words can be accommodated into the classical, semantic framework of *walī* mentioned previously.

Therefore, semantic analysis reveals the complex nature of the concept of *awliyā'*. In this respect al-Aṣfahānī provides a crucial key for understanding this concept when he remarks that the notion of *awliyā'* pertains to different spheres of socio-cultural life. Al-Aṣfahānī's remark suggests that the concept of *awliyā'* in the case of verse 5:51 should be observed from a particular angle related to the religious belief system, since this is the context of the verse. Consequently, the definition of *awliyā'* given by al-Jurjānī would appear to be the most suitable in explaining the meaning of the command. He writes: "*Walī* is whoever you take as a subject to unconditional obedience."[130] Adding to al-Jurjānī's definition those semantic meanings of *awliyā'* which are closely related to the belief system, the scope of the prohibition in 5:51 can be limited to the following semantic illustration in respect of Jews and Christians: religious guidance→unconditional obedience→fusion and religious melting. This semantic illustration leads, in turn, to the conclusion that the root cause for the prohibition in 5:51 is related to the idea of preserving religious particularities, which in fact constitute an essential element of the structure of religious pluralism. At this point, it should be mentioned, therefore, that the English translation and definition of *awliyā'* as "friends" in the context of 5:51 raises much concern about the methodology applied to draw such a conclusion.[131] Indeed, if we were to determine a single English word to express all these meanings of *awliyā'*, then that word would seem to be "patron" which conveys most suitably the meaning of that Arabic word considered in the particular context of 5:51. This is because, in addition to the meaning of a protector, the word "patron" etymologically means lord, master, father, and patron saint.[132]

The Historical Context of Verse 5:51

The historical context of verse 5:51 is determined by the occasion of its revelation. In this respect, Ibn Abī Ḥātim reports the following:

> We were told by my father, who said: We were told by Abū al-Aṣbagh al-Ḥarrānī, who said: We were told by Muḥammad ibn Salamah, who narrated from Muḥammad ibn Isḥāq, who said: I was told by my father Isḥāq ibn Yasār, who narrated from ʿUbādah ibn al-Walīd, who narrated from ʿUbādah ibn al-Ṣāmit that: It was not until the Jewish tribe of Banū Qaynuqāʿ waged war [on the Prophet and Muslims in Madinah], when ʿUbādah ibn al-Ṣāmit went to the Prophet and announced that he did disown the tribe of Banū Qaynuqāʿ, whereas ʿAbdullāh ibn Ubay ibn Salūl insisted on sticking by his alliance with Banū Qaynuqāʿ. ʿUbādah ibn al-Ṣāmit was one of Banū ʿAwf ibn al-Khazraj [Arab tribe allied with Banū Qaynuqāʿ, and the chief of which was ʿAbdullah ibn Ubay ibn Salūl], but when Banū Qaynuqāʿ turned against the Prophet, ʿUbādah ibn al-Ṣāmit terminated his alliance with them, and said: I take Allah, the Prophet, and the believers as my *awliyā'*. This event was the occasion of revelation of the verse 5:51 "O ye who believe! Take not the Jews and the Christians for your allies and protectors; they are but allies and protectors to each other."[133]

The content of this narration is also transmitted by al-Wāḥidī as well as al-Ṭabarī, but both exegetes narrate it from ʿAṭiyyah al-ʿAwfī, who, in addition to his controversial status as a transmitter, had not met ʿUbādah ibn al-Ṣāmit[134] nor had he mentioned the mediator between him and ʿUbādah. Therefore, the narration presented by Ibn Abī Ḥātim in his *Tafsīr*, appears as the only authentic one in terms of its content, which comes in accordance to the Qur'anic textual context of the verse. In addition its chain of transmission consists of purely reliable transmitters and thus is defined as authentic.[135]

However, two objections might be raised with regard to it. The first is related to the chain of transmission, where one can claim that ʿUbādah ibn al-Walīd ibn ʿUbādah ibn al-Ṣāmit did not hear hadith from ʿUbādah ibn al-Ṣāmit. At this point, it should be noted that ʿUbādah ibn al-Ṣāmit was the grandfather of ʿUbādah ibn al-Walīd, and thus it is very likely that the latter did hear hadith from the former. Furthermore, in *Musnad al-Imām Aḥmad ibn Ḥanbal*, Sufyān ibn ʿUyaynah states that ʿUbādah ibn al-Walīd did hear his grandfather ʿUbādah ibn al-Ṣāmit. But then, commenting on Sufyān's statement, Ibn Ḥanbal states: "Another time Sufyān said: *from*[136] his grandfather ʿUbādah,"[137] meaning that ʿUbādah ibn al-Walīd was narrating from his grandfather through a mediator between them. The mediator in this case is known. This is al-Walīd ibn ʿUbādah ibn al-Ṣāmit, the father of the young ʿUbādah, and the son of the old ʿUbādah ibn al-Ṣāmit. This relation in terms of transmission is confirmed by Ibn Abī Ḥātim in his *al-Jarḥ wa al-Taʿdīl*, where he declares that ʿUbādah ibn al-Walīd was transmitting hadith from his father al-Walīd ibn ʿUbādah ibn al-Ṣāmit.[138] Therefore, any objection as to the chain of transmission seems untenable.

With regard to the second possible objection, this pertains to the content of the narration. How can the narration refer to a historical event which occurred between the Jews of Banū Qaynuqāʿ and the Muslims in around the year 623-624 C.E./2-3 AH in Madinah, as being the occasion for revelation of the verse which note occurs in surah *al-Mā'idah* known as the last Qur'anic surah to have been revealed?

In order to dispel this objection, it should be emphasized that the revelation of some Madinan surahs lasted for several years, including surah *al-Mā'idah* which took a long period of time. Evidence to support this statement can be found in al-Bukhārī in which he transmits a narration from the Prophet's wife ᶜĀ'ishah who asserts explicitly that verse 6 of *al-Mā'idah* was revealed when she lost her necklace in the region of al-Baydā' near Madinah.[139] Historically, according to Ibn Ḥajar, this incident happened in 626 C.E./5 AH during the event known as the battle of *Banū Muṣṭalaq* which occurred in the region of the springs of al-Muraysīᶜ.[140] This evidence witnesses that certain verses of *al-Mā'idah* were revealed during the early Madinan period. Therefore, it seems that the opening of *al-Mā'idah* commenced at the end of the second and beginning of the third Hijri year, as indicated by the occasion of the revelation of 5:51, and continued until the end of the Qur'anic revelation, when the largest part of *al-Mā'idah* was revealed.

Now, after proving the occasion of the revelation of 5:51 as sound, it becomes clear that the imperative prohibiting Muslims from taking the Jews and Christians as their patrons (*awliyā'*) has been based on a specific historical event, which plays a paramount role in understanding the cause and the scope of this imperative. The prohibition therefore emerged from the historical context of the first religious conflict which took place between the Muslims and Jews following the Muslim victory over the Makkan polytheists at the battle of Badr. At this stage, as the oldest monotheists in the region, the Jews of Madinah were expected to show support for Islam. However, instead of supporting the Muslims, the Jews of Banū Qainuqāᶜ chose to transgress their covenants, threaten the Prophet, make a mockery of the Muslims, and violate the dignity of a Muslim woman.[141] Consequently, all these provocations led to a war between the Muslims and Jews of Banū Qaynuqāᶜ. But, since the axis of that war was religious, with allies and enemies grouped along religious lines, the Muslims were forbidden to team up with the Jews of Banū Qaynuqāᶜ against the Prophet and his followers. In other words the verse is telling Muslims not to trust and take as protectors those who were their enemies. Therefore, the different attitudes each of ʿUbādah ibn al-Ṣāmit and ʿAbdullah ibn Ubay ibn Salūl, in the context of religious conflict, served as an occasion to prohibit all Muslims in all times to take Jews and Christians as religious patrons, or to team up with them against Muslims.

In summary, as historical analysis shows the reason for the prohibition in verse 5:51 was to caution Muslims at a time of religious conflict which aimed to involve the Islamic faith in religious turmoil and also to exterminate it. Accordingly, the scope of the prohibition pertains only to those among the Jews and Christians attempting to religiously fuse Muslims or engage them in a religious conflict against the followers of Islam. These reasons aside, it has also been historically proven that the Prophet himself, both before and after the conflict with the Jews of Banū Qaynuqāʿ, engaged with the Jews and Christians in mutual understanding, mutual co-operation in all that is good, and mutual support against all that is evil.

Textual and Intertextual Study of Verse 5:51

An inseparable and integral part of Qur'anic exegesis is (methodologically speaking) the examination of both the textual and intertextual contexts of content. Failure to do so makes determining the precise meaning of any verse impossible. For this reason, a selective approach, which disregards the different contexts of Qur'anic verses, tends to distort the true meanings of those verses. Thus, in accordance with this stipulation, and to complete our analysis, we next examine verse 5:51in terms of textual and intertextual context.

With regard to the textual aspect, it should be noted that the verse's linguistic structure consists of an imperative addressed to all believers applicable for all times: "O ye who believe! Take not the Jews and the Christians for your patrons" (5:51). Grammatically the subject, that is the addressees, of the imperative cannot be limited to a certain historical period, as Osman seems to suggest,[142] since the particularity of the occasion of the revelation does not restrict the general sense of the Qur'anic words. However, what is subject to limitation is the grammatical object of the imperative, namely "the Jews and the Christians as *awliyā'*." Just as not all meanings of the term *awliyā'* can be accommodated to serve as the object of the imperative in this particular context, so neither can all Jews and Christians be considered as the object of this imperative. This is largely clear from Qur'anic principles which call for universal moral values, as well as from the example of the Prophet concerning interfaith relations.

Now, it is worth quoting al-Ṭabarī's conclusion on this verse, wherein he states: "God has forbidden all believers to take the Jews and the Christians as supporters and allies against those who have belief in God and His Messenger."[143] It is obvious from this that al-Ṭabarī limits the meaning of *awliyā'* to "supporters" and "allies" *against* the followers of Islam. Moreover, al-Ṭabarī refers to this meaning of *awliyā'* as forming partisanship, that is favoring the Jews and the Christians against the Muslims, *taḥazzub*.[144] Hence, according to al-Ṭabarī's understanding of the verse, the prohibition concerns only that kind of support and alliance with the Jews and Christians which is directed against God, His Messenger, and the believers. He goes further however to regard this, what is in effect betrayal if you like, as apostasy. For this reason, he literally interprets the statement "And he amongst you that turns to them [for protection] is of them" (5:51).[145] Hence, grammatically the object of the imperative "Take not" (in the 2nd person masculine plural (form VIII) imperfect verb, jussive mood) is limited in al-Ṭabarī's interpretation to partisanship with the Jews and the Christians against Islam and thus to the realm of religious apostasy.

Two centuries after al-Ṭabarī's relevantly liberal conclusion, al-Zamakhsharī chose to expand the focus of the prohibition to such a degree that he derives a "legal norm" from the verse of "obligation to avoid religiously different others and to isolate them."[146] Of course, this generalisation underpinned by the legal term obligation conflicts not only with the normative teachings of Islam towards others, but also with the history of interfaith relations and any constructive reasoning. And it is this, al-Zamakhsharī's conclusion, which may have provided good reason (if not ammunition) for certain parties to understand the term *awliyā'* as meaning "friends," thus allowing them to promote the view that Islam is an intolerant religion which does not make any room for religious pluralism.

Whilst citing al-Zamakhsharī's avoiding the religiously other as an obligation assumption, al-Rāzī also adds that the prohibition means neither to seek the protection of Jews or Christians or to show them affection.[147] We are left with a generalised statement which does not qualify the circumstances, if any, under which this action is to take place, opening the door wide to adverse speculation and misleading conclusion. Note for example in contrast that the Prophet himself sought the protection of the Christians in Abyssinia against Makkan oppression and persecution.

Modern sources of Qur'anic exegesis differ little, echoing much the same interpretation of the prohibition. In fact, barely a significant difference exists. For instance, Ibn Ashur states that the meaning of *awliyā'* in 5:51 pertains to notions of affection and protection.[148] In his opinion the reason for the prohibition of taking Jews and Christians as *awliyā'* can be understood in the light of the verses preceding 5:51, wherein God describes some of the People of the Book as having corrupted their holy scripture, corrupted the moral example of their prophets, and attempted to religiously misguide Muslims.[149] In fact, even though Ibn Ashur does not state so explicitly, his explanation of the cause of the prohibition implies that the scope of the imperative does not inclusively cover all People of the Book, as the descriptions provided by him are not applicable to all of them.

Another modern exegete, al-Tabataba'i, argues strongly that the meaning of *awliyā'* in 5:51 is related mainly to love and affection. He asserts that though the prohibition is specific to historical context, and has a meaning linked to alliance, this nevertheless cannot restrict application of *awliyā's* general sense which conveys a meaning of love and affection. To defend his statement, al-Tabatabai applies both textual and intertextual approaches to interpreting verse 5:51.[150] Yet, the issue once again remains of qualifying a statement, that is al-Tabatabai does not provide a clear distinction between those Jews and Christians who are not to be treated on the basis of love and affection, and those who can be. Moreover, al-Tabatabai does not seem to distinguish between different reasons for showing love and affection to People of the Book. Consequently, generalisation, deprived of accurate distinction between different notions and conceptions, tends to lead to a conclusion that claims prohibition for all Muslims to show any kind of love and affection to any Jews and Christians. If this were so, it would not explain how the Qur'an could permit a Muslim man to lawfully marry a Jewish or a Christian woman yet simultaneously prohibit him from showing any love or affection to her. It has to be emphasised, such contradictions are not becoming of any scripture, and are certainly not characteristic of the Qur'an considered by Muslims as divine revelation.

In sum, as analysis reveals, the object of the prohibition in verse 5:51 has been differently defined, fluctuating between absolute generalisation and excessive restriction. In this case, it is methodologically necessary to use a thematic approach to examine the textual as well as intertextual context of verse 5:51 in order to reconcile the different definitions.

Analyzing the content of the whole of surah *al-Mā'idah*, it becomes obvious from the very beginning that the surah encourages cooperation and thus mutual engagement with the other: "Help ye one another in righteousness and piety" (5:2). Moreover, to facilitate implementation of this, the same surah stipulates that the food and women of the People of the Book are made lawful for Muslims (5:5). Similarly, surah *al-Mā'idah* also promotes mutual contribution in the context of religious diversity through competing with the other in good works (5:48). Note however the textual context of *al-Mā'idah* also commands

Muslims to "take not for friends and protectors (*awliyā'*) those who take your religion for a mockery or sport" from among the People of the Book and disbelievers (5:57). At this point, it should be borne in mind that both verses 5:51 and 5:57 occur in the context of discussion on the issue of apostasy, which is a clear sign that the prohibition in 5:51 cannot be reduced to the issue of friendship and affection.

Moving on to the intertextual context as thematically related to verse 5:51, it is apparent that, in addition to the broad Qur'anic sphere of human brotherhood, the Qur'an fosters the objective of mutual understanding through the human initiative of knowing each other (49:13). This culminates in the Qur'an's emphasis on the need for mutual support between religions with the aim of protecting religious freedom and repelling oppression (22:40).

Additionally, another thematic circle can be traced in the Qur'an, which clearly identifies different categorisations of the People of the Book. This thematic circle seems to start from the statement that "not all of them [the People of the Book] are alike" (3:113), and ends at two different positions. The first position pertains to those among the People of the Book who when "hearing what has been revealed to the Messenger, you see their eyes overflowing with tears because of what they have recognised of the truth" (5:83), whereas the second corresponds to the following Qur'anic statement: "and that which has been revealed to you from your Lord will increase many of them [the People of the Book] in transgression and disbelief" (5:68). Of course, between these two positions, the Qur'an discusses other attitudes adopted by the People of the Book towards Muslims. However, what is essential to stress here is that the object of the prohibition in 5:51 certainly should be limited to those among the Jews and the Christians who represent the second position.

Another intertextual thematic reading explicitly shows that only those who are enemies of God, the Prophet, and Muslims are not to be taken as *awliyā'* as well as not to be treated on the basis of love and affection by Muslims. The Qur'an says: "O you who believe! Take not My enemies and yours as *awliyā'* – offering them (your) love" (60:1). The reason for this prohibition is explained in the same verse; it is because those enemies have "driven out the Prophet and yourselves (from your homes), (simply) because you believe in Allah your Lord!" (60:1). However, in the same surah it is advised that "Allah forbids you not, with regard to those who fight you not for your faith nor drive you out of your homes, from dealing kindly and justly with them" (60:8). The Arabic word for "dealing kindly and justly with them" is *tabarrūhum*, which carries the meaning of honest treatment on the basis of love and compassion.

Therefore, all these foregoing elements[151] thematically related to verse 5:51 construct necessary limitations to our understanding of the grammatical object of the command. In other words, a thematic reading of the Qur'an does not allow for generalisation of the prohibition stipulated in 5:51 to include reference to all People of the Book, claiming that any kind of friendship, alliance, mutual support, and protection in respect of the Jews and Christians is not allowed for Muslims.

Overall, based on semantic, historical, and textual study, analysis of verse 5:51 reveals that the Qur'an's command to not take the Jews and Christians as *awliyā'* is limited to two aspects. The first is purely theological, wherein the prohibition is related to Muslims' reliance on the Jews and Christians as a source of religious guidance aiming at religious fusion, and thus leading to apostasy. The root cause of the prohibition in this aspect is related to the idea of preserving religious particularities, which, in fact, constitute an essential element of the structure of religious pluralism. The second aspect pertains to any involvement in partisanship with the Jews and the Christians against Islam. The reason behind the prohibition in this respect is enmity and transgression. Consequently, the scope of the prohibition in this second aspect is limited to those among the Jews and the Christians who are people of transgression, aggression, and enmity towards the Muslims. Apart from these two aspects, any kind of friendship with Jews and Christian based on love and affection, and any kind of alliance with them seeking to spread all that is good and fight all that is evil, is not subject to prohibition in the case of verse 5:51.

[3]
Conclusion

In summary, analysis reveals that Qur'anic exegesis sources do not systematically present the Qur'an's concept of fighting against, or alliance with, non-Muslims contextualised to inter-faith relations. Misinterpretation and confusion characterise understanding of the prohibitions stipulated, primarily their root cause, scope and objective, as reflected in the inconsistency of statements and conclusions scattered throughout the sources. This in turn creates a vast area for speculation and misleading conclusions. By employing a holistic-thematic approach to systematically examine the historical, linguistic, and contextual aspects of, in this case, the command to fight non-Muslims and not take them as *awliyā'*, we discover no contradiction to exist between the Qur'anic conception of normative religious pluralism and the command to fight. This is because the root cause for this command is not the belief system of others, but their initiation of war on peaceful people. Thus, the scope of the Qur'anic imperative to fight refers only to people of war.

Similarly analysis of verse 5:51 and the prohibition against taking the Jews and Christians as *awliyā'* reveals that it is limited to two aspects. The first is purely theological, whereby Muslims are forbidden to rely on Jews and Christians as a source of religious guidance aiming at religious fusion, and thus leading to apostasy. The second pertains to any involvement in partisanship with the Jews and Christians against Islam. The reason for the prohibition in this respect is enmity and transgression. Consequently, the scope of the prohibition here is limited to those among the Jews and Christians who are hostile to Muslims and their faith, in other words people of transgression, aggression, and enmity towards Muslims. Putting these two aspects aside, and keeping commitment to their faith, in relation to verse 5:51 Muslims are not barred from any kind of friendship with the Jews and Christian based on love and affection, and any kind of alliance with them seeking to spread all that is good and fight all that is evil.

It is clear Qur'anic prescriptions play an important role in preventing the process of the normative religious pluralism from corruption, and remain as relevant today in our fractured times as when first revealed, since these prescriptions are related to issues such as aggression and transgression, but not to the belief systems of non-Muslims and not to people of peace.

Conclusion

Religious pluralism is a complex concept accommodating a multiplicity of definitions, each containing considerable discrepancy between them in terms of their themes, scope, and areas of contention. Inability to distinguish between the different types of religious pluralism and to adopt hence a relevant approach corresponding to its appropriate type pave the way for misleading conclusions to be drawn which can impact how we perceive, tolerate, and co-exist with different Others. One of the results of this inability has been the emergence of mutually exclusive theories concerning interfaith relations.

Yet for Muslims religious pluralism and interfaith relations is nothing new. In fact, being the final Revelation, the Qur'an encompassed earlier religious traditions, centuries ahead of its time, giving precise guidance on not only how to live with the Other, including those of other faiths, but also how to conduct discourse with intelligence and respect. It was unique in doing so. A cardinal principle has been to establish and maintain peace, after all as the Qur'an itself states we have been created to "know" each other, not fight or cause turmoil and oppression. "O mankind, indeed We have created you from a male and a female and made you peoples and tribes that you may know one another. Indeed, the most noble of you in the sight of Allah is the most righteous of you. Indeed, Allah is Knowing and Acquainted" (Qur'an 49:13).

This sense of community, of shared humanity, is so integral to the Muslim sense of itself, and of its non-Muslim neighbors, that it forms a crucial part of how Muslims approach the social, cultural, religious and geographical boundaries of the Other and interact on the basis of a shared humanity and shared values.

Even animals are referred to in the Qur'an as living in communities, such is the importance of the concept. What is to be borne in mind is that religious pluralism can be interpreted in a number of ways and in the Islamic context we need to be clear as to the requirements of the Qur'an interpreting its injunctions correctly. In reference to the Qur'an, religious pluralism has largely been historically challenged by two factors: socio-political context and the hermeneutical process. The relationship between the two is inseparable and has created different exegetical paradigms with respect to religious pluralism one of which is pure exclusivism and a reluctance to interact with those outside our religious boundaries.

This persistent exclusivist attitude seems to have been shaped by historical circumstance, forming the specific historical context in which exegetical literature was produced. It is no coincidence that the socio-political context and formative period of this literature – and thus the most influential part of it – coincided with a time of religious conflict, persecution and warfare, which commenced during the time of the Prophet and peaked during the Crusades. For instance, key exegetes such as al-Zamakhsharī, Ibn ʿAṭiyyah, al-Rāzī, Ibn ʿArabī, al-Qurṭubī, etc. spent their entire lives in the context of the first Crusades and hence witnessed interfaith relations from that particular backdrop of religiously motivated war.

As a consequence, Qur'anic hermeneutics came to be negatively affected in the shape of two claims. The first was abrogation of those Qur'anic verses prescribing a positive attitude towards non-Muslims. The second was to specify the general sense of verses relating positively to non-Muslims, and hence restrict their meaning exclusively only to Muslims. Embedded in the atomistic approach to Qur'anic exegesis, which naturally prevents crystallisation of understanding based on thematic coherence of a topic, the two claims have left little chance for the humanistic view to flourish in Qur'anic exegesis.

As a result, Qur'anic guidance on self-defence in the context of war and oppression has been emphasised and given greater precedence over its message of peace and universal ethical teachings. The repercussion being that religious exclusivism has failed to distinguish between the Qur'an's theological view on the beliefs of others and its ethical view on the followers of other beliefs. The natural result of this failure was the division of people into believers and unbelievers, which is tantamount to the territories of peace and war, respectively. Or in a better case scenario, it resulted in a definition of the relationship between Muslims and non-Muslims as being based on *daᶜwah*, which would appear as a strategy of embrace.

There exist different types of pluralisms as mentioned earlier. Normative Religious Pluralism, Soteriological Religious Pluralism, Epistemological Religious Pluralism, and Alethic Religious Pluralism. For Muslims, and with regards to the Qur'an, confusion about soteriological, alethic, and normative religious pluralism has led to the emergence of an exclusivist approach. This position developed as a theological stance firstly historically against the backdrop of conflict constantly necessitating Muslim defence and secondly, through using an atomistic approach in Qur'anic exegesis. Misleading *theological*, note *not Qur'anic* as is the contention of this study, conclusions emerged which were radical or hardline in nature, claiming that Muslims had no obligations towards non-Muslims. Moreover, claims that non-Muslims should be deprived of their rights, have their dignity violated, their property taken, and even their blood shed often appear in *tafsīr* literature. In other words Muslims closed ranks in reaction to constant hostility.

However – and given the current civilisational context of diversity – adopting a thematic approach to understanding Qur'anic texts we note fundamental differences between its findings and those of the exclusivists, the primary being that there is ample room for accommodation of normative religious pluralism. Unlike soteriological and alethic pluralism, whose issues are inherently irreconcilable for Muslims as they concern core aspects of religious truth and salvation which Muslims cannot concede to, normative religious pluralism concentrates on terrestrial dimensions and ramifications allowing for a genuine discourse whose objective is understanding and peacebuilding.

The legitimacy of normative religious pluralism in Islam largely emerges from the Qur'an's ethical system and in particular its recognition of the universality of freedom of belief and respect for human dignity. In this case, the Qur'anic ethical system cannot be regarded as subject to abrogation or restriction on the basis of religious affiliation. It's teachings of the universality of freedom of belief and respect for human dignity rejects the exclusive ethico-behavioral position. In fact, the ethical system repeatedly outlined in the Qur'an is inseparably related to belief in God and the Day of Judgement suggesting that the ethico-behavioral pattern prescribed for Muslims is not limited to its outward aspect only, but also penetrates to the inward dimensions of human behavior. Thus the principles of normative religious pluralism are not alien to Islam, and the Qur'an in fact sets the highest standards, rejecting any mutual understanding based on false diplomacy or hidden strategies of embrace.

Accordingly, the objectives of the human relationship universally prescribed in the Qur'an cannot be restricted exclusively to a particular religious group nor can they be directed to serve nefarious goals. However, since four of these universal objectives are mentioned in Madinan surahs (that is revealed in a multicultural society as well as in the textual context of religious diversity) they can be employed to serve as main objectives of normative religious pluralism. Arranged in the following ascending order: mutual understanding-*taʿāruf*; mutual engagement-*taʿāwun*; mutual contribution-*istibāq al-khayrāt*; and mutual support-*tadāfuʿ*, these objectives construct the axis of the peacebuilding process and encourage the achievement of universal righteousness and excellence in the context of diversity.

Furthermore, the two main, dialectical elements of normative religious pluralism, namely diversity and commonality, are presented in the Qur'an as a fact of nature and unchangeable law inherent in the universe and human nature. Thus, the process of normative religious pluralism cannot be regarded in the light of the Qur'an as a theory or mere idea, in fact such a process is advanced as a divine law emerging from God's creation of mankind with free will, the natural result of which is diversity. Consequently, both the exclusivist's approach, which refuses to accept the different other, and that of the relativists, which disregards particularities, contradict not only the Qur'anic worldview, but also natural laws and human nature. Moreover, prescribed by the Qur'an as an essential vehicle for communication between all people at every stage of the socio-political development of a society, constructive conversation is expected to strike a right balance between elements of religious commonality and those of particularity. This prevents their being employed as a means of religious dilution or seclusion, respectively. In other words, the function of constructive conversation is to keep the process of normative religious pluralism on an even path, away from extremes.

This Qur'anic conception of normative religious pluralism, an important facet of developing and promoting peacebuilding, has been seriously threatened by exclusive interpretations which seemingly contradict the overall message of the Qur'an, and which misinterpret Qur'anic prescriptions such as fighting non-Muslims and not taking them as friends (*awliyā'*), to lend scriptural credibility to this exclusivist position, when in reality they have failed to determine the root cause and scope of these prescriptions. For example, the basis for the imperative to fight is not rooted in the belief system of others, but their initiation of war on people of peace, meaning that the scope of the imperative falls only on people of war. The Qur'anic prescription of not taking the Jews and Christians as *awliyā'* is governed by two aspects. The first is purely theological, where the prohibition is related to Muslim reliance on Jews and Christians as sources of religious guidance aiming at religious fusion, and thus leading to apostasy. The basis for the prohibition in this case is rooted in preserving religious particularities, which constitute an essential element of the structure of religious pluralism. The second aspect relates to any involvement in partisanship with the Jews and

Christians against Islam. The reason for the prohibition being enmity and transgression. Thus the basis for the prohibition in this case is rooted in, and limited to, those Jews and Christians bent on transgression, aggression, and enmity towards Muslims. These two aspects aside, any kind of friendship with Jews and Christian based on love and affection, as well as any kind of alliance with them seeking to spread all that is good and fight all that is evil, is not subject to prohibition. Thus, providing that these Qur'anic prescriptions are related to issues such as aggression and transgression, but not to the belief systems of non-Muslims, it appears that the prescriptions can play an important role in preventing the process of the normative religious pluralism from suffering any corruption.

Finally, the Qur'anic conception of normative religious pluralism perfectly corresponds to both the prophetic ethico-behavioral pattern of dealing with non-Muslims and universal human values. In this way, the dynamic nature of the Qur'anic text establishes a right balance between authenticity and modernity. In doing so it thus, on the one hand, preserves human particularities as a source of dignity, and on the other provides a vast common ground for the promotion of normative religious pluralism as a value system on an environmental, moral, and spiritual basis.

Therefore, the real danger appears to be the substantial paradox of claiming to emulate the Prophet, claim the universality of Islam, yet threaten division by remaining committed to an exclusivist perspective which pays lip service to peaceful co-existence and respect of other faith traditions, of being created into "peoples and tribes that you may know one another" and which when all is said and done is based on only a few select verses of the Qur'an.

Notes

Introduction

1. The classical method of Qur'anic exegesis, which explains the Qur'an on a verse-by-verse basis, commencing from the first chapter and moving towards the end, without considering the thematic coherence of the verses.
2. The humanistic approach of Qur'anic exegesis concentrates on universally accepted human values and thus emphasises the universality of the Qur'anic ethical system.
3. Mustafa Muslim, *Mabāḥith fī al-Tafsīr al-Mawḍūʿī* (Damascus: Dār al-Qalam, 2000), p. 16.
4. Muhammad A. Draz, *The Moral World of the Qur'an* (London: I.B. Tauris, 2008), p. 3.
5. Fadl Abbas, *Itqān al-Burhān fī ʿUlūm al-Qur'ān* (Amman: Dār al-Furqān, 1997), pp. 11-12.
6. Abū ʿUthmān al-Jāḥiẓ, *Kitāb al-Ḥayawān* (Beirut: Dār al-Jīl, 1988), vol.4, p. 461.
7. Samir Rashwani, *Manhaj al-Tafsīr al-Mawḍūʿī li al-Qur'ān al-Karīm* (Ḥalab: Dār al-Multaqā, 2009), pp. 80-99.
8. Probably one of the significant reasons that the thematic exegetical method, which is based on reasoning, did not flourish was the perception of some medieval scholars that reason and revelation are contradictory or as Amin states controversially: "After the ban on the Muʿtazilah, Muslims remained under the influence of the Conservatives for approximately 1000 years." Ahmad Amin, *Ḍuḥā al-Islām* (Cairo: Maktabah al-Nahḍah al-Miṣriyyah, 1978), vol.3, p.207.
9. Muhammad A. Draz, *The Moral World of the Qur'an* (London: I.B. Tauris, 2008), p. 2.
10. Samir Rashwani, *Manhaj al-Tafsīr al-Mawḍūʿī li al-Qur'ān al-Karīm* (Ḥalab: Dār al-Multaqā, 2009), p. 110.
11. Ibid., p. 111.
12. Nikki Keddie, *An Islamic Response to Imperialism* (Los Angeles: University of California Press, 1968), p. 107.

13. Samir Rashwani, *Manhaj al-Tafsīr al-Mawḍūʿī li al-Qur'ān al-Karīm* (Ḥalab: Dār al-Multaqā, 2009), p. 113.
14. Jane D. McAuliffe, *Qur'anic Christians* (Cambridge: Cambridge, 1991), p. 292.
15. Toshihiko Izutsu, *Ethico-Religious Concepts in the Qur'an* (McGill-Queen's University Press, 2002), p. 252.
16. Abd al-Sattar Said, *Al-Madkhal ilā al-Tafsīr al-Mawḍūʿī* (Cairo: Dār al-Tawzīʿ wa al-Nashr al-Islāmiyyah, 1991), pp. 58-59.
17. Muhammad Baqir al-Sadr, *Al-Madrasah al-Qur'āniyyah* (Markaz al-Abḥāth wa al-Dirāsāt al-Takhaṣṣuṣiyyah li al-Shahīd al-Ṣadr, 1421 AH), pp. 26-36.
18. Mehmet S. Aydin, *Islam and the Challenges of Pluralism*, (http://www.cie.ugent.be/maydinen1.htm, 2005).
19. Muhammad A. Draz, *The Moral World of the Qur'an* (London: I.B. Tauris, 2008), pp. 13-116.
20. Samir Rashwani, *Manhaj al-Tafsīr al-Mawḍūʿī li al-Qur'ān al-Karīm* (Ḥalab: Dār al-Multaqā, 2009), p. 214.
21. Muhammad Baqir al-Sadr, *Al-Madrasah al-Qur'āniyyah* (Markaz al-Abḥāth wa al-Dirāsāt al-Takhaṣṣuṣiyyah li al-Shahīd al-Ṣadr, 1421 AH), p. 29.
22. Muhammad A. Draz, *The Moral World of the Qur'an* (London: I.B. Tauris, 2008), p. 3.

Chapter 1

1. Gavin D'Costa, *Theology and Religious Pluralism:The Challenge of Other Religions* (Oxford: Basil Blackwell Ltd, 1986), p. 40.
2. Ibid., p. 111.
3. T.S. Eliot, *The Complete Poems and Plays of T.S.Eliot* (London: Faber and Faber, 1969), p. 197.
4. Hans Küng, *Global Responsibility:In Search of a New World Ethic* (London: SCM Press Ltd, 1991), p. 80.
5. Ibid., p. 81.
6. Ibid., p. 85.
7. Ibid., p. 81.
8. Jonathan Sacks, *The Dignity of Difference:How to Avoid the Clash of Civilizations* (London: Continuum, 2002), p. 21.
9. Hossein S. Nasr, *The Heart of Islam: Enduring Values for Humanity* (New York: HarperCollins Publishers, 2002), p. 8.
10. Ibid., p. 43.

11. ('a) is the abbreviation for "peace be upon them."
12. (s) is the abbreviation for "may the peace and blessings of God be upon him."
13. Muhammad Legenhausen, "A Muslim's Non-Reductive Religious Pluralism" In *Islam and Global Dialogue: Religious Pluralism and the Pursuit of Peace*, ed. Roger Boase, pp.51-73 (Aldershot: Ashgate, 2005), here p. 66.
14. Ibid., pp. 65-66.
15. Ibid., pp. 53-56.
16. Ibid., p. 70.
17. Hassan Hanafi, *Religious Dialogue and Revolution* (Cairo: The Anglo-Egyptian Bookshop, 1976), p. 1.
18. Muhammad Legenhausen, "A Muslim's Non-Reductive Religious Pluralism" In *Islam and Global Dialogue*, pp. 60-63.
19. Douglas Harper, *Online Etymology Dictionary*. 10 10 2008. http://www.etymonline.com (accessed 12 8, 2011). The reference includes all eight etymological definitions of the word "religion."
20. Malory Nye, *Religion the Basics* (London and New York: Routledge, 2008), p. 21.
21. Syed al-Attas, *Islam and Secularism* (Kuala Lumpur: International Institute of Islamic Thought and Civlization, 1993), p. 54.
22. Ismāʿīl al-Fārūqī, *Toward Islamization of Disciplines* (Herndon: International Institute of Islamic Thought, 1989), p. 410.
23. Douglas Harper, *Online Etymology Dictionary*. 10 10 2008. http://www.etymonline.com (accessed 12 8, 2011). The reference includes all four etymological definitions of the word "pluralism."
24. Paul B. Clarke and Joe Foweraker, *Encyclopedia of Democratic Thought* (London: Routledge, 2001), p. 515.
25. Muhammad Legenhausen, "A Muslim's Non-Reductive Religious Pluralism" In *Islam and Global Dialogue*, p. 56.
26. B. A. Roibnson, *Religious Tolerance*. 20 May 2001. http://www.religious-tolerance.org (accessed March 17, 2010).
27. Karl Rahner, *Theological Investigations*, translated by Karl-H. Kruger (London: Darton, Longman and Todd, 1966), vol.5, p. 116.
28. Shailer Mathews and Gerald Smith, *A Dictionary of Religion and Ethics* (London: Waverley Book Company, LTD., 1921), p. 370.
29. Paul Copan, *True for You, But Not for Me* (Minneapolis: Bethany House Publishers, 1998), p. 19.

30. John Hick, *Problems of Religious Pluralism* (Hampshire: The Macmillan Press LTD, 1985), p. 34.
31. J.A. Simpson and E.S.C. Weiner, *The Oxford English Dictionary*, 2nd edn. (Oxford: Clarendon Press, 2004), vol.xvii, p. 475.
32. Ibid.
33. David B. Barrett, *World Christian Encyclopedia*, 2nd edn. (Oxford: Oxford University Press, 2001), vol.2, p. 675.
34. Hossein S. Nasr, *The Heart of Islam: Enduring Values for Humanity* (New York: HarperCollins Publishers, 2002), p. 39.
35. Ibid., p. 43.
36. There will be further discussion on this issue in the second section of the current chapter.
37. Pope Leo XIII, V.G.R. *Immortale Dei.* 1885.
38. David B. Barrett, *World Christian Encyclopedia*, 2nd edn. (Oxford: Oxford University Press, 2001), vol.2, p. 659.
39. Hans Küng, *Global Responsibility: In Search of a New World Ethic* (London: SCM Press Ltd, 1991).
40. David B. Barrett, *World Christian Encyclopedia*, 2nd edn. (Oxford: Oxford University Press, 2001), vol.2, p. 672.
41. Ibid.
42. Diana L. Eck, *The Pluralism Project at Harvard University.* 2006. http://pluralism.org (accessed March 25, 2010).
43. Muhammad Legenhausen, "A Muslim's Non-Reductive Religious Pluralism" In *Islam and Global Dialogue*, pp.51-73.
44. Ibid., p. 65.
45. All quotations from the English translation of the Qur'an are from Yusuf Ali.
46. Muhammad Legenhausen, "A Muslim's Non-Reductive Religious Pluralism" In *Islam and Global Dialogue*, p. 66.
47. Abū al-Ḥusayn Muslim, *Ṣaḥiḥ Muslim*, vol.1, translated by Abdul Hamid Siddiqi (Lahore: Ashraf Islamic Publishers, 1990), p. 103, no. 153.
48. Yaḥyā al-Nawawī, *Sharḥ Ṣaḥīḥ Muslim* (Beirut: Dār al-Fikr, 1996), vol.1, p. 889.
49. Sulaymān al-Ṭabarānī, *Al-Muʿjam al-Kabīr*, 2nd edn., edited by Hamdi al-Salafi, n.d., vol.2, p. 87, no. 1388.
50. ʿAlī al-Haythamī, *Majmaʿ al-Zawā'id wa Manbaʿ al-Fawā'id*, edited by Muhammad Ata (Beirut: Dār al-Kutub al-ʿIlmiyyah, 2001), vol.7, pp. 32-33, no. 10899.

51. Muhammad Legenhausen, "A Muslim's Non-Reductive Religious Pluralism" In *Islam and Global Dialogue*, pp. 64-70.
52. Fakhr al-Dīn al-Rāzī, *Mafātīḥ al-Ghayb* (Beirut: Dār al-Fikr, 2002), vol.13, p. 197.
53. Sulaymān al-Ṭabarānī, *Al-Muʿjam al-Kabīr*, 2nd edn., edited by Hamdi al-Salafi (n.p., n.d.), vol.2, p. 87, no. 1388.
54. Ibn Jarīr al-Ṭabarī, *Tafsīr al-Ṭabarī* (Beirut: Dār al-Kutub al-ʿIlmiyyah, 1999), vol.1, p. 360.
55. Fakhr al-Dīn al-Rāzī, *Mafātīḥ al-Ghayb* (Beirut: Dār al-Fikr, 2002), vol.2, p. 113.
56. Hossein S. Nasr, *The Heart of Islam: Enduring Values for Humanity* (New York: HarperCollins Publishers, 2002), p. 43.
57. See: Ibn Jarīr al-Ṭabarī, *Tafsīr al-Ṭabarī* (Beirut: Dār al-Kutub al-ʿIlmiyyah, 1999), vol.1, p. 358; Maḥmūd al-Zamakhsharī, *Al-Kashshāf ʿan Ḥaqā'iq al-Tanzīl* (Beirut: Dār al-Kutub al-ʿIlmiyyah, 1995), vol.1, p. 149; Muḥammad al-Qurṭubī, *Al-Jāmiʿ li Aḥkām al-Qur'ān* (Beirut: Dār al-Fikr, 1998) vol.1, p. 404; Ismāʿīl ibn Kathīr, *Tafsīr al-Qur'ān al-ʿAẓīm* (Beirut: Mu'assasah al-Rayyān, 1998), vol.1, p. 139; Muhammad ibn Ashur, *Tafsīr al-Taḥrīr wa al-Tanwīr* (Tunis: Maison Souhnoun, n.d.), vol.1, p. 539; Muhammad al-Sharawi, *Tafsīr al-Shaʿrāwī* (Cairo: Akhbār al-Yawm, 1991), vol.20, pp. 370-371.
58. ʿAbdullah Yūsuf ʿAlī, *The Meaning of The Holy Qur'an* (Beltsville, Maryland, U.S.A.: Amana Publications, 2008), p. 271.
59. Abd al-Aziz Atiq, *ʿIlm al-Maʿānī* (Beirut: Dār al-Nahḍah al-ʿArabiyyah, 1985), p. 161; Fadl Abbas, *Al-Balāghah: Funūnuhā wa* 'Afnānuhā (Amman: Dār al-Furqān, 1992), p. 405.
60. ʿAbdullah Yūsuf ʿAlī, *The Meaning of The Holy Qur'an* (Beltsville, Maryland, U.S.A.: Amana Publications, 2008), p. 390.
61. Abū Naṣr al-Fārābī, *Kitāb Ārā' Ahl al-Madīnah al-Fāḍilah* (Beirut: Dār al-Mashriq, 1968), pp. 114-116.
62. Ibn Jarīr al-Ṭabarī, *The History of al-Ṭabarī*, translated by W.M Watt and M.V. McDonald, (Albany: State University of New York Press, 1988), vol.6, p. 98.
63. Martin Lings, *Muhammad – His Life Based on the Earliest Sources* (Cambridge: The Islamic Text Society, 1991), p. 81.
64. Although Yusuf al-Ish in his book *The Arabic State and Its Decline, Al-Dawlah al-ʿArabiyyah wa Suqūṭuha,* suggests that the document is a fabrication (see Akram al-Umari, *Madinan Society at the Time of the Prophet*, (Herndon: The International Institute of Islamic Thought, 1995), p. 100.),

Akram al-Umari after studying thoroughly all chains of transmission, *asānīd,* of "The Constitution of Madinah" dispelled all doubts surrounding the authenticity of the document. See Akram al-Umari, *Al-Sīrah al-Nabawiyyah al-Ṣaḥīḥah* (Madinah: Maktabah al-ʿUlūm wa al-Ḥikam, 1994, p. 274.

65. William M. Watt and Richard Bell, *Introduction to the Qur'an* (Edinburgh: University Press, 1970), p. 7.
66. Muḥammad ibn al-ʿArabī, *Aḥkām al-Qur'ān* (Beirut: Dār al-Fikr, n.d.), vol.6, p. 486.
67. Muḥammad Abū al-Suʿūd, *Irshād al-ʿAql al-Salīm ilā Mazāyā al-Kitāb al-Karīm* (Beirut: Dār al-Fikr, n.d.), vol.4, p. 198.
68. Muhammad Qalahji and Hamid Qunaibi, *Muʿjam Lughah al-Fuqahā'* (Beirut: Dār al-Nafā'is, 1985), p. 62.
69. Carl Brockelmann, *History of the Islamic Peoples* (London: Routledge and Kegan Paul, 1949), p. 4.
70. Jawad Ali, *Al-Mufaṣṣal fī Tārīkh al-ʿArab Qabl al-Islām* (Baghdad: University of Baghdad, 1993), vol.1, p. 266.
71. Badr al-Dīn al-Zarkashī, *Al-Burhān fī ʿUlūm al-Qur'ān* (Beirut: Al-Maktabah al-ʿAṣriyyah, 1972), vol.1, p. 206.
72. Muhammad ibn Ashur, *Tafsīr al-Taḥrīr wa al-Tanwīr* (Tunis: Maison Souhnoun, n.d.), vol.12, p. 447.
73. Ibn Hishām al-Anṣārī, *Mughnī al-Labīb ʿan Kutub al-Aʿārīb* (Dār Iḥyā' al-Turāth al-ʿArabī, n.d.), vol.2, p. 690.
74. Abū Jahl (lit. "father of ignorance"). A prominent enemy of Islam among the Quraysh. His hostility earned him the appellation of father of ignorance from the Muslims, but his real name was ʿAmr ibn Hishām. He was killed in the Battle of Badr in 2/624. See Cyril Glasse, *The New Encyclopaedia of Islam* (Walnut Creek: AltaMira Press, 2002), p. 23.
75. ʿAbd al-Ḥaq ibn ʿAṭiyyah, *Al-Muḥarrar al-Wajīz fī Tafsīr al-Kitāb al-ʿAzīz* (Beirut: Dār al-Kutub al-ʿIlmiyyah, 2001), vol.5, p. 502.
76. Muḥammad Abū Ḥayyān al-Andalusī, *Tafsīr al-Baḥr al-Muḥīṭ* (Beirut: Dār al-Kutub al-ʿIlmiyyah, 2001), vol.8, p. 489.
77. Ḍiyā' al-Dīn ibn al-Athīr, *Al-Mathal al-Sā'ir* (Dār Nahḍah Miṣr, n.d.), vol.2, p. 169.
78. Maḥmūd al-Zamakhsharī, *Al-Kashshāf ʿan Ḥaqā'iq al-Tanzīl* (Beirut: Dār al-Kutub al-ʿIlmiyyah, 1995), vol.1, p. 24.
79. Ḍiyā' al-Dīn ibn al-Athīr, *Al-Mathal al-Sā'ir* (Dār Nahḍah Miṣr, n.d.), vol.2, p. 167.
80. It seems that the subtle meanings conveyed by the linguistic approach of

iltifāt in the Qur'an, were not always clear for Theodor Nöldeke, who states that: "*Die grammatischen Personen wechseln im Korān zuweilen in ungewöhnlicher undnicht schöner Weise*": "the grammatical persons change from time to time in the Qur'an in an unusual and not beautiful way." See Theodor Nöldeke, *Neue Beiträge zur Semitischen* Sprachwissenashaft, (Strassburg: Karl J. Trubner, 1910), p. 13.

81. Akram al-Umari, *Al-Sīrah al-Nabawiyyah al-Ṣaḥīḥah* (Madinah: Maktabah al-ʿUlūm wa al-Ḥikam, 1994), p. 284.

82. Abū Muḥammad ʿAbd al-Malik ibn Hishām, *Al-Sīrah al-Nabawiyyah*, (Miṣr: Muṣṭafā al-Bābī al-Ḥalabī wa Awlāduh, 1955), vol.2, p. 574. The arrival of the Christian delegation from Najran to the Prophet Muhammad in Madinah is authentically documented in both collections of hadith: al-Bukhārī, no. 4380 and Muslim, no. 2420, according to Abd al-Baqi's numbering. However, some details of the event and particularly the Prophet's permission for Christians to pray in the mosque does not exist at all in al-Bukhārī and Muslim. Actually, the source of the detailed information is Muḥammad ibn Isḥāq, who narrates it from Muḥammad ibn Jaʿfar ibn al-Zubayr, but this chain of transmission is problematic in terms of its discontinuity, since Muḥammad ibn Jaʿfar ibn al-Zubayr was from the generation succeeding the Successors, *al-Tābiʿūn* (See Ibn Ḥajar al-ʿAsqalānī, *Taqrīb al-Tahdhīb*, edited by Abu al-Ashbal Sagir Ahmad Shagif al-Bakistani, (Dār al-ʿĀṣimah, n.d.), p. 832.) Nevertheless, there is a possibility for the detailed narration to be an authentic one because in his commentary on verse 61 of surah *Āl ʿImrān*, after mentioning the detailed content transmitted by Muḥammad ibn Jaʿfar ibn al-Zubayr, Ibn Kathīr states: "Ibn Mardawayh narrates from Muḥammad ibn Isḥāq, from ʿĀṣim ibn ʿUmar ibn Qatādah, from Maḥmūd ibn Labīd, from Rāfiʿ ibn Khadīj that: 'the delegation from Najran came to the Prophet, peace be upon him...' and then mentions the same story (narrated by Muḥammad ibn Jaʿfar ibn al-Zubayr)...in greater detail." (see Ismāʿīl ibn Kathīr, *Tafsīr al-Qur'ān al-ʿAẓīm* (Beirut: Mu'assasah al-Rayyān, 1998), vol.1, p. 481). The chain of transmission through which Ibn Mardawayh narrates the information is connected and authentic, since, apart from Muḥammad ibn Isḥāq who is generally defined as a trustworthy narrator (see Ibn Ḥajar al-ʿAsqalānī, *Taqrīb al-Tahdhīb*, edited by Abu al-Ashbal Sagir Ahmad Shagif al-Bakistani (Dār al-ʿĀṣimah, n.d.), p. 825.), the rest of the narrators appear in the collections of al-Shaykhayn: al-Bukhārī's and Muslim (see the conclusion of Shuaib al-Arnaut regarding the above chain in Aḥmad ibn Ḥanbal, *Musnad al-Imām Aḥmad*, edited by Shuaib al-Arnaut (Beirut: Mu'assasah

al-Risālah, 2001),vol.25, p. 133). So, the narration of Ibn Mardawayh might have been the reason for some classical sources of Islamic jurespru-dance to accept the information about the Prophet's permission for Christians to pray in the mosque as authentic. For example, Ibn Qayyim al-Jawziyyah in his *Aḥkām Ahl al-Dhimmah* states the following: "It is **authentically** transmitted from the Prophet, peace be upon him, that he received the Christian delegation from Najran in his mosque and when the time for their prayer came they prayed in the mosque." (See Ibn Qayyim al-Jawziyyah, *Aḥkām Ahl al-Dhimmah* (al-Dammām: Ramādī li al al-Nashr, 1997), p. 397). Yet, the works of Ibn Mardawayh, in which he transmits the information, are unfortunately not available to us, having become lost down the centuries.

83. S.H. Griffith, *Disputing with Islam in Syriac: The Case of the Monk of Bêt Hālê and a Muslim Emir* (*Hugoye: Journal of Syriac Studies*, January, pp. 1-45), vol.3, para. 6.
84. S.H. Griffith, *Arabic Christianity in the Monasteries of Ninth-Century Palestine* (Hampshire: Variorum, 1992), p. 102.
85. S.H. Griffith, *The Beginnings of Christian Theology in Arabic* (Hampshire: Ashgate, 2002), p. 271.
86. Mark Swanson, "The Christian al-Mamun Tradition." In *Christians at the Heart of Islamic Rule*, edited by David Thomas, 63-92, (Leiden-Boston: Brill, 2003), p. 65.
87. Ibid. The words "by that which is better" come from surah *Al-ʿAnkabūt*: "And dispute ye not with the People of the Book, except with means better (than mere disputation)...." (Qur'an *al-ʿAnkabūt* 29: 46).
88. Ibid., pp. 67-68.
89. Hilary Kilpatrick, "Monasteries Through Muslim Eyes: The Diyārāt Books." In *Christians at the Heart of Islamic Rule: Church Life and Scholarship in ʿAbbasid Iraq*, edited by David Thomas, 19-37, (Leiden: Brill, 2003), p. 19.
90. Ibid., p. 23.
91. Muhammad Legenhausen, "A Muslim's Non-Reductive Religious Pluralism" In *Islam and Global Dialogue*, p. 54.
92. Fathi Osman, *The Other* (USA: Pharos Foundation, 2008), p. 37.
93. Muhammad al-Buti, *Fiqh al-Sīrah al-Nabawiyyah* (Damascus: Dār al-Salām, 2004), pp. 258-259.
94. Muhammad A. Bakhit, *The Fourth International Conference on the History of Bilad al-Sham During the Umayyad Period*, vols. Arabic Section-1, (Amman: University of Jordan, 1989), p. 415.

Notes

Chapter 2

1. Toshihiko Izutsu, *Ethico-Religious Concepts in the Qur'an* (McGill-Queen's University Press, 2002), p. 252.
2. ᶜAlī al-Muttaqī al-Hindī, *Kanz al-ᶜUmmāl fī Sunan al-Aqwāl wa al-Afᶜāl* (Beirut: Mu'assasah al-Risālah, 1985), vol.12, pp. 660-661.
3. Jean-Jacques Rousseau, *The Social Contract and The First and Second Discourses*, edited by Susan Dunn (New Haven and London: Yale University Press, 2002), p. 156.
4. Ibid., p. 159.
5. Said Nursi, *Münazarat* (Istanbul: Envâr Ne riyat, 1993), pp. 24-25 cited in T.S.J. Michel, "Muslim-Christian Dialogue and Cooperation in the Thought of Bediuzzaman Said Nursi." *The Muslim World* 89, no. 3-4 (1999): 325-335, pp. 329-331.
6. See Franz Rosenthal, *The Muslim Concept of Freedom* (Leiden: E. J. Brill, 1960).
7. Abū al-Ḥusayn ibn Fāris, *Muᶜjam al-Maqāyīs fī al-Lughah* (Beirut: Dār al-Fikr, 1998), p. 240.
8. Ibid.
9. The sentence in the quotation is translated in Franz Rosenthal, *The Muslim Concept of Freedom* (Leiden: E. J. Brill, 1960), p. 24.
10. Al-Rāghib al-Aṣfahānī, *Mufradāt Alfāẓ al-Qur'ān*, edited by Safwan Daudi (Damascus: Dār al-Qalam, 2002), pp. 224-225.
11. Fakhr al-Dīn al-Rāzī, *Al-Mabāḥith al-Sharqiyyah* (Hyderabad: Majlis Dā'irah al-Maᶜārif, 1343 AH), vol.2, p. 414; translated in Franz Rosenthal, *The Muslim Concept of Freedom* (Leiden: E. J. Brill, 1960), p. 25.
12. Muḥammad al-Bukhārī, *Ṣaḥīḥ al-Bukhārī*, translated by Muhammad Muhsin Khan (Beirut: Dār al-ᶜArabiyyah, 1985), vol.8, p. 296.
13. Abū Ḥāmid al-Ghazālī, *Iḥyā' ᶜUlūm al-Dīn* (Beirut: Dār al-Kutub al-ᶜIlmiyyah, 2001), vol.3, p. 247.
14. Franz Rosenthal, *The Muslim Concept of Freedom* (Leiden: E. J. Brill, 1960), p. 11.
15. Abū al-Ḥasan al-Wāḥidī, *Asbāb al-Nuzūl* (Cairo: Maktabah al-Mutanabbī, n.d.), p. 47.
16. Muhammad al-Albani, *Ṣaḥīḥ Sunan Abī Dāwūd* (Riyad: Maktabah al-Maᶜārif, 2000),vol.3, p. 148, no. 2682.
17. Ibn Jarīr al-Ṭabarī, *Tafsīr al-Ṭabarī* (Beirut: Dār al-Kutub al-ᶜIlmiyyah, 1999), vol.3, p. 17.
18. Abū Jaᶜfar al-Nuḥās, *Kitāb al-Nāsikh wa al-Mansūkh fī al-Qur'ān al-Karīm* (Al-Maktabah al-ᶜĀlamiyyah, 1938), p. 81.

19. Muhammad ibn Ashur, *Tafsīr al-Taḥrīr wa al-Tanwīr* (Tunis: Maison Souhnoun, n.d.), vol.2, p. 26.
20. Abū Ja'far al-Nuḥās, *Al-Nāsikh wa al-Mansūkh*, edited by Sulaiman al-Lahim (Beirut: Mu'assasah al-Risālah, 1991), vol.1, pp. 102-114.
21. Fadl Abbass, *Itqān al-Burhān fī 'Ulūm al-Qur'ān* (Amman: Dār al-Furqān, 1997), vol.2, pp. 11-12.
22. Muhammad abu Zahrah, *Zahrah al-Tafāsīr* (Dār al-Fikr al-'Arabī, n.d.), vol.1, p. 41.
23. Ibid.
24. Muslim scholar (d. 934), and by whom Fakhr al-Dīn al-Rāzī was influenced.
25. Muhammad Abu Zahrah, *Zahrah al-*Tafāsīr (Dār al-Fikr al-'Arabī, n.d.), vol.1, p. 41.
26. Muhammad al-Ghazali, *Naẓarāt fī al-Qur'ān* (Cairo: Nahḍah Miṣr, 2005), p. 194.
27. 'Alī al-Rummānī, Ḥamd al-Khaṭṭābī and 'Abd al-Qādir al-Jurjānī, *Thalāth Rasā'il fī I'jāz al-Qurān* (Cairo: Dār al-Ma'ārif, n.d.), p. 77.
28. Muhammad ibn Ashur, *Tafsīr al-Taḥrīr wa al-Tanwīr* (Tunis: Maison Souhnoun, n.d.), vol.2, p. 26.
29. Ibn Jarīr al-Ṭabarī, *Tafsīr al-Ṭabarī* (Beirut: Dār al-Kutub al-'Ilmiyyah, 1999), vol.3, p. 18.
30. Fakhr al-Dīn al-Rāzī, *Mafātīḥ al-Ghayb* (Beirut: Dār al-Fikr, 2002), vol.4, p. 16.
31. Ibn Jarīr al-Ṭabarī, *Tafsīr al-Ṭabarī* (Beirut: Dār al-Kutub al-'Ilmiyyah, 1999), vol.6, p. 349.
32. Muhammad al-Buti, *Fiqh al-Sīrah al-Nabawiyyah* (Damascus: Dār al-Salām, 2004), p. 190.
33. The root cause of the Qur'anic imperative to fight will be discussed in detail in chapter five.
34. Muhammad ibn Ashur, *Tafsīr al-Taḥrīr wa al-Tanwīr* (Tunis: Maison Souhnoun, n.d.), vol.2, p. 28.
35. Ibid., p. 25.
36. Arnold Toynbee, *A Study of History-Abridgement of Volumes VII-X*, edited by D.C. Somervell (Oxford: Oxford University Press, 1985), p. 312.
37. Badr al-Dīn al-Zarkashī, *Al-Burhān fī 'Ulūm al-Qur'ān* (Beirut: Dār al-Jīl, 1988), vol.1, p. 195.
38. Subhi al-Salih, *Mabāḥith fī 'Ulūm al-Qur'ān* (Beirut: Dār al-'Ilm li al-Malāyīn, 2002), p. 141.
39. Ibid., p. 157.

40. Ibn Jarīr al-Ṭabarī, *Tafsīr al-Ṭabarī* (Beirut: Dār al-Kutub al-ʿIlmiyyah, 1999), vol.10, p. 342.
41. Maḥmūd al-Zamakhsharī, *Al-Kashshāf ʿan Ḥaqā'iq al-Tanzīl* (Beirut: Dār al-Kutub al-ʿIlmiyyah, 1995), vol.3, p. 546.
42. Fakhr al-Dīn al-Rāzī, *Mafātīḥ al-Ghayb* (Beirut: Dār al-Fikr, 2002), vol.13, p. 235.
43. Shihāb al-Dīn al-Ālūsī, *Rūḥ al-Maʿānī* (Beirut: Dār al-Kutub al-ʿIlmiyyah, 1994), vol.11, p. 270.
44. Muhammad ibn Ashur, *Tafsīr al-Taḥrīr wa al-Tanwīr* (Tunis: Maison Souhnoun, n.d.), vol.9, p. 127.
45. Muhammad al-Sharawi, *Tafsīr al-Shaʿrāwī* (Cairo: Akhbār al-Yawm, 1991), vol 20, p. 12212.
46. Fakhr al-Dīn al-Rāzī, *Mafātīḥ al-Ghayb* (Beirut: Dār al-Fikr, 2002), vol.13, p. 235.
47. Muhammad ibn Ashur, *Tafsīr al-Taḥrīr wa al-Tanwīr* (Tunis: Maison Souhnoun, n.d.), vol.9, p. 16.
48. See Muhammad ibn Ashur, *Maqāṣid al-Sharīʿah al-Islāmiyyah* (Doha: Wizārah al-Awqāf wa al-Shu'ūn al-Islamiyyah Qatar, 2004), p. 380; Ṭaha J. al-Alwani, *lā Ikrāh fī al-Dīn* (Cairo: Maktabah al-Shurūq al-Dawliyyah, 2006), p. 90; Jamāl al-Dīn ʿAṭiyyah, *Naḥwū Tafʿīl Maqāṣid al-Sharīʿah* (Damascus: Dār al-Fikr, 2001), pp. 170-171.
49. Jurgen Moltmann, *On Human Dignity*, translated by M. Douglas Meeks (London: SCM Press Ltd, 1984), p. ix.
50. Immanuel Kant, *Grounding for the Metaphysics of Moral*, translated by James W. Ellington (Indianapolis: Hackett Publishing Company, Inc, 1993), p. vii.
51. Fakhr al-Dīn al-Rāzī, *Mafātīḥ al-Ghayb* (Beirut: Dār al-Fikr, 2002), vol.16, pp. 11-12.
52. Muḥammad al-Albani, *Silsilāh al-Aḥādīth al-Ṣaḥīḥah* (Riyadh: Maktabah al-Maʿārif, 1995), vol.1, p. 787, no. 426.
53. Muḥammad al-Bukhārī, *Ṣaḥīḥ al-Bukhārī*, translated by Muhammad Muhsin Khan (Beirut: Dār al-Arabiyyah, 1985), vol.8, p. 224, no. 398.
54. Ibid., no. 399.
55. Abbas M. al-Aqqad, *Al-Insān fī al-Qur'ān* (Cairo: Dār al-Hilāl, n.d.), p. 57.
56. Jaudat Said, *Iqra' wa Rabbuka al-Akram* (Damascus: Dār al-Fikr, 1998).
57. Jonathan Sacks, *The Dignity of Difference: How to Avoid the Clash of Civilizations* (London: Continuum, 2002), p. 15.
58. Jasser Auda, *Maqasid al-Shariah as Philosophy of Islamic Law* (London: The International Institute of Islamic Thought, 2008), p. 23.

59. Badr al-Dīn al-Zarkashī, *Al-Burhān fī ʿUlūm al-Qur'ān* (Beirut: Dār al-Jīl, 1988), vol.1, p. 193.
60. Maḥmūd al-Zamakhsharī, *Al-Kashshāf ʿan Ḥaqā'iq al-Tanzīl* (Beirut: Dār al-Kutub al-ʿIlmiyyah, 1995), vol.2, p. 81.
61. Muhammad R. Rida, *Tafsīr al-Manār* (Beirut: Dār al-Kutub al-ʿIlmiyyah, 1999), vol.8 p. 215.
62. Jonathan Sacks, *The Dignity of Difference: How to Avoid the Clash of Civilizations* (London: Continuum, 2002), pp. 67-86.
63. Muhammad al-Sharawi, *Tafsīr al-Shaʿrāwī* (Cairo: Akhbār al-Yawm, 1991), vol.1, p. 229.
64. Muḥammad Abū Ḥayyān al-Andalusī, *Tafsīr al-Baḥr al-Muḥīṭ* (Beirut: Dār al-Kutub al-ʿIlmiyyah, 2001), vol.1, p. 279.
65. Muhammad al-Sharawi, *Tafsīr al-Shaʿrāwī* (Cairo: Akhbār al-Yawm, 1991), vol.1, p. 583.
66. Burhān al-Dīn al-Biqāʿī, *Naẓmu al-Durar fī Tanāsub al-Āyāt wa al-Suwar* (Beirut: Dār al-Kutub al-ʿIlmiyyah, 1995), vol.1, p. 241.
67. Fakhr al-Dīn al-Rāzī, *Mafātīḥ al-Ghayb* (Beirut: Dār al-Fikr, 2002),vol.10, p. 183.
68. The Holy Qur'an: English Translation of the Meanings and Commentary. The Presidency of Islamic Researches, Ifta, Call and Guidance.
69. M.A.S. Abdel Haleem, *The Qur'an: A New Translation* (New York: Oxford University Press Inc., 2004), p. 81.
70. Ibn Jarīr al-Ṭabarī, *Tafsīr al-Ṭabarī* (Beirut: Dār al-Kutub al-ʿIlmiyyah, 1999), vol.2, p. 164.
71. Muhammad R. Rida, *Tafsīr al-Manār* (Beirut: Dār al-Kutub al-ʿIlmiyyah, 1999), vol.2, p. 134.
72. Henry Coribn, *History of Islamic Philosofy,* translated by Liadain Sherrard (London: Kegan Paul International, n.d.), p. 2.
73. Muhammad ibn Ashur, *Tafsīr al-Taḥrīr wa al-Tanwīr* (Tunis: Maison Souhnoun, n.d.), vol.9, p. 40.
74. Ibn Jarīr al-Ṭabarī, *Tafsīr al-Ṭabarī* (Beirut: Dār al-Kutub al-ʿIlmiyyah, 1999), vol.12, p. 63.
75. Ibid.
76. Abū Jaʿfar al-Nuḥās, *Al-Nāsikh wa al-Mansūkh*, edited by Sulaiman al-Lahim, (Beirut: Mu'assasah al-Risālah, 1991), vol.1, pp. 102-114.
77. Ibn Jarīr al-Ṭabarī, *Tafsīr al-Ṭabarī* (Beirut: Dār al-Kutub al-ʿIlmiyyah, 1999), vol.12, p. 63.
78. Muhammad Abu Zahrah, *Zahrah al-Tafāsīr* (Dār al-Fikr al-ʿArabī, n.d.), vol.1, p. 41.

79. Ibid.
80. Muhammad Abd al-Salam Abu al-Nail, *Tafsīr al-Imām Mujāhid ibn Jabr*, (Naṣr: Dār al-Fikr al-Islāmī al-Ḥadīthah, 1989), p. 655.
81. Fakhr al-Dīn al-Rāzī, *Mafātīḥ al-Ghayb* (Beirut: Dār al-Fikr, 2002), vol.15, pp. 304-305.
82. Ibid., p. 305.
83. Musaid al-Taiar, *Maqālāt fī ʿUlūm al-Qur'ān wa Usūl al-Tafsīr* (Riad: Dār al-Muḥaddith, 1425 AH-2004), pp. 22-30.
84. Ibn Jarīr al-Ṭabarī, *Tafsīr al-Ṭabarī* (Beirut: Dār al-Kutub al-ʿIlmiyyah, 1999), vol.12, p. 63.
85. See Maḥmūd al-Zamakhsharī, *Al-Kashshāf ʿan Ḥaqā'iq al-Tanzīl* (Beirut: Dār al-Kutub al-ʿIlmiyyah, 1995), vol.4, p. 503; Muhammad ibn Ashur, *Tafsīr al-Taḥrīr wa al-Tanwīr* (Tunis: Maison Souhnoun, n.d.), vol.11, pp. 151-152.
86. Muhammad Asad, *The Message of the Qur'an* (Bristol: The Book Foundation, 2003), vol.1, p. 46.
87. Ibn Jarīr al-Ṭabarī, *Tafsīr al-Ṭabarī* (Beirut: Dār al-Kutub al-ʿIlmiyyah, 1999), vol.2, pp. 192-193.
88. Abū al-Ḥusayn ibn Fāris, *Muʿjam al-Maqāyīs fī al-Lughah* (Beirut: Dār al-Jīl, 1999), vol.1, p. 177-178.
89. Muḥammad al-Bukhārī, *Ṣaḥīḥ al-Bukhārī*, translated by Muhammad Muhsin Khan (Beirut: Dār al-ʿArabiyyah, 1985), vol.3, p. 395, no. 656.
90. Ibid., vol.5, p. 406, no. 583.
91. Ibid., p. 413, no. 595.
92. Muhammad al-Buti, *Fiqh al-Sīrah al-Nabawiyyah* (Damascus: Dār al-Salām, 2004), p. 265.
93. Muḥammad al-Bukhārī, *Ṣaḥīḥ al-Bukhārī*, translated by Muhammad Muhsin Khan, vol.5, p. 421, no. 605.
94. Ibid., p. 406, no. 584.
95. William Watt, *A Short History of Islam* (Oxford: Oneworld Publications, 1996), p. 9.
96. Muhammad al-Tabatabai, *Al-Mīzān fī Tafsīr al-Qur'ān* (Beirut: Mu'assasah al-Aʿlamī, 1997), vol.7, p. 325.
97. Muḥammad al-Qurṭubī, *Al-Jāmiʿ li Aḥkām al-Qur'an* (Beirut: Dār al-Fikr, 1998), vol.4, p. 56.
98. Maḥmūd al-Zamakhsharī, *Al-Kashshāf ʿan Ḥaqā'iq al-Tanzīl* (Beirut: Dār al-Kutub al-ʿIlmiyyah, 1995), vol.2, p. 53.
99. Fakhr al-Dīn al-Rāzī, *Mafātīḥ al-Ghayb* (Beirut: Dār al-Fikr, 2002), vol.7, p. 147.

100. Muḥammad al-Qurṭubī, *Al-Jāmiᶜ li Aḥkām al-Qur'ān* (Beirut: Dār al-Fikr, 1998), vol.4, p. 56.
101. Muhammad ibn Ashur, *Tafsīr al-Taḥrīr wa al-Tanwīr* (Tunis: Maison Souhnoun, n.d.), vol.3, pp. 427-432.
102. Muhammad al-Sharawi, *Tafsīr al-Shaᶜrāwī* (Cairo: Akhbār al-Yawm, 1991), vol.6, pp. 3855-3863.
103. Muhammad ibn Ashur, *Tafsīr al-Taḥrīr wa al-Tanwīr* (Tunis: Maison Souhnoun, n.d.), vol.3, p. 427.
104. Ibid., p. 428.
105. ᶜAbd al-Ḥaq ibn ᶜAṭiyyah, *Al-Muḥarrar al-Wajīz fī Tafsīr al-Kitāb al-ᶜAzīz* (Beirut: Dār al-Kutub al-ᶜIlmiyyah, 2001), vol.2, p. 332.
106. Sayyid Qutub, *In the Shade of the Qur'an*, edited by M.A. Salahi, translated by M.A. Salahi and A.A. Shamis (Leicester: The Islamic Foundation, 2002), vol.5, p. 271.
107. Muhammad Asad, *The Message of the Qur'an* (Bristol: The Book Foundation, 2003), vol.2, p. 216.
108. Muhammad al-Tabatabai, *Al-Mīzān fī Tafsīr al-Qur'ān* (Beirut: Mu'assasah al-Aᶜlamī, 1997), vol.7, p. 325.
109. Muhammad R. Rida, *Tafsīr al-Manār* (Beirut: Dār al-Kutub al-ᶜIlmiyyah, 1999), vol.7, p. 548.
110. Ibid., p. 549.
111. Muḥammad al-Bukhārī, *Ṣaḥīḥ al-Bukhārī*, translated by Muhammad Muhsin Khan (Beirut: Dār al-ᶜArabiyyah, 1985), vol.8, p. 44, no. 72.
112. Abū al-Ḥusayn Muslim, *Ṣaḥīḥ Muslim*, translated by Abdul Hamid Siddiqi, (Lahore: Ashraf Islamic Publishers, 1990), vol.iv, p. 187, no. 2599.
113. Abū al-Ḥusayn ibn Fāris, *Muᶜjam al-Maqāyīs fī al-Lughah* (Beirut: Dār al-Fikr, 1998), p. 801.
114. Al-Rāghib al-Aṣfahānī, *Mufradāt Alfāẓ al-Qur'ān*, edited by Safwan Dawudi (Damascus: Dār al-Qalam, 2002), p. 609.
115. Ibid.
116. Abū al-Ḥusayn ibn Fāris, *Muᶜjam al-Maqāyīs fī al-Lughah* (Beirut: Dār al-Fikr, 1998), p. 667.
117. Al-Rāghib al-Aṣfahānī, *Mufradāt Alfāẓ al-Qur'ān*, edited by Safwan Dawudi (Damascus: Dār al-Qalam, 2002), p. 574.
118. Abū al-Ḥusayn ibn Fāris, *Muᶜjam al-Maqāyīs fī al-Lughah* (Beirut: Dār al-Fikr, 1998), p. 569.
119. Al-Rāghib al-Aṣfahānī, *Mufradāt Alfāẓ al-Qur'ān*, edited by Safwan Dawudi (Damascus: Dār al-Qalam, 2002), p. 486.

120. Ibn Jarīr al-Ṭabarī, *Tafsīr al-Ṭabarī* (Beirut: Dār al-Kutub al-ʿIlmiyyah, 1999), vol.11, p. 256.
121. See the verse 45:14 in Isam al-Humaidan, *Al-Ṣaḥīḥ min Asbāb al-Nuzūl* (Beirut: Mu'assasah al-Rayyān, 1999) and Muqbil al-Wadii, *Al-Ṣaḥīḥ al-Musnad min Asbāb al-Nuzūl* (Ṣanʿā': Maktabah Ṣanʿā' al-Athariyyah, 2004).
122. See the verse 45:14 in Abd al-Aziz al-Humaidi, *Tafsīr Ibn ʿAbbās wa Marwiyyātuhu fī al-Tafsīr min Kutub al-Sunnah* (Makkah al-Mukarramah: Jāmiʿah Umm al-Qurā, n.d.).
123. Ibn Jarīr al-Ṭabarī, *Tafsīr al-Ṭabarī* (Beirut: Dār al-Kutub al-ʿIlmiyyah, 1999), vol.11, p. 256.
124. Ibn Jarīr al-Ṭabarī, *Tafsīr al-Ṭabarī*, edited by Ahmad Shakir and Mahmud Shakir (Cairo: Maktabah Ibn Taymiyyah, n.d.), vol.1.
125. Maḥmūd al-Zamakhsharī, *Al-Kashshāf ʿan Ḥaqā'iq al-Tanzīl* (Beirut: Dār al-Kutub al-ʿIlmiyyah, 1995), vol.4, p. 281.
126. Fakhr al-Dīn al-Rāzī, *Mafātīḥ al-Ghayb* (Beirut: Dār al-Fikr, 2002), vol.14, p. 264.
127. See Muhammad ibn Ashur, *Tafsīr al-Taḥrīr wa al-Tanwīr* (Tunis: Maison Souhnoun, n.d.), vol.10, pp. 338-343; Muhammad al-Tabatabai, *Al-Mīzān fī Tafsīr al-Qur'ān* (Beirut: Mu'assasah al-Aʿlamī, 1972), vol.18, pp. 163-164.
128. Ibn Jarīr al-Ṭabarī, *Tafsīr al-Ṭabarī* (Beirut: Dār al-Kutub al-ʿIlmiyyah, 1999), vol.7, p. 533.
129. Fadl Abbas, *Itqān al-Burhān fī ʿUlūm al-Qur'ān* (Amman: Dār al-Furqān, 1997), vol.2, pp. 11-12.
130. Muhammad Abu al-Nail, *Tafsīr al-Imām Mujāhid ibn Jabr* (Naṣr: Dār al-Fikr al-Islāmī al-Ḥadīthah, 1989), pp. 84-85.
131. Emphasis mine.
132. Ibn Jarīr al-Ṭabarī, *Tafsīr al-Ṭabarī* (Beirut: Dār al-Kutub al-ʿIlmiyyah, 1999), vol.7, p. 533.
133. Shams al-Dīn al-Dhahabī, *Mīzān al-Iʿtidāl fī Naqd al-Rijāl* (Dār al-Fikr al-ʿArabī), n.d.), vol.2, p. 363.
134. Ibn Ḥajar al-ʿAsqalānī, *Tahdhīb al-Tahdhīb* (Beirut: Mu'assasah al-Risālah, 2001), vol.2, p. 62.
135. Shams al-Dīn al-Dhahabī, *Mīzān al-Iʿtidāl fī Naqd al-Rijāl* (Dār al-Fikr al-ʿArabī), n.d.), vol.2, p. 363.
136. Ibn Jarīr al-Ṭabarī, *The History of al-Ṭabarī: General Introduction and From Creation to the Flood,* translated by Franz Rosenthal (Albany: State University of New York, 1989), vol.1, pp. 19-20.

137. Some scholars are of the opinion that "the verse of the sword" is 9:5, but others claim that every verse commanding jihad is called "the verse of the sword"; further explanation of this issue is provided in the last chapter.
138. Maḥmūd al-Zamakhsharī, *Al-Kashshāf ʿan Ḥaqā'iq al-Tanzīl* (Beirut: Dār al-Kutub al-ʿIlmiyyah, 1995), vol.2, p. 564.
139. Fakhr al-Dīn al-Rāzī, *Mafātīḥ al-Ghayb* (Beirut: Dār al-Fikr, 2002), vol.10, p. 215.
140. See Muhammad ibn Ashur, *Tafsīr al-Taḥrīr wa al-Tanwīr* (Tunis: Maison Souhnoun, n.d.), vol.6, p. 78; Muhammad al-Tabatabai, *Al-Mīzān fī Tafsīr al-Qur'ān* (Beirut: Mu'assasah al-Aʿlamī, 1972), vol.12, pp. 198-201; Muhammad al-Sharawi, *Tafsīr al-Shaʿrāwī* (Cairo: Akhbār al-Yawm, 1991), vol.13, pp. 7757-7758.
141. Ibn Jarīr al-Ṭabarī, *Tafsīr al-Ṭabarī* (Beirut: Dār al-Kutub al-ʿIlmiyyah, 1999), vol.11, p. 220.
142. Muhammad ibn Ashur, *Tafsīr al-Taḥrīr wa al-Tanwīr* (Tunis: Maison Souhnoun, n.d.), vol.10, p. 273.
143. Ibn Jarīr al-Ṭabarī, *Tafsīr al-Ṭabarī* (Beirut: Dār al-Kutub al-ʿIlmiyyah, 1999), vol.4, p. 498.
144. Ibid., p. 499.
145. Muhammad Abu Zahrah, *Zahrah al-Tafāsīr* (Dār al-Fikr al-ʿArabī, n.d.), vol.1, p. 41.
146. Maḥmūd al-Zamakhsharī, *Al-Kashshāf ʿan Ḥaqā'iq al-Tanzīl* (Beirut: Dār al-Kutub al-ʿIlmiyyah, 1995), vol.1, p. 604; Muhammad ibn Ashur, *Tafsīr al-Taḥrīr wa al-Tanwīr* (Tunis: Maison Souhnoun, n.d.), vol.3, p. 145.
147. Nāṣir al-Dīn al-Bayḍāwī, *Anwār al-Tanzīl wa Asrār al-Ta'wīl* (Beirut: Dār al-Kutub al-ʿIlmiyyah, 1988), vol.1, p. 259.
148. Muhammad al-Sharawi, *Tafsīr al-Shaʿrāwī* (Cairo: Akhbār al-Yawm, 1991), vol.1, pp. 524-525.
149. Ibn Jarīr al-Ṭabarī, *Tafsīr al-Ṭabarī* (Beirut: Dār al-Kutub al-ʿIlmiyyah, 1999), vol.1, p. 536.
150. Ibid., pp. 536-537.
151. Abū Yaʿlā al-Khalīlī, *Kitāb al-Irshād fī Maʿrifah ʿUlamā' al-Ḥadīth*, edited by Muhammad Idris, (Riad: Maktabah al-Rushd, n.d.), vol.1, p. 394.
152. Abū Bakr al-Baghdādī, *Tārīkh Baghdād* (Beirut: Dār al-Kutub al-ʿIlmiyyah, n.d.), vol.11, p. 429.
153. Ibn Manjuwayh al-Aṣbahānī, *Rijāl Ṣaḥīḥ Muslim*, edited by Abdullah al-Laithi (Beirut: Dār al-Maʿrifah, 1987), vol.2, p. 56.
154. Ibn Ḥajar al-ʿAsqalānī, *Tahdhīb al-Tahdhīb* (Beirut: Mu'assasah al-Risālah, 2001), vol.3, p. 171.

155. Ibid.
156. See note 137.
157. Nāṣir al-Dīn al-Bayḍāwī, *Anwār al-Tanzīl wa Asrār al-Ta'wīl* (Beirut: Dār al-Kutub al-ʿIlmiyyah, 1988), vol.1, p. 81.
158. Muhammad al-Amin al-Shanqiti, *Aḍwā' al-Bayān fī Īḍāḥ al-Qur'ān bi al-Qur'ān* (Cairo: Dār al-Ḥadīth, 2006), vol.1, p. 88.
159. Muhammad ibn Ashur, *Tafsīr al-Taḥrīr wa al-Tanwīr* (Tunis: Maison Souhnoun, n.d.), vol.1, pp. 670-671.
160. Muḥammad al-Bukhārī, *Ṣaḥīḥ al-Bukhārī*, translated by Muhammad Muhsin Khan (Beirut: Dār al-ʿArabiyyah, 1985), vol.6, pp. 261-267, no. 281.
161. Fadl Abbas, *Itqān al-Burhān fī ʿUlūm al-Qur'ān* (Amman: Dār al-Furqān, 1997), vol.1, p. 345.

Chapter 3

1. Muhammad Amarah, *Al-Islām wa al-Taʿaddudiyyah* (Cairo: Dār al-Rashād, 1997), p. 22.
2. Fuad Baali, *Society, State, and Urbanism: Ibn Khaldun's Sociological Thought* (Albany: State University of New York Press, 1988), p. 48.
3. Abū al-Ḥusayn ibn Fāris, *Muʿjam al-Maqāyīs fī al-Lughah* (Beirut: Dār al-Jīl, 1999), vol.4, p. 336.
4. Fuad Baali, *Society, State, and Urbanism: Ibn Khaldun's Sociological Thought* (Albany: State University of New York Press, 1988), p. 43.
5. Ibid., pp. 45-46.
6. Maurice Bucaille, *Al-Tawrāh wa al-Injīl wa al-Qur'ān wa al-ʿIlm* (Beirut: Al-Maktab al-Islāmī, 1987), p. 171.
7. Muhammad ibn Ashur, *Tafsīr al-Taḥrīr wa al-Tanwīr* (Tunis: Maison Souhnoun, n.d.), vol.7, p. 55.
8. Ibid., p. 56.
9. Al-Rāghib al-Aṣfahānī, *Mufradāt Alfāẓ al-Qur'ān* (Beirut: Dār al-Kutub al-ʿImiyyah, 1997), p. 350.
10. Fakhr al-Dīn al-Rāzī, *Mafātīḥ al-Ghayb* (Beirut: Dār al-Fikr, 2002), vol.4, p. 135.
11. ʿAbdullah Yūsuf ʿAlī, *The Meaning of The Holy Qur'an* (Beltsville, Maryland, U.S.A.: Amana Publications, 2008), p. 985.
12. Imad al-Din Khalil, *Ḥawla Tashkīl al-ʿAql al-Muslim* (Herndon: The International Institute of Islamic Thought, 1991), pp. 150-152.
13. Kenneth Cragg, *The Qur'an and the West* (London: Melisend, 2006).

14. Muhammad R. Rida, *Tafsīr al-Manār* (Beirut: Dār al-Kutub al-ʿIlmiyyah, 1999), vol.4, p. 263.
15. Fakhr al-Dīn al-Rāzī, *Mafātīḥ al-Ghayb* (Beirut: Dār al-Fikr, 2002), vol.5, p. 167.
16. Ibid.
17. Abū al-Ḥusayn ibn Fāris, *Muʿjam al-Maqāyīs fī al-Lughah* (Beirut: Dār al-Jīl, 1999), vol.2, p. 110.
18. Muhammad ibn Ashur, *Tafsīr al-Taḥrīr wa al-Tanwīr* (Tunis: Maison Souhnoun, n.d.), vol.8, p. 89.
19. Ibid.
20. ʿAbdullah Yūsuf ʿAlī, *The Meaning of The Holy Qur'an* (Beltsville, Maryland, U.S.A.: Amana Publications, 2008), p. 1655.
21. Ibid.
22. Romans 2:15, *New American Standard Bible* (1995).
23. J. Budziszewski, "Act Naturally," *Australian Presbyterian*, June 2005: 4-8.
24. Fakhr al-Dīn al-Rāzī, *Mafātīḥ al-Ghayb* (Beirut: Dār al-Fikr, 2002), vol.15, p. 223.
25. Henry Coribn, *History of Islamic Philosofy*, translated by Liadain Sherrard (London: Kegan Paul International, n.d.), p. 3.
26. Seyyed H. Nasr, *The Heart of Islam: Enduring Values for Humanity* (New York: Harper Collins Publishers, 2002), p. 8.
27. "Their mothers are different, but their religion is one" means that prophets had different legislations but one religion.
28. Muḥammad al-Bukhārī, *Ṣaḥīḥ al-Bukhārī*, translated by Muhammad Muhsin Khan (Beirut: Dār al-ʿArabiyyah, 1985), vol.4, p. 434, no. 652.
29. Seyyed H. Nasr, *The Heart of Islam: Enduring Values for Humanity* (New York: Harper Collins Publishers, 2002), p. 4.
30. Abdulaziz O. Altwaijri, *Islam and Inter-religious Coexistence on the Threshold of the 21st Century* (Rabat: ISESCO, 1998), p. 31.
31. Jonathan Sacks, *The Dignity of Difference: How to Avoid the Clash of Civilizations* (London: Continuum, 2002), p. 21.
32. Abū Ḥayyān al-Tawḥīdī, *Al-Muqābasāt*, edited by Hasan al-Sandubi (Cairo: Dār Suʿād al-Ṣabāḥ, 1992), p. 142, no. 4.
33. ʿAbdullah Yūsuf ʿAlī, *The Meaning of The Holy Qur'an*, (Beltsville, Maryland, U.S.A.: Amana Publications, 2008), p.1363.
34. Jonathan Sacks, *The Dignity of Difference: How to Avoid the Clash of Civilizations* (London: Continuum, 2002), pp. 14-15.
35. Ibid., p. 21.

36. Muzammil Siddiqi, *Islam for Today*, 5 May 2001, http://www.islamforto-day.com/diversity.htm (accessed November 2, 2010).
37. Ishraq Khafagi, Amira Zakaria, Ahmed Dewedar, and Khaled al-Zahdany, "A Voyage in the World of Plants as Mentioned in the Holy Quran." *International Journal of Botany*, 2 March 2006, pp.242-251.
38. Maḥmūd al-Zamakhsharī, *Al-Kashshāf ͑an Ḥaqā'iq al-Tanzīl* (Beirut: Dār al-Kutub al-͑Ilmiyyah, 1995), vol.2, p. 493.
39. Muhammad ibn Ashur, *Tafsīr al-Taḥrīr wa al-Tanwīr* (Tunis: Maison Souhnoun, n.d.), vol.6, p. 86.
40. Ibn Jarīr al-Ṭabarī, *Tafsīr al-Ṭabarī* (Beirut: Dār al-Kutub al-͑Ilmiyyah, 1999), vol.7, p. 336.
41. Ibid., pp. 338-339.
42. Muhammad ibn Ashur, *Tafsīr al-Taḥrīr wa al-Tanwīr* (Tunis: Maison Souhnoun, n.d.), vol.9, pp. 300-304.
43. Ibid., vol.3, p. 206.
44. Ibid., p. 213.
45. Maḥmūd al-Zamakhsharī, *Al-Kashshāf ͑an Ḥaqā'iq al-Tanzīl* (Beirut: Dār al-Kutub al-͑Ilmiyyah, 1995), vol.3, p. 586.
46. Ibn Jarīr al-Ṭabarī, *Tafsīr al-Ṭabarī* (Beirut: Dār al-Kutub al-͑Ilmiyyah, 1999), vol.1, p. 558.
47. Maḥmūd al-Zamakhsharī, *Al-Kashshāf ͑an Ḥaqā'iq al-Tanzīl* (Beirut: Dār al-Kutub al-͑Ilmiyyah, 1995), vol.3, p. 587.
48. Said Nursi, *Ṣayqal al-Islām*, translated by Ihsan Qasim al-Salihi (Cairo: Sharikah Sūzlar, 2004), p. 339.
49. Fakhr al-Dīn al-Rāzī, *Mafātīḥ al-Ghayb* (Beirut: Dār al-Fikr, 2002), vol.13, pp. 11-12.
50. Muhammad ibn Ashur, *Tafsīr al-Taḥrīr wa al-Tanwīr* (Tunis: Maison Souhnoun, n.d.), vol.9, p. 279.
51. Multiplicity of perceptions towards religious truth is a terrestrial fact which should not be misused as a reason for mutual judgement and accusations, since such actions exclusively pertain to God in the eschatological context of human accountability.
52. Ibn Jarīr al-Ṭabarī, *Tafsīr al-Ṭabarī* (Beirut: Dār al-Kutub al-͑Ilmiyyah, 1999), vol.7, p. 141; Muḥammad al-Qurṭubī, *Al-Jāmi͑ li Aḥkām al-Qur'ān* (Beirut: Dār al-Fikr, 1998), vol.5, p. 101; Muhammad ibn Ashur, *Tafsīr al-Taḥrīr wa al-Tanwīr*, vol.5 (Tunis: Maison Souhnoun, n.d.), pp. 189-190.
53. Ibn Jarīr al-Ṭabarī, *Tafsīr al-Ṭabarī* (Beirut: Dār al-Kutub al-͑Ilmiyyah, 1999), vol.4, p. 610; Fakhr al-Dīn al-Rāzī, *Mafātīḥ al-Ghayb* (Beirut: Dār al-Fikr, 2002), vol.6, p. 14.

54. Ibn Jarīr al-Ṭabarī, *Tafsīr al-Ṭabarī* (Beirut: Dār al-Kutub al-ʿIlmiyyah, 1999), vol.4, p. 610.
55. Ibid., vol.2, p. 5.
56. Sayyid Qutub, *In the Shade of the Qur'an*, edited by M.A. Salahi, translated by M.A. Salahi and A.A. Shamis (Leicester: The Islamic Foundation, 1999), vol.1, p. 134.
57. This is the alternative translation given by ʿAbdullah Yūsuf ʿAlī.
58. Muhammad ibn Ashur, *Tafsīr al-Taḥrīr wa al-Tanwīr* (Tunis: Maison Souhnoun, n.d.), vol.1, p. 42.
59. Fakhr al-Dīn al-Rāzī, *Mafātīḥ al-Ghayb* (Beirut: Dār al-Fikr, 2002)vol.2, p. 146.
60. Ibn Jarīr al-Ṭabarī, *Tafsīr al-Ṭabarī* (Beirut: Dār al-Kutub al-ʿIlmiyyah, 1999), vol.8, p. 140.
61. Maḥmūd al-Zamakhsharī, *Al-Kashshāf ʿan Ḥaqā'iq al-Tanzīl* (Beirut: Dār al-Kutub al-ʿIlmiyyah, 1995), vol.2, p. 663.
62. Muhammad ibn Ashur, *Tafsīr al-Taḥrīr wa al-Tanwīr* (Tunis: Maison Souhnoun, n.d.), vol.6, p. 194.
63. *Q-w-l* taken as a noun *qawl*, means "a word" the plural of which is *aqwāl*, "words", whereas taken as a verb *qāl-yaqūl*, it means "to say, to utter words".
64. Abu Zayd al-Idrisi, *Dirāsāt Qur'āniyyah*, 15 10 2008, http://www.almulta-ka.net (accessed 01 17, 2011).
65. ʿAlī al-Rummānī; Ḥamd al-Khaṭṭābī and ʿAbd al-Qādir al-Jurjānī, *Thalāth Rasā'il Fī Iʿjāz al-Qur'ān* (Cairo: Dār al-Maʿārif, n.d.), pp. 21-27.
66. Fakhr al-Dīn al-Rāzī, *Mafātīḥ al-Ghayb* (Beirut: Dār al-Fikr, 2002), vol.11, p. 59.
67. Ibid.
68. Ibid.
69. Badr al-Dīn al-Zarkashī, *Al-Burhān fī ʿUlūm al-Qur'ān* (Beirut: Dār al-Jīl, 1988), vol.1, p. 193.
70. Muhammad ibn Ashur, *Tafsīr al-Taḥrīr wa al-Tanwīr* (Tunis: Maison Souhnoun, n.d.), vol.7, p. 224.
71. Ibid., p. 225.
72. In the researcher's opinion "forgive them" is more appropriate than "keep clear of them" as a meaning of *"fa'aʿriḍ ʿanhum"* in this particular verse.
73. In the researcher's opinion "advise them" is more appropriate than "admonish them" as a meaning of *"wa ʿiẓhum"* in this particular verse.
74. Toshihiko Izutsu, *Ethico-Religious Concepts in the Qur'an*, (McGill-Queen's University Press, 2002).

75. Fakhr al-Dīn al-Rāzī, *Mafātīḥ al-Ghayb* (Beirut: Dār al-Fikr, 2002), vol.5, p. 164.
76. Muhammad ibn Ashur, *Tafsīr al-Taḥrīr wa al-Tanwīr* (Tunis: Maison Souhnoun, n.d.), vol.2, p. 108.
77. Maḥmūd al-Zamakhsharī, *Al-Kashshāf ʿan Ḥaqā'iq al-Tanzīl* (Beirut: Dār al-Kutub al-ʿIlmiyyah, 1995), vol.1, p. 516.
78. Fakhr al-Dīn al-Rāzī, *Mafātīḥ al-Ghayb* (Beirut: Dār al-Fikr, 2002), vol.5, p. 165.
79. Ibn Jarīr al-Ṭabarī, *Tafsīr al-Ṭabarī* (Beirut: Dār al-Kutub al-ʿIlmiyyah, 1999), vol.7, p. 473; Fakhr al-Dīn al-Rāzī, *Mafātīḥ al-Ghayb* (Beirut: Dār al-Fikr, 2002), vol.10, pp. 123-128.
80. According to all sources of Qur'anic exegesis the meaning of *kalimah sawā'* is either "a just word" or "a common word." In the researcher's opinion the most accurate meaning of *kalimah sawā'* seems to be "an equitable word" which combines between "just" and "common."
81. Muhammad ibn Ashur, *Tafsīr al-Taḥrīr wa al-Tanwīr* (Tunis: Maison Souhnoun, n.d.), vol.2, p. 268.
82. ʿAbd al-Ḥaq ibn ʿAṭiyyah, *Al-Muḥarrar al-Wajīz fī Tafsīr al-Kitāb al-ʿAzīz* (Beirut: Dār al-Kutub al-ʿIlmiyyah, 2001), vol.1, p. 449.
83. Hassan Hanafi, *Religious Dialogue and Revolution* (Cairo: The Anglo-Egyptian Bookshop, 1976), p. 1.
84. Ibid.
85. Isam al-Humaidan, *Al-Ṣaḥīḥ min Asbāb al-Nuzūl* (Beirut: Mu'assasah al-Rayyān, 1999), pp. 27-28.
86. Abū al-Ḥasan al-Wāḥidī, *Asbāb al-Nuzūl* (Cairo: Maktabah al-Mutanabbī, n.d.), p. 23. Trans. Mokrane Guezzou, http://www.altafsir.com/asbabalnuzol.asp?soraname=1&ayah=0&img=a&languageid=2
87. Ibn Jarīr al-Ṭabarī, *Tafsīr al-Ṭabarī* (Beirut: Dār al-Kutub al-ʿIlmiyyah, 1999), vol.1, p. 542.
88. Fakhr al-Dīn al-Rāzī, *Mafātīḥ al-Ghayb* (Beirut: Dār al-Fikr, 2002), vol.2, p. 10.
89. Ibn Jarīr al-Ṭabarī, *Tafsīr al-Ṭabarī* (Beirut: Dār al-Kutub al-ʿIlmiyyah, 1999), vol.1, p. 615. Al-Humaidan judged the narration's chain of transmission as *ḥasan*, good, which falls into the category of acceptable hadith. See Isam al-Humaidan, *Al-Ṣaḥīḥ min Asbāb al-Nuzūl* (Beirut: Mu'assasah al-Rayyān, 1999), p. 31.

Chapter 4

1. Muhammad Amarah, *Al-Taʿaddudiyyah: Al-Ru'yah al-Islāmiyyah wa al-Taḥaddiyāt al-Gharbiyyah* (Cairo: Dār Nahḍah Miṣr, 1997).
2. Muhammad Legenhausen, "A Muslim's Non-Reductive Religious Pluralism." In *Islam and Global Dialogue*, p. 60.
3. Abdulaziz O. Altwaijri, *Islam and Inter-religious Coexistence on the Threshold of the 21st Century* (Rabat: ISESCO, 1998), p. 37.
4. Ali Asani, "So That You May Know One Another: A Muslim American Reflects on Pluralism and Islam." *Annals of the American Academy of Political and Social Science*, July 2003: 40-51, p. 42.
5. Badr al-Dīn al-Zarkashī, *Al-Burhān fī ʿUlūm al-Qur'ān* (Beirut: Dār al-Jīl, 1988), vol.1, p. 194.
6. Fadl Abbas, *Itqān al-Burhān fī ʿUlūm al-Qur'ān* (Amman: Dār al-Furqān, 1997), vol.1, p. 380.
7. *Bāhilī* is a person belonging to the Arab tribe of *Bāhilah*, which was perceived as a tribe of low social status among the Arabs.
8. Muhammad ibn Ashur, *Tafsīr al-Taḥrīr wa al-Tanwīr* (Tunis: Maison Souhnoun, n.d.), vol.10, p. 258.
9. Sayyid Qutub, *In the Shade of the Qur'an*, edited by M.A. Salahi, translated by M.A. Salahi and A.A. Shamis, (Leicester: The Islamic Foundation, 2009), vol.xvi, p. 69.
10. Muhammad M. Hijazi, *Al-Tafsīr al-Wāḍiḥ* (Al-Zaqāzīq: Dār al-Tafsīr, 2003), vol.3, p. 498.
11. Burhān al-Dīn al-Biqāʿī, *Naẓmu al-Durar fī Tanāsub al-Āyāt wa al-Suwar* (Beirut: Dār al-Kutub al-ʿIlmiyyah, 1995), vol.7, p. 235.
12. Muhammad ibn Ashur, *Tafsīr al-Taḥrīr wa al-Tanwīr* (Tunis: Maison Souhnoun, n.d.), vol.10, p. 258.
13. Said Nursi, *Ṣayqal al-Islām*, translated by Ihsan Qasim al-Salihi (Cairo: Sharikah Sūzlar, 2004), p. 339.
14. Ibn Ḥajar al-ʿAsqalānī, *Fatḥ al-Bārī: Sharḥ Ṣaḥīḥ al-Bukhārī* (Damascus: Dār al-Fayḥā', 1997), vol.6, p. 642, no. 3489.
15. Muhammad Abu al-Nail, *Tafsīr al-Imām Mujāhid ibn Jabr* (Naṣr: Dār al-Fikr al-Islāmī al-Ḥadīthah, 1989), p. 610.
16. Ibn Jarīr al-Ṭabarī, *Tafsīr al-Ṭabarī* (Beirut: Dār al-Kutub al-ʿIlmiyyah, 1999), vol.11, p. 397; Maḥmūd al-Zamakhsharī, *Al-Kashshāf ʿan Ḥaqā'iq al-Tanzīl* (Beirut: Dār al-Kutub al-ʿIlmiyyah, 1995), vol.4, p. 365.
17. Fakhr al-Dīn al-Rāzī, *Mafātīḥ al-Ghayb* (Beirut: Dār al-Fikr, 2002),vol.14, p. 137.

18. Ibid., p. 138.
19. Ibid., pp. 140-141.
20. Sayyid Qutub, *In the Shade of the Qur'an*, edited by M.A. Salahi, translated by M.A. Salahi and A.A. Shamis (Leicester: The Islamic Foundation, 2009), vol.xvi, p. 97.
21. Sayyid Qutub *Fī Ẓilāl al-Qur'ān* (Beirut: Dār al-Shurūq, 1996), vol.6, p. 3348.
22. Muhammad ibn Ashur, *Tafsīr al-Taḥrīr wa al-Tanwīr* (Tunis: Maison Souhnoun, n.d.), vol.10, pp. 259-260.
23. Ibid., p. 260.
24. Muhammad al-Tabatabai, *Al-Mīzān fī Tafsīr al-Qur'ān* (Beirut: Mu'assasah al-Aᶜlamī, 1972), vol.18, p. 326.
25. Tariq Ramadan, "Interreligious Dialogue from an Islamic Perspective." In *How to Conquer the Barriers to Intercultural Dialogue: Christianity, Islam and Judaism*, by Timmerman Christiane and Barbara Segaert, 85-104, (Brussels: P.I.E, Peter Lang, 2007).
26. Abdelmajid Najar, *The Islamic Civilizing Process* (Beirut: Dār al-Gharb al-Islāmī, 1999), vol.1, pp. 59-63.
27. Jeremy Henzell-Thomas, *The Challenge of Pluralism and the Middle Way of Islam* (Richmond, UK: AMSS, 2002), p. 2.
28. Ibn Jarīr al-Ṭabarī, *Tafsīr al-Ṭabarī* (Beirut: Dār al-Kutub al-ᶜIlmiyyah, 1999), vol.4, p. 398.
29. Muhammad al-Zawaiti, *Tafsīr al-Ḍaḥḥāk* (Cairo: Dār al-Salām, 1999), vol.1, p. 316.
30. Muhammad Abu al-Nail, *Tafsīr al-Imām Mujāhid ibn Jabr* (Naṣr: Dār al-Fikr al-Islāmī al-Ḥadīthah, 1989), p. 299.
31. Ibn Jarīr al-Ṭabarī, *Tafsīr al-Ṭabarī* (Beirut: Dār al-Kutub al-ᶜIlmiyyah, 1999), vol.4, p. 400.
32. Muhammad al-Zawaiti, *Tafsīr al-Ḍaḥḥāk* (Cairo: Dār al-Salām, 1999), vol.1, p. 398.
33. Badr al-Dīn al-Zarkashī, *Al-Burhān fī ᶜUlūm al-Qur'ān* (Beirut: Dār al-Jīl, 1988), vol.1, p. 194.
34. Underlined by the researcher.
35. Ibn Jarīr al-Ṭabarī, *Tafsīr al-Ṭabarī* (Beirut: Dār al-Kutub al-ᶜIlmiyyah, 1999), vol.4, pp. 400-401.
36. Maḥmūd al-Zamakhsharī, *Al-Kashshāf ᶜan Ḥaqā'iq al-Tanzīl* (Beirut: Dār al-Kutub al-ᶜIlmiyyah, 1995), vol.1, p. 590.
37. Ibid.

38. Ibid.
39. Al-Qāsim ibn Salām, *Faḍā'l al-Qur'ān wa Ma'ālimuh wa Ādābuh*, edited by Ahmad al-Khaiati (The Kingdom of Morocco: Wizārah al-Awqāf wa al-Shu'ūn al-Islāmiyyh, 1995), vol.2, p. 45, no. 444.
40. Ibn Ḥajar al-'Asqalānī, *Tahdhīb al-Tahdhīb* (Beirut: Mu'assasah al-Risālah, 2001), vol.2, p. 229.
41. Ibid., vol.3, pp. 115-116.
42. Ibid., vol.4, p. 490.
43. Aḥmad ibn Ḥanbal, *Al-Musnad* (Cairo: Dār al-Ḥadīth, 1995), vol.17, p. 623, no. 25424.
44. Aḥmad ibn Ḥanbal, *Musnad al-Imām Aḥmad*, edited by Shuaib al-Arnaut, (Beirut: Mu'assasah al-Risālah, 2001), vol.42, p. 353, no. 57425.
45. By the term "the Two Shaikhs," in the field of Hadith, are meant al-Bukhārī and Muslim.
46. Muḥammad al-Ḥākim, *Al-Mustadrak 'alā al-Ṣaḥīḥayn*, edited by Mustafa Ata (Beirut: Dār al-Kutub al-'Imiyyah, 1990), vol.2, p. 340, no. 3210.
47. Badr al-Dīn al-Zarkashī, *Al-Burhān fī 'Ulūm al-Qur'ān* (Beirut: Dār al-Jīl, 1988), vol.1, p. 194.
48. Muḥammad al-Bukhārī, *Ṣaḥīḥ al-Bukhārī*, translated by Muhammad Muhsin Khan (Beirut: Dār al-'Arabiyyah, 1985), vol.1, p. 38, no. 43.
49. Muslim scholar (d. 934), and by who Fakhr al-Dīn al-Rāzī was influenced.
50. Muhammad Abu Zahrah, *Zahrah al-Tafāsīr* (Dār al-Fikr al-'Arabī, n.d.), vol.1, p. 41.
51. Muhammad al-Ghazali, *Naẓarāt fī al-Qur'ān* (Cairo: Nahḍah Miṣr, 2005), p. 194.
52. Ibn Jarīr al-Ṭabarī, *Tafsīr al-Ṭabarī* (Beirut: Dār al-Kutub al-'Ilmiyyah, 1999), vol.4, p. 405.
53. Muhammad ibn Ashur, *Tafsīr al-Taḥrīr wa al-Tanwīr* (Tunis: Maison Souhnoun, n.d.), vol.3, p. 74.
54. The subtle nuances of the conjunction *wāw al-'aṭf* are lost in the process of English translation.
55. Maḥmūd al-Zamakhsharī, *Al-Kashshāf 'an Ḥaqā'iq al-Tanzīl* (Beirut: Dār al-Kutub al-'Ilmiyyah, 1995), vol.1, p. 591.
56. Muhammad ibn Ashur, *Tafsīr al-Taḥrīr wa al-Tanwīr* (Tunis: Maison Souhnoun, n.d.), vol.3, p. 87.
57. Muḥammad al-Qurṭubī, *Al-Jāmi' li Aḥkām al-Qur'ān* (Beirut: Dār al-Fikr, 1998), vol.3, p. 18.
58. Ibn al-Qayyim al-Jawziyyah, *Zād al-Muhājir*, edited by Said Ibrahim Sadiq (Cairo: Dār al-Ḥadīth, n.d.), p. 10.

59. Muhammad R. Rida, *Tafsīr al-Manār* (Beirut: Dār al-Kutub al-ʿIlmiyyah, 1999), vol.6, p. 107.
60. Abd al-Rahman al-Sadi, *Taysīr al-Karīm al-Raḥmān fī Tafsīr Kalām al-Mannān* (Beirut: Mu'assasah al-Risālah, 2000), p. 219.
61. Ibid.
62. Muhammad al-Tabatabai, *Al-Mīzān fī Tafsīr al-Qur'ān* (Beirut: Mu'assasah al-Aʿlamī, 1997), vol.5, p. 166.
63. Muhammad al-Sharawi, *Tafsīr al-Shaʿrāwī* (Cairo: Akhbār al-Yawm, 1991), vol.5, p. 2906.
64. This is the alternative translation given by Abdullah Yusuf Ali.
65. Ibn Jarīr al-Ṭabarī, *Tafsīr al-Ṭabarī* (Beirut: Dār al-Kutub al-ʿIlmiyyah, 1999), vol.2, p. 33.
66. Ibid.
67. Emphasis mine.
68. Ibn Jarīr al-Ṭabarī, *Tafsīr al-Ṭabarī* (Beirut: Dār al-Kutub al-ʿIlmiyyah, 1999), vol.4, p. 614.
69. Muhammad ibn Ashur, *Tafsīr al-Taḥrīr wa al-Tanwīr* (Tunis: Maison Souhnoun, n.d.), vol.1, p. 42.
70. Ibid., vol.3, p. 224.
71. Ibid., vol.1, p. 42.
72. Muhammad al-Sharawi, *Tafsīr al-Shaʿrāwī* (Cairo: Akhbār al-Yawm, 1991), vol.1, p. 638.
73. Fakhr al-Dīn al-Rāzī, *Mafātīḥ al-Ghayb* (Beirut: Dār al-Fikr, 2002), vol.6, p. 14.
74. *ʿAzīz:* title of a nobleman or officer of Court, of high rank.
75. Muhammad al-Sharawi, *Tafsīr al-Shaʿrāwī* (Cairo: Akhbār al-Yawm, 1991), vol.11, pp. 6884-6885.
76. Stanislaw Grodz, "'Vie with Each Other in Good Works': What Can a Roman Catholic Missionary Order Learn from Entering into Closer Contact with Muslims?," *Islam and Christian-Muslim Relations* (Routledge) 18 (2007): 205-218, p. 207.
77. Ibid.
78. Muhammad Asad, *The Message of the Qur'an* (Bristol: The Book Foundation, 2003), vol.4, p. 570.
79. Maḥmūd al-Zamakhsharī, *Al-Kashshāf ʿan Ḥaqā'iq al-Tanzīl* (Beirut: Dār al-Kutub al-ʿIlmiyyah, 1995), vol.3, p. 157.
80. Fakhr al-Dīn al-Rāzī, *Mafātīḥ al-Ghayb* (Beirut: Dār al-Fikr, 2002), vol.12, p. 40.

81. Muhammad al-Said Tantawi, *Al-Tafsīr al-Wasīṭ li al al-Qur'ān al-Karīm* (Cairo: Maṭbaʿah al-Saʿādah, 1985), vol.9, p. 72.
82. Badr al-Dīn al-Zarkashī, *Al-Burhān fī ʿUlūm al-Qur'ān* (Beirut: Dār al-Jīl, 1988), vol.1, p. 194.
83. Ibn Jarīr al-Ṭabarī, *Tafsīr al-Ṭabarī* (Beirut: Dār al-Kutub al-ʿIlmiyyah, 1999), vol.9, p. 162.
84. Muḥammad al-Bukhārī, *Ṣaḥīḥ al-Bukhārī*, translated by Muhammad Muhsin Khan (Beirut: Dār al-ʿArabiyyah, 1985), vol.1, p. 4, no. 3.
85. Ibn Jarīr al-Ṭabarī, *Tafsīr al-Ṭabarī* (Beirut: Dār al-Kutub al-ʿIlmiyyah, 1999), vol.9, pp. 163-164.
86. Muhammad al-Sharawi, *Tafsīr al-Shaʿrāwī* (Cairo: Akhbār al-Yawm, 1991), vol.16, pp. 9838-9840.
87. Muhammad al-Tabatabai, *Al-Mīzān fī Tafsīr al-Qur'ān* (Beirut: Mu'assasah al-Aʿlamī, 1972), vol.14, pp. 385-386.
88. Muhammad Asad, *The Message of the Qur'an* (Bristol: The Book Foundation, 2003), vol.1, p. 68.
89. Muhammad Abu Zahrah, *Tanẓīm al-Islam lī al-Mujtamaʿ* (Cairo: Dār al-Fikr al-ʿArabī, n.d.), p. 60.

Chapter 5

1. David Marshall, *God, Muhammad and the Unbelievers* (London: Curzon Press, 1999).
2. ʿAbd al-Raḥmān ibn Khaldūn, *The Muqaddimah: An Introduction to History,* translated by Franz Rosenthal (Princeton: Princeton University Press, 1967), vol.1, p. 302.
3. ʿAbd al-Raḥmān ibn Khaldūn, *The Muqaddimah: An Introduction to History,* translated by Franz Rosenthal (Princeton and Oxford: Princeton University Press, 2005), p. 119.
4. Carl Brockelmann, *History of the Islamic Peoples* (London: Routledge and Kegan Paul, 1949), p. 4.
5. Ibid.
6. Ḥājjī Khalīfah, *Kashf al-Ẓunūn* (Dār al-Fikr, 1982), vol.1, p. 204.
7. ʿAlī ibn al-Athīr, *Al-Kāmil fī al-Tārīkh* (Beirut: Dār al-Kutub al-ʿIlmiyyah, 1998), vol.1, p. 410.
8. Ignaz Goldziher, *Muslim Studies*, translated by C.R. and Stern, S.M. Barber, (London: George Allen and Unwin Ltd, 1967), p. 21.
9. Fathi Osman, *The Other* (USA: Pharos Foundation, 2008), p. 37.
10. Muhammad Asad, *The Message of the Qur'an* (Bristol: The Book Foundation, 2003), vol.4, p. 570.

11. Muhammad al-Sharawi, *Tafsīr al-Shaᶜrāwī* (Cairo: Akhbār al-Yawm, 1991), vol.16, pp. 9838-9840.
12. Abū al-Ḥusayn ibn Fāris, *Muᶜjam al-Maqāyīs fī al-Lughah* (Beirut: Dār al-Fikr, 1998), p. 874.
13. Al-Rāghib al-Aṣfahānī, *Mufradāt Alfāẓ al-*Qur'ān, edited by Safwan Dawudi (Damascus: Dār al-Qalam, 2002), p. 655.
14. Muḥammad ibn Manẓūr, *Lisān al-ᶜArab* (Beirut: Dār Iḥyā' al-Turāth al-ᶜArabī, Mu'assasah al-Tārīkh al-ᶜArabī, 1999), vol.11, p. 33; Abū al-Ḥusayn ibn Fāris, *Muᶜjam al-Maqāyīs fī al-Lughah* (Beirut: Dār al-Fikr, 1998), p. 874.
15. Rohi Baalbaki, *Al-Mawrid: A Modern Arabic-English Dictionary* (Beirut: Dār al-ᶜIlm li al-malāyīn, 2001), p. 850.
16. Muḥammad ibn Manẓūr, *Lisān al-ᶜArab* (Beirut: Dār Iḥyā' al-Turāth al-ᶜArabī, Mu'assasah al-Tārīkh al-ᶜArabī, 1999), vol.11, p. 35; ᶜUthmān ibn Jinnī, *Al-Munṣif* (Al-Jumhuriyyah al-ᶜArabiyyah al-Muttaḥidah: Al-Idārah al-ᶜĀmmah li al-Thaqāfah, 1960), vol.3, p. 277.
17. Rohi Baalbaki, *Al-Mawrid: A Modern Arabic-English Dictionary* (Beirut: Dār al-ᶜIlm li al-Malāyīn, 2001), p. 841.
18. The second source noun *muqātalah* does not exist in the Qur'an.
19. Jamal Abu Hassan, "Al-ᶜAlāqah bayn al-Muslimīn wa Ahl al-Kitāb fī Ḍaw' al-Aḥkām al-Qur'āniyyah." An Unpublished Essay.
20. It seems that the expression "the verse of the sword" was not applied among the Companions and their Successors. Even exegetes such as al-Ṭabarī (d. 610 AH), al-Zamakhsharī (d. 538 AH), and al-Rāzī (d. 606 AH), do not mention the expression "the verse of the sword." It appears that Ibn Kathīr (d. 774 AH) emphasised this expression where in relation to 9:5 he states "and this precious verse is the verse of the sword." See Ismāᶜīl ibn Kathīr, *Tafsīr al-Qur'ān al-ᶜAẓīm* (Beirut: Mu'assasah al-Rayyān, 1998), vol.2, p. 443. On the other hand, Ibn Taymiyyah (d. 728 AH) is of the opinion that "every verse in the Qur'an containing an imperative of jihad is called 'the verse of the sword.'" See Aḥmad ibn Taymiyyah, *Qāᶜidah Mukhtaṣarah fī Qitāl al-Kuffār wa Muhādanatihim wa Taḥrīm Qatlihim li Mujarrad Kufrihim*, edited by Abd al-Aziz Abdullah al-Zair Al Hamd (Riyad: Maktabah al-Malik Fahd al-Waṭaniyyah, 2004), pp. 115-116.
21. ᶜAbd al-Raḥmān ibn Abī Ḥātim, *Al-Tafsīr bi al-Ma'thūr* (Beirut: Dār al-Kutub al-ᶜIlmiyyah, 2006), vol.5, p. 10.
22. Jalāl al-Dīn al-Suyūṭī, *Al-Durr al-Manthūr fī al-Tafsīr bi al-Ma'thūr* (Beirut: Dār al-Kutub al-ᶜIlmiyyah, 2000), vol.3, p. 384.

23. ʿAbd al-Ḥaq ibn ʿAṭiyyah, *Al-Muḥarrar al-Wajīz fī Tafsīr al-Kitāb al-ʿAzīz* (Beirut: Dār al-Kutub al-ʿIlmiyyah, 2001), vol.3, p. 8.
24. Ibn Ḥajar al-ʿAsqalānī, *Tahdhīb al-Tahdhīb* (Beirut: Mu'assasah al-Risālah, 2001), vol.1, p. 320.
25. Ibid., p. 321.
26. Ibn Ḥajar al-ʿAsqalānī, *Taqrīb al-Tahdhīb*, edited by Abu al-Ashbal Sagir Ahmad Shagif al-Bakistani (Dār al-ʿĀṣimah, n.d.), p. 205.
27. Italics mine.
28. Muḥammad al-Samarqandī, *Tafsīr al-Samarqandī – Baḥr al-ʿUlūm*, edited by Mahmud Matraji (Beirut: Dār al-Fikr, 1997),vol.2, p. 39.
29. Al-Ḥusayn ibn al-Faḍl (d. 282H-895 C.E.) was a prominent scholar of Qur'anic exegesis. His particular area of expertise was in the field of linguistic exegesis. See Shams al-Dīn M. al-Dāwudī, *Ṭabaqāt al-Mufassirīn*, edited by Ali Muhammad Umar (Cairo: Maktabah Wahbah, 1994), vol.1, p. 156. He was praised by Ibn Ḥajar who said that Al-Ḥusayn ibn al-Faḍl "is one of the senior and noble scholars." See Ibn Ḥajar al-ʿAsqalānī, *Lisān al-Mīzān*, edited by Adil Ahmad Abd al-Mawjud and Ali Muhammad Muawwad (Beirut: Dār al-Kutub al-ʿIlmiyyah, 1996), vol.2, p. 353.
30. Al-Ḥusayn al-Bagawī, *Maʿālim al-Tanzīl fī al-Tafsīr wa al-Ta'wīl* (Beirut: Dār al-Fikr, 2002), vol.3, p. 7.
31. Muḥammad al-Qurṭubī, *Al-Jāmiʿ li Aḥkām al-Qur'ān* (Beirut: Dār al-Fikr, 1998), vol.4, p. 13.
32. Ismāʿīl ibn Kathīr, *Tafsīr al-Qur'ān al-ʿAẓīm* (Beirut: Mu'assasah al-Rayyān, 1998), vol.2, p. 443.
33. Ibn Jarīr al-Ṭabarī, *Tafsīr al-Ṭabarī*, edited by Ahmad Shakir Mahmud Shakir (Cairo: Maktabah Ibn Taymiyyah, n.d.), vol.1, p. 263.
34. Ibn Manjuwayh al-Aṣbahānī, *Rijāl Ṣaḥīḥ Muslim*, edited by Abdullah al-Laithi (Beirut: Dār al-Maʿrifah, 1987), vol.2, p. 56.
35. See chapter two, the section on forgiveness, the discussion following verse 2:109, for more details of ʿAlī ibn Abī Ṭalḥah's chain of transmission.
36. Abū Jaʿfar al-Nuḥās, *Kitāb al-Nāsikh wa al-Mansūkh fī al-Qur'ān al-Karīm* (Al-Maktabah al-ʿĀlamiyyah, 1938), p. 166.
37. Fakhr al-Dīn al-Rāzī, *Mafātīḥ al-Ghayb* (Beirut: Dār al-Fikr, 2002), vol.8, p. 234.
38. Muhammad ibn Ashur, *Tafsīr al-Taḥrīr wa al-Tanwīr* (Tunis: Maison Souhnoun, n.d.), vol.5, p. 115.
39. Muhammad al-Sharawi, *Tafsīr al-Shaʿrāwī* (Cairo: Akhbār al-Yawm, 1991), vol.8, p. 4875.

40. Ibid.
41. Ibn Jarīr al-Ṭabarī, *Tafsīr al-Ṭabarī* (Beirut: Dār al-Kutub al-ʿIlmiyyah, 1999), vol.6, p. 305.
42. Ibid.
43. Ibid.
44. At this point, it should be mentioned that al-Ṭabarī is one of the earliest exegetes to employ the textual context as a crucially important means for weighing the most precise meaning of Qur'anic words and verses.
45. Ibn Jarīr al-Ṭabarī, *Tafsīr al-Ṭabarī* (Beirut: Dār al-Kutub al-ʿIlmiyyah, 1999), vol.6, p. 320.
46. In respect of the chain of transmission, it is the most reliable and authentic chain through which Qatādah's exegetical opinions are transmitted. This is because Saʿīd ibn Abī ʿArūbah in addition to being a reliable transmitter, *thiqah ḥāfiẓ*, is also one of the most reliable and accurate sources of Qatādah's *tafsīr*. See Ibn Ḥajar al-ʿAsqalānī, *Taqrīb al-Tahdhīb*, edited by Abu al-Ashbal Sagir Ahmad Shagif al-Bakistani (Dār al-ʿĀṣimah, n.d.), p. 384. In the same way, Yazīd ibn Zurayʿ is a reliable, firm transmitter, *thiqah thabat* (ibid., p. 1074), as well as Bishr ibn Muʿādh al-ʿAqadī who is defined as trustworthy transmitter, *ṣadūq* (Ibid., p. 171).
47. Aḥmad ibn Taymiyyah, *Qāʿidah Mukhtaṣarah fī Qitāl al-Kuffār wa Muhādanatihim wa Taḥrīm Qatlihim li Mujarrad Kufrihim*, edited by Abd al-Aziz Abdullh al-Zair Al Hamd (Riyad: Maktabah al-Malik Fahd al-Waṭaniyyah, 2004), pp. 116-117.
48. Muhammad Asad, *The Message of the Qur'an* (Bristol: The Book Foundation, 2003), vol.2, p. 289.
49. Muhammad Abu Zahrah, *Naẓariyyah al-Ḥarb fī al-Islām* (Cairo: Al-Majlis al-Aʿlā li al-Shu'ūn al-Islāmiyyah, 2008), p. 23.
50. Muhammad al-Sharawi, *Tafsīr al-Shaʿrāwī* (Cairo: Akhbār al-Yawm, 1991), vol.8, p. 4875-4876.
51. The other most common Arabic conditional word is *idhā* which indicates likeness, exactly the opposite indication of *in*, but the English translation refers to both as "if." This shows how the nuances and the beauty of the original Arabic text are lost through the process of translation.
52. Fadl Abbas, *Al-Balāghah: Funūnuhā wa Afnānuhā* (Amman: Dār al-Furqān, 1992), p. 338.
53. In the English language it is different, since the conditional word "if" is usually followed by the subject, and then the verb.
54. The inversion exists in the original Arabic text, not in the translation, where the original syntactic order has been re-organised.

55. Ibn Jarīr al-Ṭabarī, *Tafsīr al-Ṭabarī* (Beirut: Dār al-Kutub al-ʿIlmiyyah, 1999), vol.6, p. 349; Maḥmūd al-Zamakhsharī, *Al-Kashshāf ʿan Ḥaqā'iq al-Tanzīl* (Beirut: Dār al-Kutub al-ʿIlmiyyah, 1995), vol.2, p. 254.
56. Fakhr al-Dīn al-Rāzī, *Mafātīḥ al-Ghayb* (Beirut: Dār al-Fikr, 2002), vol.8, pp. 29-31.
57. Muhammad R. Rida, *Tafsīr al-Manār* (Beirut: Dār al-Kutub al-ʿIlmiyyah, 1999), vol.10, p. 259.
58. Muhammad ibn Ashur, *Tafsīr al-Taḥrīr wa al-Tanwīr* (Tunis: Maison Souhnoun, n.d.), vol.5, pp. 163-164.
59. Fathi Osman, *The Other* (USA: Pharos Foundation, 2008), p. 37.
60. The area of Karak in today's Southern Jordan.
61. Muḥammad al-Wāqidī, *Kitāb al-Maghāzī*, edited by Marsden Jones (ʿĀlam al-Kutub, 1984), p. 755.
62. Ibn Ḥajar al-ʿAsqalānī, *Taqrīb al-Tahdhīb*, edited by Abu al-Ashbal Sagir Ahmad Shagif al-Bakistani (Dār al-ʿĀṣimah, n.d.), p. 716.
63. Ibid., p. 322.
64. Abū Bakr al-Baghdādī, *Tārīkh Baghdād* (Beirut: Dār al-Kutub al-ʿIlmiyyah, n.d.), vol.3, p. 3.
65. Nur al-Din Itr, *Manhaj al-Naqd fī ʿUlūm al-Ḥadīth* (Damascus: Dār al-Fikr, 1981), p. 100.
66. Ibn Ḥajar al-ʿAsqalānī, *Taqrīb al-Tahdhīb*, edited by Abu al-Ashbal Sagir Ahmad Shagif al-Bakistani (Dār al-ʿĀṣimah, n.d.), p. 882.
67. Abd al-Aziz al-Salumi, *Al-Wāqidī wa Kitābuhu al-Maghāzī: Manhajuhu wa Maṣādiruhu* (Al-Madīnah al-Munawwarah: Al-Jāmiʿah al-Islāmiyyah, 2004), vol.2, p. 847.
68. The name of the springs where the battle of *Banū Muṣṭalaq* occurred in the year 626 C.E./5 AH.
69. Abū Bakr al-Baghdādī, *Tārīkh Baghdād* (Beirut: Dār al-Kutub al-ʿIlmiyyah, n.d.), vol.3, p. 6; ʿAlī ibn ʿAsākir, *Tārīkh Madīnah Dimashq*, edited by Umar al-Amrawi (Beirut: Dār al-Fikr, 1997), vol.54, p. 445.
70. Abd al-Aziz al-Salumi, *Al-Wāqidī wa Kitābuhu al-Maghāzī: Manhajuhu wa Maṣādiruhu* (Al-Madīnah al-Munawwarah: Al-Jāmiʿah al-Islāmiyyah, 2004), vol.2, p. 848.
71. Muḥammad ibn Saʿd, *Al-Ṭabaqāt al-Kubrā*, edited by Muhammad Ata (Beirut: Dār al-Kutub al-ʿIlmiyyah, 1997), vol.2, p. 97.
72. Yūsuf ibn ʿAbd al-Barr, *Al-Istīʿāb fī Maʿrifah al-Aṣḥāb*, edited by Ali Muawwad and Adil Abd al-Mawjud (Beirut: Dār al-Kutub al-ʿIlmiyyah, 2002), vol.1, p. 361.
73. ʿIzz al-Dīn ibn al-Athīr, *'Usud al-Ghābah fī Maʿrifah al-Ṣaḥābah*, edited by

Ali Muawwad and Adil Abd al-Mawjud (Beirut: Dār al-Kutub al-ʿIlmiyyah, 1994), vol.1, p. 628.

74. Ibn Ḥajar al-ʿAsqalānī, *Al-Iṣābah fī Tamyīz al-Ṣaḥābah*, edited by Ali al-Bajawi (Beirut: Dār al-Jīl, 1992), vol.1, p. 589.
75. Ibn Ḥajar al-ʿAsqalānī, *Fatḥ al-Bārī: Sharḥ Ṣaḥīḥ al-Bukhārī* (Damascus: Dār al-Fayḥā', 1997), vol.7, p. 639.
76. Muhammad al-Buti, *Fiqh al-Sīrah al-Nabawiyyah* (Damascus: Dār al-Salām, 2004), p. 258.
77. Ibid., p. 259.
78. Muḥammad al-Bukhārī, *Ṣaḥīḥ al-Bukhārī*, translated by Muhammad Muhsin Khan, vol.6 (Beirut: Dār al-ʿArabiyyah, 1985), p. 407, no. 435.
79. In the original Arabic text, the expression appears as *kunnā taḥaddathnā*, the connotation of which is different from "it was rumoured" which indicates doubt and uncertainty.
80. Muḥammad al-Bukhārī, *Ṣaḥīḥ al-Bukhārī*, translated by Muhammad Muhsin Khan (Beirut: Dār al-ʿArabiyyah, 1985), vol.3, pp. 388-389, no. 648.
81. The region of today's Southern Jordan.
82. Aḥmad ibn Taymiyyah, *Qāʿidah Mukhtaṣarah fī Qitāl al-Kuffār wa Muhādanatihim wa Taḥrīm Qatlihim li Mujarrad Kufrihim*, edited by Abd al-Aziz Abdullah al-Zair Al Hamd (Riyad: Maktabah al-Malik Fahd al-Waṭaniyyah, 2004), p. 136.
83. Ibn Ḥajar al-ʿAsqalānī, *Al-Iṣābah fī Tamyīz al-Ṣaḥābah*, edited by Alī al-Bajawi (Beirut: Dār al-Jīl, 1992), vol.5, p. 387.
84. Muhammad al-Buti, *Fiqh al-Sīrah al-Nabawiyyah* (Damascus: Dār al-Salām, 2004), pp. 300-301.
85. The borders between Jordan and Saudi Arabia today or more precisely the city of Tabūk in Saudi Arabia.
86. Muhammad al-Buti, *Fiqh al-Sīrah al-Nabawiyyah* (Damascus: Dār al-Salām, 2004), p. 300.
87. Muḥammad ibn Saʿd, *Al-Ṭabaqāt al-Kubrā*, edited by Muhammad Ata (Beirut: Dār al-Kutub al-ʿIlmiyyah, 1997), vol.2, p. 125.
88. Ibn Ḥajar al-ʿAsqalānī, *Fatḥ al-Bārī: Sharḥ Ṣaḥīḥ al-Bukhārī* (Damascus: Dār al-Fayḥā', 1997), vol.8, p. 139.
89. Ibn Jarīr al-Ṭabarī, *Tafsīr al-Ṭabarī* (Beirut: Dār al-Kutub al-ʿIlmiyyah, 1999), vol.6, p. 349.
90. Abū Bakr al-Baghdādī, *Tārīkh Baghdād* (Beirut: Dār al-Kutub al-ʿIlmiyyah, n.d.), vol.3, p. 127.

91. Ibn Ḥajar al-ʿAsqalānī, *Taqrīb al-Tahdhīb*, edited by Abu al-Ashbal Sagir Ahmad Shagif al-Bakistani (Dār al-ʿĀṣimah, n.d.), p. 459.
92. Ibid., p. 772.
93. Ibid., p. 552.
94. Ibid., p. 921.
95. Muḥammad ibn Ḥibbān, *Kitāb al-Thiqāt* (Hyderabad: Dā'irah al-Maʿārif al-ʿUthmāniyyah, 1978), vol.7, p. 5.
96. Ṣalāḥ al-Dīn al-ʿAlā'ī, *Jāmiʿ al-Taḥṣīl fī Aḥkām al-Marāsīl*, edited by Hamdi Al-Salaifa (Beirut: ʿĀlam al-Kutub, 1986), p. 218.
97. Sufyān's father was a governor for Khālid ibn ʿAbd Allāh al-Qasrī in Iraq, but when Yūsuf ibn ʿUmar al-Thaqafī was appointed by al-Hishām ibn ʿAbd al-Malik as a new ruler of Iraq in 737-738 C.E./120-121 AH, Sufyān's father fled to Makkah and settled there. See Muḥammad ibn Saʿd, *Al-Ṭabaqāt al-Kubrā*, edited by Muhammad Ata (Beirut: Dār al-Kutub al-ʿIlmiyyah, 1997), vol.6, p. 41; Aḥmad ibn Khalkān, *Wafayāt al-Aʿyān wa Anbā' Abnā' al-Zamān* (Beirut: Dār al-Kutub al-ʿIlmiyyah, 1997), vol.2, pp. 191-196.
98. Muḥammad ibn Saʿd, *Al-Ṭabaqāt al-Kubrā*, edited by Muhammad Ata (Beirut: Dār al-Kutub al-ʿIlmiyyah, 1997), vol.6, p. 42.
99. Ibid., p. 31.
100. Shams al-Dīn al-Dhahabī, *Siyar Aʿlām al-Nubalā'*, edited by Shuaib al-Arnaut and Husain Al-Asad (Beirut: Mu'assasah al-Risālah, 2001), vol.6, p. 126.
101. Italics mine.
102. Muḥammad al-Bukhārī, *Kitāb al-Tārīkh al-Kabīr*, edited by Mustafa Ata (Beirut: Dār al-Kutub al-ʿIlmiyyah, 2001), vol.5, p. 130.
103. Shams al-Dīn al-Dhahabī, *Siyar Aʿlām al-Nubalā'*, edited by Shuaib al-Arnaut and Husain Al-Asad (Beirut: Mu'assasah al-Risālah, 2001), vol.6, p. 126.
104. Ṣalāḥ al-Dīn al-ʿAlā'ī, *Jāmiʿ al-Taḥṣīl fī Aḥkām al-Marāsīl*, edited by Hamdi Al-Salaifa (Beirut: ʿĀlam al-Kutub, 1986), p. 218.
105. See Muḥammad ibn Ḥibbān, *Kitāb al-Thiqāt* (Hyderabad: Dā'irah al-Maʿārif al-ʿUthmāniyyah, 1978), vol.7, p. 5, p. 331; Ṣalāḥ al-Dīn al-ʿAlā'ī, *Jāmiʿ al-Taḥṣīl fī Aḥkām al-Marāsīl*, edited by Hamdi Al-Salaifa (Beirut: ʿĀlam al-Kutub, 1986), p. 218; Ibn Ḥajar al-ʿAsqalānī, *Tahdhīb al-Tahdhīb* (Beirut: Mu'assasah al-Risālih, 2001), vol.2, p. 445.
106. Muḥammad ibn Ḥibbān, *Kitāb al-Thiqāt* (Hyderabad: Dā'irah al-Maʿārif al-ʿUthmāniyyah, 1978), vol.7, p. 331; Ibn Ḥajar al-ʿAsqalānī, *Taqrīb al-Tahdhīb*, edited by Abu al-Ashbal Sagir Ahmad Shagif al-Bakistani (Dār al-ʿĀṣimah, n.d.), p. 790.

107. Muhammad H. al-Dhahabi, *Al-Tafsīr wa al-Mufassirūn* (Cairo: Maktabah Wahbah, 2000), vol.1, p. 79.
108. Ibn Jarīr al-Ṭabarī, *Tafsīr al-Ṭabarī* (Beirut: Dār al-Kutub al-ʿIlmiyyah, 1999), vol.6, p. 349.
109. The existence of the imperative *uqtulū*, slay or kill, prescribed to Muslims in four Qur'anic verses (2:191; 4:89, 91; 9:5) does not contradict my statement, since the imperative of the first morphological form *qatala* in all those verses is prescribed within the context of initially waged war on Muslims. For this reason, all four verses occur in a textual context of the third form *qātala*.
110. Ibn Hishām al-Anṣārī, *Mughnī al-Labīb ʿan Kutub al-Aʿārīb* (Dār Iḥyā' al-Turāth al-ʿArabī, n.d.), vol.1, p. 122.
111. Abū Bishr ʿAmrū Sībawayh, *Al-Kitāb: Kitāb Sībawayh*, vol.3, edited by Abd al-Salam Harun (Cairo: Maktabah al-Khānjī, n.d.), p. 17.
112. Italics and emphasis mine.
113. Ibn al-Qayyim al-Jawziyyah, *Aḥkām Ahl al-Dhimmah*, 1, edited by Yusuf Al-Bakri and Shakir Al-Aruri (Al-Dammām: Ramādī li al-Nashr, 1997), p. 122.
114. Fathi Osman, *The Other* (USA: Pharos Foundation, 2008), p. 174.
115. Thomas Arnold, *The Preaching of Islam: A History of the Propagation of the Muslim Faith* (London: Darf Publishers Limited, 1986), pp. 60-61.
116. William Watt, *Muhammad at Medina* (London: Oxford University Press, 1962), pp. 319-320.
117. It seems that the word "patrons" is a more accurate English translation of the Arabic word *awliyā'*, in this particular context, than the words "allies" and "protectors."
118. Maḥmūd al-Zamakhsharī, *Al-Kashshāf ʿan Ḥaqā'iq al-Tanzīl* (Beirut: Dār al-Kutub al-ʿIlmiyyah, 1995), vol.1, p. 629; Fakhr al-Dīn al-Rāzī, *Mafātīḥ al-Ghayb* (Beirut: Dār al-Fikr, 2002), vol.6, p. 18.
119. Al-Qarāfī in his work *al-Furūq* argues that the People of the Book should be treated on the basis of justice in respect of their human rights, but not on the basis of love and affection. See Aḥmad al-Qarāfī, *Al-Furūq* (Beirut: Dār al-Kutub al-ʿImiyyah, 1998), vol.3, pp. 29-33.
120. Abū al-Ḥusayn ibn Fāris, *Muʿjam al-Maqāyīs fī al-Lughah* (Beirut: Dār al-Fikr, 1998), p. 1104.
121. Ibid.
122. Ibid.
123. Al-Rāghib al-Aṣfahānī, *Mufradāt Alfāẓ al-Qur'ān*, edited by Safwan Dawudi (Damascus: Dār al-Qalam, 2002), p. 885.

124. Ibid.
125. Muḥammad ibn Manẓūr, *Lisān al-ʿArab* (Beirut: Dār Iḥyā' al-Turāth al-ʿArabī, Mu'assasah al-Tārīkh al-ʿArabī, 1999), vol.15, p. 403.
126. Ibid., p. 402.
127. Ibid., p. 404.
128. Al-Sharīf al-Jurjānī, *Kitāb al-Taʿrīfāt* (Beirut: Lubnān, 1985), p. 275.
129. Rohi Baalbaki, *Al-Mawrid: A Modern Arabic-English Dictionary* (Beirut: Dar al-ʿIlm li al-Malayīn, 2001), p. 1248.
130. Al-Sharīf al-Jurjānī, *Kitāb al-Taʿrīfāt* (Beirut: Lubnān, 1985), p. 275.
131. In an essay entitled "Christians in the Qur'an and Tafsir", the author excessively underlines the word "friends" as the English equivalent for the Arabic word *awliyā'* in the case of Qur'anic verse 5:51. See Jane McAuliffe, "Christians in the Qur'an and Tafsir." In *Muslim Perceptions of Other Religions*, by Jacques Waardenburg, pp. 105-121 (New York: Oxford University Press, 1999).
132. Douglas Harper, *Online Etymology Dictionary*, 10 October 2008. http://www.etymonline.com (accessed March 10, 2010).
133. ʿAbd al-Raḥmān ibn Abī Ḥātim, *Al-Tafsīr bi al-Ma'thūr* (Beirut: Dār al-Kutub al-ʿIlmiyyah, 2006), vol.3, p. 221.
134. ʿUbādah ibn al-Ṣāmit died 654 C.E./34 AH, see Ibn Ḥajar al-ʿAsqalānī, *Taqrīb al-Tahdhīb*, edited by Abu al-Ashbal Sagir Ahmad Shagif al-Bakistani (Dār al-ʿĀṣimah, n.d.), p. 484; whereas ʿAṭiyyah al-ʿAwfī was born during the reign of Khalīfah ʿAlī ibn Abī Ṭālib 655-660 C.E./35-40 AH, see Ibn Jarīr al-Ṭabarī, *The History of al-Ṭabarī*, translated by Ella Landau-Tasseron (New York: State University of New York Press, 1998), vol.xxxix, p. 228.
135. Ibn Abī Ḥātim reliable transmitter, *ḥāfiẓ*, see Shams al-Dīn al-Dhahabī, *Mīzān al-Iʿtidāl fī Naqd al-Rijāl* (Dār al-Fikral-ʿArabī, n.d.), vol.3, p. 301; Abī Ḥātim Muḥammad ibn Idrīs reliable transmitter, *ḥāfiẓ*, see Ibn Ḥajar al-ʿAsqalānī, *Taqrīb al-Tahdhīb*, edited by Abu al-Ashbal Sagir Ahmad Shagif al-Bakistani (Dār al-ʿĀṣimah, n.d.), p. 824; Abū al-Aṣbagh al-Ḥarrānī, his name is ʿAbd al-ʿAzīz ibn Yaḥyā ibn Yūsuf al-Bukā'ī reliable transmitter, see Muḥammad ibn Ḥibbān, *Kitāb al-Thiqāt* (Hyderabad: Dā'irah al-Maʿārif al-ʿUthmāniyyah, 1978), vol.8, p. 397; Muḥammad ibn Salamah al-Ḥarrānī al-Bāhilī reliable transmitter, ibid., vol.9, p. 40; Muḥammad ibn Isḥāq ibn Yasār reliable transmitter, ibid., vol.7, p. 380; Isḥāq ibn Yasār reliable transmitter, ibid., vol.6, p. 48; ʿUbādah ibn al-Walīd ibn ʿUbādah ibn al-Ṣāmit reliable transmitter, see Ibn Ḥajar al-ʿAsqalānī, *Taqrīb al-Tahdhīb*, edited by Abu al-Ashbal Sagir Ahmad Shagif al-Bakistani (Dār al-ʿĀṣimah, n.d.),

p. 485; ʿUbādah ibn al-Ṣāmit, he is the well known Companion of the Prophet, ibid., p. 484.

136. Italics mine.
137. Aḥmad ibn Ḥanbal, *Musnad al-Imām Aḥmad*, edited by Shuaib al-Arnaut (Beirut: Mu'assasah al-Risālah, 2001), vol.37, p. 353.
138. ʿAbd al-Raḥmān ibn Abī Ḥātim, *Kitāb al-Jarḥ wa al-Taʿdīl* (Dār al-Fikr, 1952), vol.6, p. 96.
139. Muḥammad al-Bukhārī, *Ṣaḥīḥ al-Bukhārī*, translated by Muhammad Muhsin Khan (Beirut: Dār al-ʿArabiyyah, 1985), vol.6, p. 205, no. 132.
140. Ibn Ḥajar al-ʿAsqalānī, *Fatḥ al-Bārī: Sharḥ Ṣaḥīḥ al-Bukhārī* (Damascus: Dār al-Fayḥā', 1997), vol.1, pp. 560-561.
141. Muhammad al-Buti, *Fiqh al-Sīrah al-Nabawiyyah* (Damascus: Dār al-Salām, 2004), pp. 167-171.
142. Fathi Osman, *The Other* (USA: Pharos Foundation, 2008), p. 112.
143. Ibn Jarīr al-Ṭabarī, *Tafsīr al-Ṭabarī* (Beirut: Dār al-Kutub al-ʿIlmiyyah, 1999), vol.4, p. 616.
144. Ibid.
145. Ibid., p. 617.
146. Maḥmūd al-Zamakhsharī, *Al-Kashshāf ʿan Ḥaqā'iq al-Tanzīl* (Beirut: Dār al-Kutub al-ʿIlmiyyah, 1995), vol.1, p. 629.
147. Fakhr al-Dīn al-Rāzī, *Mafātīḥ al-Ghayb* (Beirut: Dār al-Fikr, 2002), vol.6, p. 18.
148. Muhammad ibn Ashur, *Tafsīr al-Taḥrīr wa al-Tanwīr* (Tunis: Maison Souhnoun, n.d.), vol.3, p. 229.
149. Ibid., pp. 228-229.
150. Muhammad al-Tabatabai, *Al-Mīzān fī Tafsīr al-Qur'ān* (Beirut: Mu'assasah al-Aʿlamī, 1997), vol.5, pp. 377-378.
151. All these thematic elements are discussed thoroughly throughout the book.

Bibliography

Abbas, Fadl. *Itqān al-Burhān fī ᶜUlūm al-Qur'ān* (Amman: Dār al-Furqān, 1997).

—. *Al-Balāghah: Funūnuhā wa Afnānuhā* (Amman: Dār al-Furqān, 1992).

Abdel Haleem, M.A.S. *The Qur'an: A New Translation* (New York: Oxford University Press Inc., 2004).

Abu Hassan, Jamal. "Al-ᶜAlāqah bayn al-Muslimīn wa Ahl al-Kitāb fī Ḍaw' al-Aḥkām al-Qur'āniyyah." Unpublished essay.

Abū Ḥayyān al-Andalusī, Muḥammad. *Tafsīr al-Baḥr al-Muḥīṭ* (Beirut: Dār al-Kutub al-ᶜIlmiyyah, 2001).

Abu al-Nail, Muhammad Abd al-Salam. *Tafsīr al-Imām Mujāhid ibn Jabr* (Naṣr: Dār al-Fikr al-Islāmī al-Ḥadīthah, 1989).

Abu al-Suᶜud, Muhammad. *Irshād al-ᶜAql al-Salīm ilā Mazāyā al-Kitāb al-Karīm* (Beirut: Dar al-Fikr, n.d.).

Abu Zahrah, Muhammad. *Naẓariyyah al-Ḥarb fī al-Islām* (Cairo: Al-Majlis al-Aᶜlā li al-Shu'ūn al-Islāmiyyah, 2008).

—. *Tanẓīm al-Islām lī al-Mujtamaᶜ* (Cairo: Dār al-Fikr al-ᶜArabī, n.d.).

—. *Zahrah al-Tafāsīr* (Dār al-Fikral-ᶜArabī, n.d.).

ᶜAlā'ī (al-), Ṣalāḥ al-Dīn. *Jāmiᶜ al-Taḥṣīl fī Aḥkām al-Marāsīl.* Edited by Hamdi Al-Salaifa (Beirut: ᶜĀlam al-Kutub, 1986).

Albānī (al-), Muḥammad. *Ṣaḥīḥ Sunan Abī Dāwūd* (Riyadh: Maktabah al-Maᶜārif, 2000).

—. *Silsilah al-Aḥādīth al-Ḍaᶜīfah wa al-Mawḍūᶜah* (Riyadh: Maktabah al-Maᶜārif, 1988).

—. *Silsilāh al-Aḥādīth al-Ṣaḥīḥah* (Riyadh: Maktabah al-Maᶜārif, 1995).

ᶜAlī, ᶜAbdullah Yūsuf. *The Meaning of The Holy Qur'an* (Beltsville, Maryland, U.S.A.: Amana Publications, 2008).

Ali, Jawad. *Al-Mufaṣṣal fī Tārīkh al-ᶜArab qabl al-Islām* (Baghdad: University of Baghdad, 1993).

Altwaijri, Abdulaziz Othman. *Islam and Inter-religious Coexistence on the Threshold of the 21st Century* (Rabat: ISESCO, 1998).

Ālūsī (al-), Shihāb al-Dīn. *Rūḥ al-Maᶜānī.* (Beirut: Dār al-Kutub al-ᶜIlmiyyah, 1994).

Alwani (al-), Taha Jabir. *Lā Ikrāh fī al-Dīn* (Cairo: Maktabah al-Shurūq al-Dawliyyah, 2006).

Amarah, Muhammad. *Al-Islām wa al-Taʿaddudiyyah* (Cairo: Dār al-Rashād, 1997).

—. *Al-Taʿaddudiyyah: Al-Ru'yah al-Islāmiyyah wa al-Taḥaddiyāt al-Gharbiyyah* (Cairo: Dār Nahḍah Miṣr, 1997).

Amin, Ahmad. *Ḍuḥā al-Islām* (Cairo: Maktabah al-Nahḍah al-Miṣriyyah, 1979).

—. *Ḍuḥā al-Islām* (Cairo: Maktabah al-Nahḍah al-Miṣriyyah, 1978).

—. *Ḍuḥā al-Islām* (Al-Nahḍah al-Miṣriyyah, n.d.).

—. *Zuʿamā' al-Iṣlāḥ fī al-ʿAṣr al-Ḥadīth* (Beirut: Dār al-Kitāb al-ʿArabī, n.d.).

Andalusī (al-), Ibn ʿAbd Rabbah. *Kitāb al-ʿAqd al-Farīd* (Cairo: Lajnah al-Ta'līf wa al-Tarjumah wa al-Nashr, 1969).

Andalusī (al-), Ibn Ḥazm. *Al-Fiṣl fī al-Milal wa al-Ahwā' wa al-Niḥal* (Cairo: Al-Maṭbaʿah al-Adabiyyah, 1317 AH).

—. *Ṭawq al-Ḥamāmah* (Damascus: Dār al-Bayān, 2002).

Anṣārī (al-), Ibn Hishām. *Mughnī al-Labīb ʿan Kutub al-Aʿārīb* (Dār Iḥyā' al-Turāth al-ʿArabī, n.d.).

Aqqad (al-), Abbas Mahmud. *Al-Insān fī al-Qur'ān* (Cairo: Dār al-Hilāl, n.d.).

Aquinas, Thomas. *Summa Theologiae-Man Made to God's Image*. Edited by Edmund O.P. Hill (Blackfriars, 1964).

Arnold, Thomas. *The Preaching of Islam: A History of the Propagation of the Muslim Faith* (London: Darf Publishers Limited, 1986).

Asad, Muhammad. *The Message of the Qur'an* (Bristol: The Book Foundation, 2003).

Asani, Ali. "So That You May Know One Another: A Muslim American Reflects on Pluralism and Islam." *Annals of the American Academy of Political and Social Science*, July 2003.

Aṣbahānī (al-), Ibn Manjuwayh. *Rijāl Ṣaḥīḥ Muslim*. Edited by Abdullah al-Laithi (Beirut: Dār al-Maʿrifah, 1987).

Aṣfahānī (al-), Abū al-Faraj. *Kitāb al-Aghānī* (Beirut: Dār al-Kutub al-ʿIlmiyyah, 2002).

Aṣfahānī (al-), al-Rāghib. *Mufradāt Alfāẓ al-Qur'ān*. Edited by Safwan Dawudi (Damascus: Dār al-Qalam, 2002).

—. *Mufradāt Alfāẓ al-Qur'ān* (Beirut: Dār al-Kutub al-ʿIlmiyyah, 1997).

Aslan, Adnan. *Religious Pluralism in Christian and Islamic Philosophy* (Surrey: Curzon, 1998).

ʿAsqalānī (al-), Ibn Ḥajar. *Al-Iṣābah fī Tamyīz al-Ṣaḥābah*. Edited by Ali al-Bajawi (Beirut: Dār al-Jīl, 1992).

—. *Fatḥ al-Bārī: Sharḥ Ṣaḥīḥ al-Bukhārī* (Damascus: Dār al-Fayḥā', 1997).

—. *Lisān al-Mīzān*. Edited by Adil Ahmad Abd al-Mawjud and Ali Muhammad Muawwad (Beirut: Dār Kutub al-ʿIlmiyyah, 1996).

—. *Tahdhīb al-Tahdhīb* (Beirut: Mu'assasah al-Risālah, 2001).

—. *Taqrīb al-Tahdhīb*. Edited by Abu al-Ashbal Sagir Ahmad Shagif al-Bakistani (Dār al-ʿĀṣimah, n.d.).

Atiq, Abd al-Aziz. *ʿIlm al-Maʿānī* (Beirut: Dār al-Nahḍah al-ʿArabiyyah, 1985).

Atiyah, Jamal al-Din. *Naḥwa Tafʿīl Maqāṣid al-Sharīʿah* (Damascus: Dār al-Fikr, 2001

Attas (al-), Syed. *Islam and Secularism* (Kuala Lumpur: International Institute of Islamic Thought and Civlization, 1993).

Auda, Jasser. *Maqasid al-Shariah as Philosophy of Islamic Law* (London: The International Institute of Islamic Thought, 2008).

Aydin, Mehmet S. "Islam and the Challenges of Pluralism." 3 November 2005. http://www.cie.ugent.be/maydinen1.htm (accessed May 11, 2013).

Baalbaki, Rohi. *Al-Mawrid: A Modern Arabic-English Dictionary* (Beirut: Dār al-ʿIlm li-Almalāyīn, 2001).

Baali, Fuad. *Society, State, and Urbanism: Ibn Khaldun's Sociological Thought* (Albany: State University of New York Press, 1988).

Badawi, Jamal. *Muslim Christian Relations*. 5 April 2005. http://www.islamawareness.net (accessed August 12, 2010).

Bagawī (al-), al-Ḥusayn. *Maʿālim al-Tanzīl fī al-Tafsīr wa al-Ta'wīl* (Beirut: Dār al-Fikr, 2002).

Baghdādī (al-), Abū Bakr. *Tārīkh Baghdād* (Beirut: Dār al-Kutub al-ʿIlmiyyah, n.d.).

Bakhit, Muhammad A. *The Fourth International Conference on the History of Bilad al-Sham During the Umayyad Period* (Amman: University of Jordan, 1989).

Baqir al-Sadr, Muhammad. *Al-Madrasah al-Qur'āniyyah*. (Markaz al-Abḥāth wa al-Dirāsāt al-Takhaṣṣuṣiyyah li al-Shahīd al-Ṣadr, 1421 AH).

Barrett, David B. *World Christian Encyclopedia*. 2nd edn. (Oxford: Oxford University Press, 2001).

Bayḍāwī (al-), Nāṣir al-Dīn. *Anwār al-Tanzīl wa Asrār al-Ta'wīl* (Beirut: Dār al-Kutub al-ʿIlmiyyah, 1988).

Bayhaqī (al-), Aḥmad. *Shuʿab al-Īmān* (Beirut: Dār al-Kutub al-ʿIlmiyyah, 2000.

Biqāʿī (al-), Burhān al-Dīn. *Naẓmu al-Durar fī Tanāsub al-Āyāt wa al-Suwar* (Beirut: Dār al-Kutub al-ʿIlmiyyah, 1995).

Bosworth, C.E,, E. van Donzel, W.P. Heinrichs, and Ch. Pellat. *The Encyclopaedia of Islam* (Leiden: E.J.Brill, 1993).

Brockelmann, Carl. *History of the Islamic Peoples* (London: Routledge and Kegan Paul, 1949).

Bucaille, Maurice. *Al-Tawrāh wa al-Injīl wa al-Qur'ān wa al-ʿIlm* (Beirut: Al-Maktab al-Islāmī, 1987).

Budziszewski, J. "Act Naturally." *Australian Presbyterian*, June 2005: 4-8.

Bukhārī (al-), Muḥammad. *Kitāb al-Tārīkh al-Kabīr*. Edited by Mustafa Ata (Beirut: Dār al-Kutub al-ʿIlmiyyah, 2001).

—. *Ṣaḥīḥ al-Bukhārī,* translated by Muhammad Muhsin Khan (Beirut: Dār al-ʿArabiyyah, 1985).

Buti (al-), Muhammad. *Fiqh al-Sīrah al-Nabawiyyah* (Damascus: Dār al-Salām, 2004.

Clarke, Paul B., and Joe Foweraker. *Encyclopedia of Democratic Thought* (London: Routledge, 2001).

Copan, Paul. *True for You, But Not for Me* (Minneapolis: Bethany House Publishers, 1998).

Coribn, Henry. *Histoire de la Philosophie Islamique,* translated by Александър Веселинов (Sofia: Maulana Djalaluddin Rumi, 2000).

—. *History of Islamic Philosophy,* translated by Liadain Sherrard (London: Kegan Paul International).

Cragg, Kenneth. *The Qur'an and the West* (London: Melisend, 2006).

Dāwūdī (al-), Shams al-Dīn Muḥammad. *Ṭabaqāt al-Mufassirīn*. Edited by Ali Muhammad Umar (Cairo: Maktabah Wahbah, 1994).

D'Costa, Gavin. *Theology and Religious Pluralism:The Challenge of Other Religions* (Oxford: Basil Blackwell Ltd, 1986).

Dhahabī (al-), Muḥammad Ḥusayn. *Al-Tafsīr wa al-Mufassirūn* (Cairo: Maktabah Wahbah, 2000).

Dhahabī (al-), Shams al-Dīn. *Mīzān al-Iʿtidāl fī Naqd al-Rijāl* (Dār al-Fikr al-ʿArabī, n.d.).

—. *Siyar Aʿlām al-Nubalā'*. Edited by Shuaib al-Arnaut and Husain Al-Asad (Beirut: Mu'assasah al-Risālah, 2001).

Draz, Muhammad A. *The Moral World of the Qur'an,* translated by Danielle Roibnson and Masterton Rebecca (London: I.B. Tauris, 2008).

Eck, Diana L. *The Pluralism Project at Harvard University*. 2006. http://pluralism.org (accessed March 25, 2010).

Eliot, T.S. *The Complete Poems and Plays of T.S.Eliot* (London: Faber and Faber, 1969).

Esack, Farid. *Qur'an,Liberation and Pluralism* (Oxford: Oneworld, 1997).

Fārābī (al-), Abū Naṣr. *Kitāb Ārā' Ahl al-Madīnah al-Fāḍilah* (Beirut: Dār al-Mashriq, 1968).

Fārūqī (al-), Ismāʿīl. *Toward Islamization of Disciplines* (Herndon: International Institute of Islamic Thought, 1989).

Ghazālī (al-), Abū Ḥāmid. *Iḥyā' ʿUlūm al-Dīn* (Beirut: Dār al-Kutub al-ʿIlmiyyah, 2001).

—. *Tahāfut al-Falāsifah*. Edited by S.J. Maurice Bouyges (Bibliotheca Arabica Scholasticorum, 1927).

Ghazali (al-), Muhammad. *Naẓarāt fī al-Qur'ān* (Cairo: Nahḍah Miṣr, 2005).

Glasse, Cyril. *The New Encyclopaedia of Islam* (Walnut Creek: AltaMira Press, 2002).

Goldziher, Ignaz. *Muslim Studies,* translated by C.R. and Stern, S.M. Barber (London: George Allen and Unwin Ltd, 1967).

Griffith, Sidney Harrison. *Arabic Christianity in the Monasteries of Ninth-Century Palestine* (Hampshire: Variorum, 1992).

—. *The Beginnings of Christian Theology in Arabic* (Hampshire: Ashgate, 2002).

—. "Disputing with Islam in Syriac: The Case of the Monk of Bêt Hālê and a Muslim Emir." *Hugoye: Journal of Syriac Studies*, January 2000s.

Grodz, Stanislaw. "'Vie with Each Other in Good Works': What Can a Roman Catholic Missionary Order Learn from Entering into Closer Contact with Muslims?" *Islam and Christian-Muslim Relations* (Routledge, 18, 2007).

Ḥākim (al-), Muḥammad. *Al-Mustadrak ʿalā al-Ṣaḥīḥayn*. Edited by Mustafa Ata (Beirut: Dār al-Kutub al-ʿIlmiyyah, 1990).

Hanafi, Hassan. *Religious Dialogue and Revolution* (Cairo: The Anglo-Egyptian Bookshop, 1976).

Harper, Douglas. *Online Etymology Dictionary*. 10 10 2008. http://www.etymonline.com (accessed 12 8, 2011).

—. *Online Etymology Dictionary*. 10 October 2008. http://www.etymonline.com (accessed March 10, 2010).

Hawting, G.R. *The First Dynasty of Islam* (London: Routledge, 2000).

Haythamī (al-), ʿAlī. *Majmaʿ al-Zawā'id wa Manbaʿ al-Fawā'id*. Edited by Muhammad Ata (Beirut: Dār al-Kutub al-ʿIlmiyyah, 2001).

Henzell-Thomas, Jeremy. *The Challenge of Pluralism and the Middle Way of Islam* (Richmond, UK: AMSS, 2002).

Hick, John. *An Interpretation of Religion: Human Responses to the Transcendent* (London: Macmillan, 1989).
—. *Problems of Religious Pluralism* (Hampshire: The Macmillan Press LTD, 1985).
Hijazi, Muhammad M. *Al-Tafsīr al-Wāḍiḥ* (Al-Zaqāzīq: Dār al-Tafsīr, 2003).
Hindī (al-), ʿAlī al-Muttaqī. *Kanz al-ʿUmmāl fī Sunan al-Aqwāl wa al-Afʿāl* (Beirut: Mu'assasah al-Risālah, 1985).
Hitti, Philip. *History of the Arabs* (London: Macmillan and Co. Ltd., 1951).
Hourani, Albert. *A History of Arab Peoples* (Croydon: CPI Bookmarque, 2005).
Humaidan (al-), Isam. *Al-Ṣaḥīḥ min Asbāb al-Nuzūl* (Beirut: Mu'assasah al-Rayyān, 1999).
Humaidi (al-), Abd al-Aziz. *Tafsīr Ibn ʿAbbās wa Marwiyyātuhu fī al-Tafsīr min Kutub al-Sunnah* (Makkah al-Mukarramah: Jāmiʿah Umm al-Qurā, n.d.).
Ibn ʿAbd al-Barr, Yūsuf. *Al-Istīʿāb fī Maʿrifah al-Aṣḥāb*. Edited by Ali Muawwad and Adil Abd al-Mawjud (Beirut: Dār al-Kutub al-ʿIlmiyyah, 2002).
Ibn Abī Ḥātim, ʿAbd al-Raḥmān. *Al-Tafsīr bi al-Ma'thūr* (Beirut: Dār al-Kutub al-ʿIlmiyyah, 2006).
Ibn al-ʿArabī, Muḥammad. *Aḥkām al-Qur'ān* (Beirut: Dār al-Fikr).
Ibn ʿArabī, Muḥy al-Dīn. *Tafsīr Ibn ʿArabī* (n.d.).
Ibn ʿAsākir, ʿAlī. *Tārīkh Madīnah Dimashq*. Edited by Umar al-Amrawi (Beirut: Dār al-Fikr, 1997).
Ibn Ashur, Muhammad. *Maqāṣid al-Sharīʿah al-Islāmiyyah* (Doha: Wizārah al-Awqāf wa al-Shu'ūn al-Islāmiyyah Qatar, 2004).
—. *Tafsīr al-Taḥrīr wa al-Tanwīr* (Tunis: Maison Souhnoun, n.d.).
Ibn ʿAṭiyyah, ʿAbd al-Ḥaq. *Al-Muḥarrar al-Wajīz fī Tafsīr al-Kitāb al-ʿAzīz* (Beirut: Dār al-Kutub al-ʿIlmiyyah, 2001).
—. *Kitāb al-Jarḥ wa al-Taʿdīl* (Dār al-Fikr, 1952).
Ibn al-Athīr, ʿAlī. *Al-Kāmil fī al-Tārīkh* (Beirut: Dār al-Kutub al-ʿIlmiyyah, 1998).
Ibn al-Athīr, Ḍiyā' al-Dīn. *Al-Mathal al-Sā'ir* (Dār Nahḍah Miṣr, n.d.).
Ibn al-Athīr, ʿIzz al-Dīn. *'Usud al-Ghābah fī Maʿrifah al-Ṣaḥābah*. Edited by Ali Muawwad and Adil Abd al-Mawjud (Beirut: Dār al-Kutub al-ʿIlmiyyah, 1994).
Ibn Fāris, Abū al-Ḥusayn. *Muʿjam al-Maqāyīs fī al-Lughah* (Beirut: Dār al-Jīl, 1999).

—. *Muᶜjam al-Maqāyīs fī al-Lughah* (Beirut: Dār al-Fikr, 1998).
Ibn Ḥanbal, Aḥmad. *Al-Musnad* (Cairo: Dār al-Ḥadīth, 1995).
—. *Musnad al-Imām Aḥmad.* Edited by Shuaib al-Arnaut (Beirut: Mu'assasah al-Risālah, 2001).
Ibn Ḥibbān, Muḥammad. *Kitāb al-Thiqāt* (Hyderabad: Dā'irah al-Maᶜārif al-ᶜUthmāniyyah, 1978.
Ibn Hishām, Abū Muḥammad ᶜAbd al-Malik. *Al-Sīrah al-Nabawiyyah* (Miṣr: Muṣṭafā al-Bābī al-Ḥalabī wa Awlāduh, 1955).
Ibn Jinnī, ᶜUthmān. *Al-Munṣif* (Al-Jumhūriyyah al-ᶜArabiyyah al-Muttaḥidah: Al-Idārah al-ᶜĀmmah li al-Thaqāfah, 1960).
Ibn Kathīr, Ismāᶜīl. *Tafsīr al-Qur'ān al-ᶜAẓīm* (Beirut: Mu'assasah al-Rayyān, 1998).
Ibn Khaldūn, ᶜAbd al-Raḥmān. *The Muqaddimah: An Introduction to History,* translated by Franz Rozenthal (Princeton and Oxford: Princeton University Press, 2005).
—. *The Muqaddimah: An Introduction to History,* translated by Franz Rosenthal (Princeton: Princeton University Press, 1967).
Ibn Khalkān, Aḥmad. *Wafiyyāt al-Aᶜyān wa Anbā' Abnā' al-Zamān* (Beirut: Dār al-Kutub al-ᶜIlmiyyah, 1997).
Ibn Manẓūr, Muḥammad. *Lisān al-ᶜArab* (Beirut: Dār Iḥyā' al-Turāth al-ᶜArabī, Mu'assasah al-Tārīkh al-ᶜArabī, 1999).
Ibn Saᶜd, Muḥammad. *Al-Ṭabaqāt al-Kubrā.* Edited by Muhammad Ata (Beirut: Dār al-Kutub al-ᶜIlmiyyah, 1997).
Ibn Salām, al-Qāsim. *Faḍā'l al-Qur'ān wa Maᶜālimuh wa Ādābuh.* Edited by Ahmad al-Khaiati (The Kingdom of Morocco: Wizārah al-Awqāf wa al-Shu'ūn al-Islāmiyyh, 1995).
Ibn Taymiyyah, Aḥmad. *Muqaddimah fī Uṣūl al-Tafsīr* (Beirut: Dār Ibn Ḥazm, 1997).
—. *Qāᶜidah Mukhtaṣarah fī Qitāl al-Kuffār wa Muhādanatihim wa Taḥrīm Qatlihim li Mujarrad Kufrihim.* Edited by Abd al-Aziz Abdullah al-Zayr Al Hamd (Riyadh: Maktabah al-Malik Fahd al-Waṭaniyyah, 2004).
Idrīsī (al-), Abū Zayd. *Dirāsāt Qur'āniyyah.* 15 10, 2008. http://www.almultaka.net (accessed 01 17, 2011).
Itr, Nur al-Din. *Manhaj al-Naqd fī ᶜUlūm al-Ḥadīth* (Damascus: Dār al-Fikr, 1981).
Izutsu, Toshihiko. *Ethico-Religious Concepts in the Qur'an* (McGill-Queen's University Press, 2002).
Jāḥiẓ (al-), Abū ᶜUthmān. *Al-Bayān wa al-Tabyīn* (Cairo: Maktabah al-Khanjī, 1975).

—. *Kitāb al-Ḥayawān* (Beirut: Dār al-Jīl, 1988).

—. *Risālah fī Banī Umayyah* (Alger: Ch. Pellat, 1952).

Jawziyyah (al-), Ibn Qayyim. *Aḥkām Ahl al-Dhimmah.* Edited by Yusuf al-Bakri and Shakir al-Aruri.(Al-Dammām: Ramādī Lilnashr, 1997).

—. *Zād al-Muhājir.* Edited by Said Ibrahim Sadiq (Cairo: Dār al-Ḥadīth, n.d.).

Jurjānī (al-), al-Sharīf. *Kitāb al-Taʿrīfāt* (Beirut: Lubnān, 1985).

Kamali, Mohammad Hashim. *The Dignity of Man: An Islamic Perspective* (Cambridge: The Islamic Texts Society, 2002).

Kant, Immanuel. *Grounding for the Metaphysics of Moral,* translated by James W. Ellington (Indianapolis: Hackett Publishing Company, Inc, 1993).

Keddie, Nikki. *An Islamic Response to Imperialism* (Los Angeles: University of California Press, 1968).

Khafagi, Ishraq, Amira Zakaria, Ahmed Dewedar, and Khaled Zahdany(al-). "A Voyage in the World of Plants as Mentioned in the Holy Quran." *International Journal of Botany* (2 March 2006).

Khalīfah, Ḥajjī. *Kashf al-Ẓunūn* (Dār al-Fikr, 1982).

Khalil, Imad al-Din,. *Ḥawla Tashkīl al-ʿAql al-Muslim* (Herndon: The International Institute of Islamic Thought, 1991).

Khalīlī (al-), Abū Yaʿlā. *Kitāb al-Irshād fī Maʿrifah ʿUlamā' al-Ḥadīth.* Edited by Muhammad Idris (Riyadh: Maktabah al-Rushd, n.d.).

Kilpatrick, Hilary. "Monasteries Through Muslim Eyes: The Diyārāt Books." In *Christians at the Heart of Islamic Rule: Church Life and Scholarship in ʿAbbasid Iraq,* edited by David Thomas, (Leiden: Brill, 2003).

Küng, Hans. *Global Responsibility:In Search of a New World Ethic* (London: SCM Press Ltd, 1991).

Legenhausen, Muhammad. "A Muslim's Non-Reductive Religious Pluralism." In *Islam and Global Dialogue: Religious Pluralism and the Pursuit of Peace,* ed. Roger Boase, (Aldershot: Ashgate, 2005).

Lings, Martin. *Muhammad – His Life Based on the Earliest Sources* (Cambridge: The Islamic Text Society, 1991).

Maimonides, Moses. *The Guide for the Perplexed* (Forgotten Books, 2008).

Maqrīzī (al-), Taqī al-Dīn. *Al-Nizāʿ wa al-Takhāṣum fīmā bayn Banī Umayyah wa Banī Hāshim* (Leiden: E.J. Brill, 1888).

Marshall, David. *God, Muhammad and the Unbelievers* (London: Curzon Press, 1999).

Masᶜūdī (al-), ᶜAlī. *Murūj al-Dhahab and Maᶜādin al-Jawhar* (Beirut: Dār al-Kutub al-ᶜIlmiyyah).

Mathews, Shailer, and Gerald Smith,. *A Dictionary of Religion and Ethics* (London: Waverley Book Company, LTD., 1921).

McAuliffe, Jane. "Christians in the Qur'an and Tafsir." In *Muslim Perseptions of Other Religions*, by Jacques Waardenburg, (New York: Oxford University Press, 1999).

—. *Qur'anic Christians* (Cambridge: Cambridge, 1991).

Michel, T.S.J. "Muslim-Christian Dialogue and Cooperation in the Thought of Bediuzzaman Said Nursi." *The Muslim World* 89, no. 3-4 (1999).

Moltmann, Jurgen. *On Human Dignity,* translated by M. Douglas Meeks (London: SCM Press Ltd, 1984).

Muslim, Abū al-Ḥusayn. *Ṣaḥiḥ Muslim,* translated by Abdul Hamid Siddiqi (Lahore: Ashraf Islamic Publishers, 1990).

Muslim, Muṣṭafā. *Mabāḥith fī al-Tafsīr al-Mawḍūᶜī* (Damascus: Dār al-Qalam, 2000).

Najar, Abdelmajid. *The Islamic Civilizing Process* (Beirut: Dār al-Gharb al-Islāmī), 1999.

Nasr, Seyyed Hossein. *The Heart of Islam: Enduring Values for Humanity* (New York: Harper Collins Publishers, 2002).

Nawawī (al-), Yaḥyā. *Sharḥ Ṣaḥīḥ Muslim* (Beirut: Dār al-Fikr, 1996).

Nettler, Ronald L, and Suha Taji-Farouki. *Muslim-Jewish Encounters Intellectual Traditions and Modern Politics* (Amsterdam: Harwood Academic Publishers, 1998).

New American Standard Bible (1995).

Nöldeke, Theodor. *Neue Beiträge zur Semitischen Sprachwissenashaft* (Strassburg: Karl J. Trubner, 1910).

Nuḥās (al-), Abū Jaᶜfar. *Al-Nāsikh wa al-Mansūkh*. Edited by Sulaiman al-Lahim (Beirut: Mu'assasah al-Risālah, 1991).

—. *Kitāb al-Nāsikh wa al-Mansūkh fī al-Qur'ān al-Karīm* (Al-Maktabah al-ᶜĀlamiyyah, 1938).

Nursi, Said. *Münazarat* (Istanbul: Envâr Neşriyat, 1993).

—. *Al-Khuṭbah al-Shāmiyyah,* translated by Ihsan Qasim al-Salihi (Cairo: Sharikah Sözler, 2005.

—. *Ṣayqal al-Islām,* translated by Ihsan Qasim al-Salihi (Cairo: Sharikah Sözler, 2004).

—. *The Damascus Sermon,* translated by Şükran Vahide (Istanbul: Sözler Neşriyat ve Sanayi A.Ş., 1996).

Nye, Malory. *Religion the Basics* (London and New York: Routledge, 2008).

O'Leary. *Arabia Before Muhammad* (1927).
Osman, Fathi. *The Other* (USA: Pharos Foundation, 2008).
Peters, F. P. *Mecca A Literary History of the Muslim Holy Land* (New Jersey: Princeton University Press, 1994).
Pope Leo XIII, V.G.R. *Immortale Dei* (1885).
Qalahji, Muhammad and Qunaibi, Hamid. *Muʿjam Lughah al-Fuqahā'* (Beirut: Dār al-Nafā'is, 1985).
Qarāfī (al-), Aḥmad. *Al-Furūq* (Beirut: Dār al-Kutub al-ʿIlmiyyah, 1998).
Qayrāwanī (al-), Ibn Rashīq. *Al-ʿUmdah fī Ṣināʿah al-Shiʿr wa Naqdih* (Cairo: Maktabah al-Khanjī, 2000).
Qurṭubī (al-), Muḥammad. *Al-Jāmiʿ li Aḥkām al-Qur'ān* (Beirut: Dār al-Fikr, 1998).
Qutub, Sayyid. *Fī Ẓilāl al-Qur'ān* (Beirut: Dār al-Shurūq, 1996).
—. *In the Shade of the Qur'an.* Edited by M.A. Salahi, translated by M.A. Salahi (Leicester: The Islamic Foundation, 2009).
Rahner, Karl. *Theological Investigations,* translated by Karl-H. Kruger, vol.5. (London: Darton, Longman and Todd, 1966).
Ramadan, Tariq. "Interreligious Dialogue from an Islamic Perspective." In *How to Conquer the Barriers to Intercultural Dialogue: Christianity, Islam and Judaism*, by Timmerman Christiane and Barbara Segaert (Brussels: P.I.E Peter Lang S.A., 2007).
Rashwani, Samir. *Manhaj al-Tafsīr al-Mawḍūʿī li al-Qur'ān al-Karīm* (Ḥalab: Dār al-Multaqā, 2009).
Rāzī (al-), Fakhr al-Dīn. *Al-Mabāḥith al-Sharqiyyah* (Hyderabad: Majlis Dā'irah al-Maʿārif, 1343 AH).
—. *Mafātīḥ al-Ghayb* (Beirut: Dār al-Fikr, 2002).
Rida, Muhammad Rashid. *Tafsīr al-Manār* (Beirut: Dār al-Kutub al-ʿIlmiyyah, 1999).
—. *Tafsīr al-Manār* (Cairo: Dār al-Manār, 1947).
Robinson, B.A. *Religious Tolerance.* 20 May 2001. http://www.religious-tolerance.org (accessed March 17, 2010).
Rosenthal, Franz. *The Muslim Concept of Freedom* (Leiden: E. J. Brill, 1960).
Rousseau, Jean-Jacques. *The Social Contract and The First and Second Discourses.* Edited by Susan Dunn (New Haven and London: Yale University Press, 2002).
Rummānī (al-), ʿAlī, Ḥamd al-Khaṭṭābī, and ʿAbd al-Qādir al-Jurjānī. *Thalāth Rasā'il fī 'Iʿjāz al-Qur'ān* (Cairo: Dār al-Maʿārif, n.d.).
Sadi (al-), Abd al-Rahman. *Taysīr al-Karīm al-Raḥmān fī Tafsīr Kalām al-Mannān* (Beirut: Mu'assasah al-Risālah, 2000).

Said, Abd al-Sattar. *Al-Madkhal Ilā al-Tafsīr al-Mawḍūʿī* (Cairo: Dār al-Tawzīʿ wa al-Nashr al-Islāmiyyah, 1991).

Said, Jaudat. *Iqra' wa Rabbuk al-Akram* (Damascus: Dār al-Fikr, 1998).

Sachedina, Abdulaziz. *The Islamic Roots of Democratic Pluralism* (New York: Oxford University Press, 2001).

Sacks, Jonathan. *The Dignity of Difference:How to Avoid the Clash of Civilizations* (London: Continuum, 2002).

Salih (al-), Subhi. *Mabāḥith fī ʿUlūm al-Qur'ān* (Beirut: Dār al-ʿIlm li al-Malāyīn, 2002).

Salumi (al-), Abd al-Aziz. *Al-Wāqidī wa Kitābuhu al-Maghāzī: Manhajuhu wa Maṣādiruhu* (Al-Madīnah al-Munawwarah: Al-Jāmiʿah al-Islāmiyyah, 2004).

Samarqandī (al-), Muḥammad. *Tafsīr al-Samarqandī – Baḥr al-ʿUlūm.* Edited by Mahmud Matraji (Beirut: Dār al-Fikr, 1997).

Shah-Kazemi, Reza. *The Other in the Light of the One* (Cambridge: Islamic Texts Society, 2006).

Shanqiti (al-), Muhammad al-Amin. *Aḍwā' al-Bayān fī Īḍāḥ al-Qur'ān bi al-Qur'ān* (Cairo: Dār al-Ḥadīth, 2006).

Sharawi (al-), Muhammad. *Tafsīr al-Shaʿrāwī* (Cairo: Akhbār al-Yawm, 1991).

Sībawayh, Abū Bishr ʿAmrū. *Al-Kitāb: Kitāb Sībawayh.* Edited by Abd al-Salam Harun (Cairo: Maktabah al-Khānjī, n.d.).

Siddiqi, Muzammil. *Islam for Today.* 5 May 2001. http://www.islamfortoday.com/diversity.htm (accessed November 2, 2010).

Simpson, J.A., and E.S.C. Weiner. *The Oxford English Dictionary* 2nd edn. (Oxford: Clarendon Press, 2004).

Suyūṭī (al-), Jalāl al-Dīn. *Al-'Itqān fī ʿUlūm al-Qur'ān* (Dār al-Fikr).

—. *Al-Durr al-Manthūr fī al-Tafsīr al-Ma'thūr* (Beirut: Dār al-Kutub al-ʿIlmiyyah, 2000).

—. *Tārīkh al-Khulafā'* (Beirut: Dār al-Kitāb al-ʿArabī, 1999).

Swanson, Mark. "The Christian al-Ma'mūn Tradition." In *Christians at the Heart of Islamic Rule*, edited by David Thomas (Leiden-Boston: Brill, 2003).

Ṭabarānī (al-), Sulaymān. *Al-Muʿjam al-Kabīr.* 2nd edn. Edited by Hamdi al-Salafi (n.d.).

Ṭabarī (al-), Ibn Jarīr. *Tafsīr al-Ṭabarī* (Beirut: Dār al-Kutub al-ʿIlmiyyah, 1999).

—. *Tafsīr al-Ṭabarī.* Edited by Ahmad Shakir Mahmud Shakir (Cairo: Maktabah Ibn Taymiyyah, n.d.).

—. *The History of al-Ṭabarī,* translated by W.M Watt and M.V.

McDonald (Albany: State University of New York Press, 1988).
—. *The History of al-Ṭabarī,* translated by Ella Landau-Tasseron (New York: State University of New York Press, 1998).
—. *The History of al-Ṭabarī,* translated by John Alden Williams, vol.xxvii, (Albany: State University of New York Press, 1985).
—. *The History of al-Ṭabarī: General Introduction and From Creation to the Flood,* translated by Franz Rosenthal (Albany: State University of New York, 1989).
Tabatabai (al-), Muhammad. *Al-Mīzān fī Tafsīr al-Qur'ān* (Beirut: Mu'assasah al-Aʿlamī, 1997).
—. *Al-Mīzān fī Tafsīr al-Qur'ān* (Beirut: Mu'assasah al-Aʿlamī, 1972).
Taiar (al-), Musaid. *Maqālāt fī ʿUlūm al-Qur'ān wa Usūl al-Tafsīr* (Riyadh: Dār al-Muḥaddith, 1425 AH-2004).
Tantawi, Muhammad al-Said. *Al-Tafsīr al-Wasīṭ li al-Qur'ān al-Karīm* (Cairo: Maṭbaʿah al-Saʿādah, 1985).
Tawḥīdī (al-), Abū Ḥayyān. *Al-Muqābasāt.* Edited by Hasan al-Sandubi (Cairo: Dār Suʿād al-Ṣabāḥ, 1992).
The Bible. American Standard Version, 1901.
Toynbee, Arnold. *A Study of History-Abridgement of Volumes VII-X.* Edited by D.C. Somervell (Oxford: Oxford University Press, 1985).
Traer, Robert. *Quest for Truth: Critical Reflections on Interfaith Cooperation* (Aurora: The Davies Group, Publishers, 1999).
Umari (al-), Akram. *Al-Sīrah al-Nabawiyyah al-Ṣaḥīḥah* (Madinah: Maktabah al-ʿUlūm wa al-Ḥikam, 1994).
—. *Madinan Society at the Time of the Prophet* (Herndon: The International Institute of Islamic Thought, 1995).
Uthaimin, Muhammad. *Sharḥ Muqaddimah al-Tafsīr* (Riyadh: Madār al-Waṭan, 1426 AH).
Waardenburg, Jacques. *Religion and Reason: Muslims and Others: Relations in Context* (Berlin: Walter de Gruyter & Co. KG Publishers, 2003).
Wadii (al-), Muqbil. *Al-Ṣaḥīḥ al-Musnad min Asbāb al-Nuzūl* (Sana: Maktabah Ṣanʿā' al-Athariyyah, 2004).
Wāḥidī (al-), Abū al-Ḥasan. *Asbāb al-Nuzūl* (Cairo: Maktabah al-Mutanabbī, n.d.).
Wāqidī (al-), Muḥammad. *Kitāb al-Maghāzī.* Edited by Marsden Jones (ʿĀlam al-Kutub, 1984).
Watt, William. *A Short History of Islam* (Oxford: Oneworld Publications, 1996).
—. *Muhammad at Medina* (London: Oxford University Press, 1962).

—. *Muhammad-Prophet and Statesman* (London: Oxford University Press, 1961).

Watt, William M. and Bell, Richard. *Introduction to the Qur'an* (Edinburgh: University Press, 1970).

Zamakhsharī (al-), Maḥmūd. *Al-Kashshāf ʿan Ḥaqā'iq al-Tanzīl* (Beirut: Dār al-Kutub al-ʿIlmiyyah, 1995).

Zarkashī (al-), Badr al-Dīn. *Al-Burhān fī ʿUlūm al-Qur'ān* (Beirut: Dār al-Jīl, 1988).

—. *Al-Burhān fī al-ʿUlūm al-Qur'ān* (Beirut: Al-Maktabah al-ʿAṣriyyah, 1972).

Zawaiti (al-), Muhammad Shukri. *Tafsīr al-Ḍaḥḥāk* (Cairo: Dār al-Salām, 1999).

Zirikli (al-), Khair al-Din. *Al-Aʿlām* (Beirut: Dār al-ʿIlm lī al-Malayīn, 2002).